The Evolution of Technical Analysis

Financial Prediction from Babylonian Tablets to Bloomberg Terminals

Andrew W. Lo

and

Jasmina Hasanhodzic

BLOOMBERG PRESS
An Imprint of
WILEY

Published by John Wiley & Sons, Inc., Hoboken, New Jersey.
Published simultaneously in Canada.

For general information on our other products and services or for technical support, please contact our Customer Care Department within the United States at (800) 762-2974, outside the United States at (317) 572-3993 or fax (317) 572-4002.

Wiley also publishes its books in a variety of electronic formats. Some content that appears in print may not be available in electronic books. For more information about Wiley products, visit our web site at www.wiley.com.

Library of Congress Cataloging-in-Publication Data:

Lo, Andrew W. (Andrew Wen-Chuan)
   The evolution of technical analysis : financial prediction from Babylonian tablets to Bloomberg terminals / Andrew W. Lo and Jasmina Hasanhodzic.
      p.   cm.
   Includes bibliographical references and index.
   ISBN 978-1-57660-349-9 (cloth)
      1. Technical analysis (Investment analysis)—History.   I. Hasanhodzic, Jasmina, 1979-   II. Title.
   HG4529.L62 2010
   332.63'2042—dc22

                                                                2010019276

Printed in the United States of America

10 9 8 7 6 5 4 3 2 1

To our mothers

Contents

Introduction   vii

Chapter 1: Ancient Roots   1

    The Beginnings   2
    Ancient Babylon   5
    Ancient Greece   11
    Ancient Rome   15
    Negative Attitudes toward Traders   18

Chapter 2: The Middle Ages and the Renaissance   21

    Western Europe   22
    Technical Analysis   32
    Societal Attitudes   39

Chapter 3: Asia   43

    Japan   44
    China   49

Chapter 4: The New World   59
    Wall Street   60
    Societal Attitudes   73

Chapter 5: A New Age for Technical Analysis   81
    Dow Theory   82
    Relative Strength   91
    Market Cycles and Waves   92
    Chart Patterns   94
    Volume of Trading   96
    Market Breadth   99
    Nontechnical Analysis   99

Chapter 6: Technical Analysis Today   105
    Trends   106
    Patterns   109
    Strength   111
    Cycles   112
    Wall Street's Reinterpretation of Technical Analysis 114

Chapter 7: A Brief History of Randomness and
              Efficient Markets   131
    Prices As Objects of Study   134
    The Emergence of Efficient Markets   137
    What Is Random?   141

Chapter 8: Academic Approaches to Technical Analysis   149
    Theoretical Underpinnings   150
    Empirical Evaluation   151
    Adaptive Markets and Technical Analysis   161

Notes   167
Bibliography   191
Acknowledgments   199
About the Authors   203
Index   205

Introduction

Technical analysis—the forecasting of prices based on patterns in past market data—is something of a black sheep in modern economics. Some skeptics view it as kissing cousins with sleazy speculation or gambling, while others regard it as a relic that is only slightly more sophisticated than the reading of chicken entrails. Proponents of quantitative analysis, who take physics as the ideal model of how economic science ought to look, view technical analysis as antiquated and contrived in its very foundations. They demand mathematical proofs of its validity and dismiss as exception bias the strong betting averages and impressive bottom lines of successful technicians. We make it no secret, then, that we regard technical analysis as a legitimate and useful discipline, tarred by spurious associations and deserving of further academic study.

Some of this skepticism is understandable in light of the historical origins (and occasional abuses) of technical analysis. Many of its methods come down to us from the days before computers and the number-crunching-intensive theories they made possible, and not all of its methods have been thoroughly explored within the quantitative frameworks now available. Many terms and concepts in technical analysis can seem abstruse or outmoded; it is easy to see how a discipline that involves eyeballing charts for patterns with names like "head and shoulders" and "cup with a handle" might seem at first blush more akin to astrology than science. However, many of these are merely heuristics developed in the precomputer age when calculating a simple statistic was a formidable task. For instance, the 10-day moving average became a fixture of technical analysis not because it was optimal, but because it was trivially easy to compute. Indeed, there are many such concepts in "classical" technical analysis that could benefit from quantitative reformulation.

Ultimately, however, both technical and quantitative analysis serve similar purposes: They both attempt to predict the future based on models of the past. One is statistical, the other is intuitive. Whereas a quant minimizes a sum of squared residuals to find the best-fitting line given the data, a technician estimates it by looking at the charts, searching for tell-tale patterns, and inferring the thoughts and feelings of other market players. Both approaches have merit. This is not to say that they are equal; clearly, quantitative methods have won hands down, dominating the investment industry because of their demonstrable value-added. But technical analysis is surprisingly resilient and persistent, and in some corners of the financial industry—such as the trading of commodities and currencies—it is still the dominant mode of analysis. This state of affairs suggests that technical analysis may have something to contribute, even to the most sophisticated quant. Fortunately, a slow but sure reconciliation is underway.

Though big strides have been made throughout history and in recent years toward developing a more systematic approach to technical analysis, technicians remain ostracized to this day. For evidence, look no further than the Financial Industry Regulatory Authority's official recognition of the Chartered Market Technician designation, which occurred only in 2005. Part of the reason is that technical analysis is often associated with the speculators, bear raiders, and market cornerers of previous eras. As Tony Tabell, a veteran technical analyst and an heir to the technical brokerage business founded by his father Edmund Tabell in the 1930s, explains:

> It's hard to visualize unless you've talked to people who were involved how difficult this was in the atmosphere of [the] 1930s and 1940s. The entire brokerage business was a basket case.

Volume on the NYSE was under a million shares. This was
the 1930s, the Great Depression, nobody had any money, and
if they did, they were very leery about investing. Furthermore,
technical analysis had been associated with the excesses of the
1920s. All of the various Securities Acts were designed to get
rid of the manipulative market operations that had characterized
the '20s. Since technical work to a great degree (certainly point
and figure charts) had been originally conceived as a means of
detecting pool operations, confessing that you were involved in
technical work at that point was sort of equivalent to confessing
that you were some kind of a low-level criminal. I saw some
[of] this, because the remainder of this attitude was still kicking
around when I started in the business in the 1950s, but I can
imagine how incredible it must have been in the '30s and '40s.[1]

The efficient markets hypothesis (EMH), formulated in the writings
of Samuelson (1965) and Fama (1965a,b; 1970), did not help much.[2]
According to this theory, there are no patterns in market data that are
exploitable through trading strategies. Ever since the advent of modern finance—a theory based on rational expectations and market efficiency—technical analysis has been dismissed in academic circles as a
mathematical impossibility. As Princeton University economist Burton
Malkiel concluded in his influential book *A Random Walk Down Wall
Street* (1973), "under scientific scrutiny, chart-reading must share a ped-
estal with alchemy."

As we recount the premature obituaries for technical analysis, it is
worth noting as an aside that recent research has not only documented
departures from the EMH—in the form of cognitive biases such as
overconfidence, overreaction, loss aversion, and herding—but has also
included new theoretical underpinnings for technical analysis and the
empirical validation of certain technical patterns and indicators.

Malkiel's lumping of technical analysis with alchemy is not entirely
coincidental, for here we come across another historical reason for the
field's questionable reputation—technical analysis was used in conjunction with astrology since the earliest times. The ancient Babylonians
would methodically record, often intraday, the prices of various
commodities, but they would also assign those same commodities to

the astrological regions of Pisces and Taurus, depending on whether they were bullish or bearish. Similarly, in addition to the very logical lists of weights, measures, and exchange rates recorded in medieval merchant manuals, they also often contained lengthy astrological appendixes and advised their readers to buy, sell, or begin anything when they were in the region of Virgo. Yet another example is provided by Christopher Kurz, a sixteenth-century Antwerp trader, who claimed to be able to forecast prices of commodities up to 20 days in advance using his technical trading system based on back-tested astrological signals.

Such close links between technical analysis and astrology are naturally a cause for suspicion and skepticism today. But for our ancestors, astrology was a way of life, applied to wide-ranging areas of human endeavor including warfare and medicine. It was no coincidence that Christopher Kurz doubled as a political astrologer—he is known for having forecasted the extinction of the papacy, among other things—while Thales of Miletus, one of the Seven Sages of ancient Greece, made meteorological predictions based on movements of the stars and planets. That societies would base their operations in part on astrology sounds absurd today, but interestingly, if we view astrology as a random number generator of the precomputer age, its prevalence becomes more understandable. Then, as now, forecasting—financial and otherwise—was a business of probabilities. Just as computer-generated random numbers are part of today's statistical forecasting models—for example, the commonly used Markov Chain Monte Carlo method for constructing Bayesian forecasts—astrology may be thought of as a random input in ancient forecasting models.

The evolution of technical analysis did not take place in isolation. The growth of markets provided one stimulus for its development. In ancient Babylon, simply writing down commodity prices on clay tablets was sufficient for tracking market action, but with the advent of financial exchanges, the need for visualizing market data became evident. By the 1830s, price charts emerged and soon became so prevalent that people like William Stanley Jevons and James Wyld made their livelihoods from producing sophisticated charts and selling them to various offices.

Speculation provided another stimulus. Though speculation and technical analysis are not synonymous, they do share a certain awareness of market psychology and of the forces of supply and demand. It was precisely when speculative techniques were ripe that technical analysis became more concrete, such as on the Dojima Rice Exchange in seventeenth-century Japan, where the legendary trader Munehisa Homma developed the "candlestick" charting method to be able to visualize open, high, low, and closing market prices over a certain period, and formulated his version of technical analysis, which remains popular to this day.

Despite the distance created by continents and thousands of years, the market wisdom of Charles Dow, the father of modern technical analysis, is astonishingly similar to that of his earliest predecessors, including the ancient Athenian practice of using price level as an indicator of market sentiment, Homma's rotation of Yang and Yin (bullishness and bearishness), and the emphasis in late imperial China on "the ultimate principle," which is that "when goods become extremely expensive, then they must become inexpensive again."[3] Such similarities reveal technical analysis as a truly universal phenomenon and highlight how deeply ingrained it is in human psychology to reason in technical terms in order to ride and reinforce the trends, as was the case with the humble tulip bulb during the 1633–1637 tulip mania in Amsterdam. As de la Vega put it, "for on this point we are all alike: when the prices rise, we think that they fly up high and, when they have risen high, that they will run away from us."[4] As long as humans, not robots, make the markets, bubbles and crashes will be a reality. This is an especially important lesson in the wake of the 2007–2009 global financial crisis, a time when many fundamentals have crumbled and in some spheres of financial practice there has been nothing left to work with other than technical analysis.

In this book, we present a broad, largely nontechnical historical survey of technical analysis, tracing its roots and evolution from ancient times through the medieval and modern eras. While neither of us is a practicing technical analyst or "technician," as they prefer to be called, we have been fascinated by this strange craft for many years, and this volume is the outgrowth of our own attempt to make sense of the discipline. As outsiders, we hope to bring a somewhat different perspective that can bridge the gap between academia and the technical analysis community. Our previous book, *The Heretics of Finance*, contained interviews with leading technicians in which they described their art in their own words. In this volume, we take a more expansive view and search for the origins of technical analysis throughout history.

This endeavor was more challenging than we anticipated because, in many cases, the historical evidence of technical analysis is indirect, and many ideas were not fully developed by their originators. This is not surprising since, in the past, the concept of technical analysis as a separate discipline did not exist; rather, it was entangled with the intuitive, sometimes whimsical, and rarely systematic way of buying and selling practiced by speculators, bankers, and merchants. Hence when we say that merchants were the liberators of the independent human spirit and the driving force behind the progress of world civilization, we mean technicians, too. It was they who put an end to solely monastic education and the use of Latin in business and private life, and who initiated lay education in the Middle Ages. It is no coincidence that some of history's great scientists were also engaged in investing, their market experiences often motivating their scientific contributions (Fibonacci being but one example). Sapori once said that medieval merchants "traced for individuals and peoples of all times to come the only way that leads to a full realization of humanity."[5] We hope this book will convey the same for technical analysts across all eras.

Chapter 1

Ancient Roots

Although there is no direct evidence of technical analysis from ancient civilizations, scattered indirect evidence can be uncovered in early market practices. Bearing in mind that technical analysis is not merely a toolbox of head-and-shoulder-like patterns and MACD-like indicators—as many think of it today—but rather the use of past prices to forecast future ones in the most general sense, we find evidence of it in Babylonian price records, Greek market sentiment assessments, and Roman seasonality patterns. Our predecessors not only followed market prices but also made conscious attempts to measure supply/demand imbalances in price data and react to them for their profit, often combining their insights with "data" from fundamental nature or astrology. It should come as no surprise that in ancient times technical forecasting methods were inextricably linked with and in some cases arose from trading and speculation; hence in this chapter we review them side by side.

The Beginnings

People trade. During the late preceramic Neolithic, which is when the settled village life began and plants and animals were domesticated, the settlers from the Jordan Valley engaged in exchange of local resources—such as salt, bitumen, and sulfur—with nomads, as well as in the long-distance trade of obsidian, and domesticated wheat and sheep with the Central Anatolian Plateau and the Zagros–Taurus arc (a mountain range situated between Europe, Asia, and the Levantine corridor to Africa).[1] In the ceramic phases of the Neolithic, settlers formed agricultural villages in the Zagros Valley while nomadic herders established encampments in the higher elevations. Although there is no evidence of markets in the Zagros during the sixth millennium B.C., the villagers traded grain, flour, fruit, vegetables, and crafts for the nomads' butter, wool, lambskins, and livestock. Long-distance trade expanded too, to include a variety of new materials such as alabaster, marble, cinnabar, wood, limestone, greenstone, and iron oxides.[2] In the later ceramic phases of the Neolithic, around 5000 B.C., villages became highly specialized, and towns or temple centers, possibly equipped with markets, came into being. Long-distance trade flourished like never before, spanning a distance of 1,500 miles and a striking variety of raw materials.[3]

During the early Bronze Age, specifically in the twenty-fourth century B.C, Sargon the Great established the first Mesopotamian empire with its capital at Agade and with the city's temple serving as the center of the empire's economic life. The merchant officially worked for the temple and pursued his private entrepreneurial activities on the side. As political power became more secular, the merchant's domain extended to the palace as well.[4] Sumerian epic literature, including the *Epic of Gilgamesh*, abounds in the allusions to the commercial realities of this period.[5] After the fall of the last one of these empires, the Third Dynasty of Ur, at around 2000 B.C., numerous and decentralized city-states emerged, each ceremonially headed by its own king but in reality run by the merchants. The same merchants established trading colonies in Anatolia, such as the famous *karum* Kanesh.[6] In the ensuing Old Babylonian period, trade was in the hands of so-called *takamaru* whose role encompassed that of merchants, brokers, merchant bankers, money lenders, and government agents. *Takamaru* dealt in slaves, foodstuffs, wool, timber, garments, textiles, grain, wine, metals, building materials, and cattle and horses. They would either do the trading themselves or loan money to others to go on trading journeys for them.[7]

The Late Bronze Age was characterized by a rigid political structure, and all trading activities were controlled by the palace.[8] In the Iron Age, political power became decentralized and the large palace-towns of the Bronze Age were replaced by numerous, diffuse settlements extending to previously unpopulated areas. Needless to say, both overland and sea trade benefited enormously. As a result, merchants became more free, both in their business activities and in their physical movement. An Iron Age merchant was no longer a palace official who pursued his own profit as a sideline; he was active mainly for his own profit, and stimulated not by royal order but by perceived market advantages.[9]

Nowhere was the focus on getting rich so pronounced as in ancient Babylon, an early hotbed of commercial innovation. For example, ancient Babylonians established a system of weights and measures, formalized business deals by introducing contracts written on clay tablets and signed by the parties involved, and invented limited partnerships where one partner would raise capital at home while the other would travel for business. Accumulation of wealth was important not just for kings and temples, but also for private individuals such as the famous Murashu family, who were wealthy bankers from Nippur of the fifth century B.C. In fact, it was at this time that trading evolved to the point of a profession—a trader acted as a middleman or a broker and dealt in products he did not produce.[10] It is under such conditions that technical analysis came into being in ancient Babylon.

Before drawing parallels between ancient Babylonian practices and modern-day technical analysis, we must first verify that prices in those times were not fixed and controlled by the prevailing rulers, but rather were determined in the market through the interaction of buyers and sellers.

First of all, the existence of markets in ancient Mesopotamia is well established. Not unlike today, the word "street" was associated with the market; for example, Sumerian tablets from the second millennium

Vase with overlapping pattern and three bands of palm trees. Mid-3rd millennium B.C. Arabian peninsula, Gulf region, or southern Iran. Chlorite, H. 23.5 cm. Gift of J. Pierpont Morgan, 1917 (17.190.106).

Source: Image copyright © The Metropolitan Museum of Art/Art Resource, NY.

Administrative tablet with cylinder seal impression of a male figure, hunting dogs, and boars. 3100–2900 B.C. Jamdat Nasr, Uruk III style, southern region, Mesopotamia. Clay, H. 2 in. (5.3 cm). Purchase, Raymond and Beverly Sackler Gift, 1988 (1988.433.1).

Source: Image copyright © The Metropolitan Museum of Art/Art Resource, NY.

document the existence of the *sūk shimātim* or "commercial street" and note that *sāchiru* (peddlers, retailers) were selling goods on the "street."[11] The Old Babylonian term *bīt machīri* "seems to refer to the stall of a merchant . . . small in size . . . and adjacent to other stalls."[12] As markets evolved from ad hoc gatherings to more established fixtures of civic life, so did the words that described them: The Akkadian term machiru, which initially had the abstract meaning "price, market value" and "commercial activity," acquired the concrete meaning "marketplace" by the beginning of the Old Assyrian and Old Babylonian periods.[13]

Moreover, literally thousands of documents from Assyrian trading stations in Anatolia record price fluctuations. For example, one trader reporting about the high price of Babylonian textiles states, "if it is possible to make a purchase which allows you a profit, we will buy for you."[14] Evidence from the third millennium B.C. suggests that prices of barley fluctuated widely. One shekel of silver at different times purchased 10, 20, or 120 quarts of barley, and based on prices, one could then distinguish between *mu-he-gal-la* or a good growing season and *mu-mi-gal-la*, a bad one.[15] Further evidence suggests that price increases were directly linked to increases in demand. When numerous merchants seeking to buy copper arrived in Anatolia, an Anatolian trader knew the impact this would have on the price of copper and wrote to his associate: "Within the next ten days they will have exhausted its [the palace's] copper. I shall then buy silver [that is, sell copper] and send it to you."[16] Prophets, too, recognized that increases in supply would lower market prices: When the ninth-century prophet Elisha forecasted the lifting of the Syrian siege, she also noted that "tomorrow about this time a measure of *soleth* [fine wheat flour] shall be sold for one shekel, and two measures of barley for a shekel in the games of Samaria."[17]

Ancient Babylon

One of the great legacies of ancient Babylon is the trove of clay tablets on which they inscribed their myths, laws, and records. For example, a large number of tablets, some dating back as far as the second millennium B.C., pose textbook-like interest rate problems and provide their solutions.[18] In another corpus of tablets, ancient Babylonians kept diaries of astronomical observations and prices of various commodities in the city for almost four centuries. Although the earliest known diary dates back to 651 B.C., it is commonly believed that most of the diaries originated between 747 and 734 B.C., during the reign of Nabonassar. The two earliest diaries, written in 651 and 567 B.C., covered 12 months each.[19] Later diaries spanned various lengths of time, ranging from days, weeks, months, or even years. A typical full-sized diary covered either an entire Babylonian year or the first half of it.[20]

Slotsky characterizes the Mesopotamian records of the market values of commodities as an old and continuous tradition that spanned not only astronomical diaries but also literary works and commemorative establishments.[21] To illustrate her point, she points to the Old Babylonian royal inscriptions that listed "ideal" commodity prices in order to "propagate the image of a prosperous reign."[22] Among her other examples are the Laws of Ešnunna and the Hittite Law Code, both of which specified legal prices for various commodities. Other sources of commodity prices include the Chronicle of Market Prices as well as literary texts such as the *Coronation Prayer of Assurbanipal* and the *Curse of Agade*.[23]

The basic unit of money was the shekel of silver, and prices were quoted as the amount of commodity that one shekel could buy. For example, one diary records the following price quotation: "This month, the equivalent for one shekel of wrought silver was barley, 2 *pān* 4 *sūt* 3 *qa*."[24] Continuously throughout the centuries, the diaries document the values of the same six commodities—barley, dates, mustard/cuscuta, cress/cardamom, sesame, and wool—a testament to their importance in ancient Babylon. As Slotsky explains:

> All six commodities were staples. Barley, dates, sesame, and wool were in widespread use since earliest times and for millennia maintained their economic role as units of payment and exchange. Mustard/cuscuta and cress/cardamom grew to become commodities of great significance, especially in the first millennium, because of their popularity in the Mesopotamian diet and their widespread use in medicine. All were of domestic

origin, all were storable, and all were raw materials from which other basics were derived.[25]

During the four hundred years of their production, the layout of the diaries did not change much. They typically start with a title, which specifies the time range covered by the diary, such as, "Diary from month I to the end of month VI of year 23 of Arses, who is called King Artaxerxes."[26] Longer diaries were produced by compiling shorter ones, and hence are divided into several distinct sections. For example, a half-year diary is divided into six or seven sections, each section corresponding to a lunar month. At the beginning of each section a scribe would record his observations of the first signs of visibility of the new moon. He would devote the body of the section to a detailed description of the moon's progress among the Normal Stars and planets during that month. He would also provide supplementary information regarding weather, comets, meteors, eclipses, equinoxes, and solstices. Toward the end of the section he would give an account of the last signs of visibility of the moon. Finally, the concluding passage would consist of the planetary positions data, the market values of the six commodities, and the water levels of the Euphrates. Sometimes, some historical notes relating to earlier months or years would be included in the conclusion.[27]

Choosing the Stocks

Now let us consider the parallels between Babylonian diaries and contemporary technical analysis. The very fact that the diaries documented the values of the same six commodities throughout centuries has some semblance to modern practices. First of all, some of the classic technical analysis manuals advise carefully choosing a small number of stocks on which to focus your attention. For example, according to Gartley, "a few well-chosen charts, religiously studied, can be of far greater use in making decisions to buy and sell stocks, than a large portfolio including several hundred stocks, which receive only casual attention."[28] Second, technical analysis teaches one to follow the chosen stocks over a long period of time. As Schabacker puts it, "understanding of the technical action of any stock or group of stocks can come only from long study of actual market action and market history."[29] By following the same six commodities over a period of four hundred years, ancient Babylonians did just that.

Diaries as a Form of Charts

To describe the ancient Babylonian custom of recording market quotations, Slotsky writes that they "were charted regularly so that fluctuations during each month of the year could be noted."[30] However, as an example of this charting practice, she gives not a graphical chart but the following statement: "until the 15th, 5½qa; the 16th and the 17th, 5 qa one-fourth and half of one-fourth."[31] Nevertheless, her labeling of the astronomical diaries as a form of charts is valid. Careful reading of Schabacker's work, which happens to be "among the most influential ever written on the technical side of the market," suggests that he would agree with this statement.[32] According to Schabacker, while a chart "may take many different forms and may be adapted in such forms to many various codes of important market factors . . . from a general standpoint . . . [it] is merely the visible record of stock market action over a period of time."[33] And a visible record of market quotations is what the Babylonian diaries undeniably were. Gartley, another one of the "illustrious names in the field of technical analysis,"[34] suggests that a chart's "primary function is to provide accurate factual data."[35] The diaries certainly provided this function. As Slotsky puts it, "To anyone who has dealt intensively with the analysis of the diaries' market data, there can be little doubt that these prices were real market values."[36]

Time Scale and Volatility

In his classic text *Stock Market Theory and Practice*, Schabacker wrote that "there are daily charts, weekly charts, monthly charts and even yearly charts."[37] He added that "the smaller the time period charted individually the more flexible the chart will be, and therefore the more valuable in tracing minor past habits and actions."[38] This would imply that higher volatility calls for a smaller time period, so that minor fluctuations can be more effectively traced. Schabacker's advice is remarkably similar to the practices of ancient Babylonian scribes. These scribes would adjust the frequency with which they recorded the market quotations in the astronomical diaries according to the level of market volatility. When volatility increased, "instead of the regular quotation at the end of each month, there might be quotations for the beginning and end of the month; the beginning, middle, and end of the month; ranges of days; or even daily."[39] When fluctuations became even more rapid, "the smallest changes would be charted."[40] For example, on a particularly volatile day, prices would be reported twice a day, both in the morning and in the afternoon.[41]

Blank Spaces

"Some charts are lined for every day in the year," wrote Schabacker, "but this means that holidays leave a blank space which distorts the chart picture."[42] Just like technical charts, astronomical diaries report "interruptions or suspensions of commodity sales . . . on explicit dates in designated places."[43] Sometimes these interruptions are confined to a single commodity. For example, one diary notes that "the 25th and 26th day, the sale of barley was cut off,"[44] while another one notes that the "[trade in bar]ley was interrupted in the streets of Babylon."[45] Other times interruptions affected several commodities: "The sale of barley and everything else was cut off in the streets of Babylon until the 5th."[46]

Forecasting with Omens

The Babylonians' celestial omen corpus records their attempts to forecast the cultivation, yield, and storage of various commodities, as well as the behavior of their market prices.[47] This forecasting was astrological in nature. For example, Slotsky notes that the flourishing of the dates and mustard/cuscuta crops "was assigned to the astrological region of Pisces when the 'benefic' planets were dim and the 'malefic' planets were bright."[48] On the other hand, "sesame was assigned to the sign of Taurus, but when the 'malefic' planets were bright and the 'benefic' planets dim, it fell into the region of Pisces." Among the six commodities, barley, dates, and sesame are mentioned most frequently in the celestial omen corpus.[49] For example, omens concerning barley include statements such as: "the cultivated barley land will prosper," "rust will affect barley," "there will be no barley, business will be reduced, there will be famine," "barley will disappear from the country," "barley will become expensive."[50] In the omens regarding dates, it is noted that "the date plantation will not prosper," "dates will not prosper," "the purchase price for dates will not be fair," and so on.[51] Similarly, in the case of sesame, it is said that "the sesame harvest will prosper," "*kurusissu* rodents will eat the sesame," "barley and sesame will increase, and the equivalent of [only] one *qa* will [have to] be paid for 1 *kur*."[52]

Diary keepers not only kept records of market prices and related phenomena but also used those data for scientific forecasting. Slotsky elaborates on this point as follows:

> The diaries' astronomical data were used not only to pro- vide the observational basis of lunar and planetary theory, but also to predict phenomena for goal years (the years it would take for the moon or a planet to return to its original starting position). Although there is no comparable evidence to show that other diary observations were used for prediction, there are signs in the diaries that both market prices and the height of the Euphrates were carefully watched and subjected to some degree of control. . . . This raises the question of whether the scribes were attempting to correlate celestial observations with terrestrial events and ultimately trying to predict and even gain control over extreme changes in weather, water level, and prices.[53]

Thus, ancient Babylonians not only charted their markets but also sought to forecast future prices based on the observed ones, just as modern-day technicians would do. And when the price forecast was not favorable, they attempted to change the future outcome by taking actions to control the future supply and demand. For example, they would shut down the market for a period of time or bring scarce com- modities into the market, increase investment in canals and irrigation or change agricultural strategies, all to ease shortages or increase future supply.[54]

Ancient Greece

The Iron Age brought an abundance of iron tools, and with them, a host of new market forces. At the most basic level, peasants and artisans desired to obtain them. In parallel, the agriculturally favorable climate of the ancient Mediterranean encouraged a lightly regulated society that rewarded individual initiative. Together, these two factors led to the birth of a new type of economy—the market-oriented economy—by the middle of the first millennium B.C.[55] The rapid development of trade and coinage widened the gap between rich and poor. Political power was divided among powerful clans and families, and the situation of the poor deteriorated. To repay debts, many

A silver coin of the Greek city of Corinth dating back to 345–307 B.C. One side of the coin shows Pegasus, the winged horse, while the other side reveals the head of the goddess Athena donning a tipped-back Corinthian helmet, and a boar running left in the background.

of the poor would sell members of their families (or even themselves) into slavery; others would sharecrop for their creditors.[56]

In efforts to alleviate the plight of poor small farmers, Pisistratus during his tyranny (561–527 B.C.) introduced institutions that would eventually entrench the new, market-oriented economic system. It was under his rule that the traditionally rural festival in honor of Dionysus, the god of wine and the patron of agriculture, turned into a popular urban phenomenon known as the City Dionysia or the Great Dionysia. Pisistratus encouraged farmers to specialize in a particular crop (for example, olives) and produce primarily for export. In addition, his construction of the great temple to Olympian Zeus further boosted the economy. As the economy grew, so did the demand for the specialized services of farmers, craftsmen, and merchants, who eventually had no time to grow their own produce, but had to obtain it from the market.[57] As Davisson and Harper put it, "For the first time in history, there appeared an urban class that made its living on the market, that needed to buy and sell in order to live."[58] Glotz vividly describes a scene from the market in Agora during the Athenian period:

> One after another, at the hours fixed by the regulations, the different markets open; there are markets for vegetables, fruit, cheese, fish, meat and sausages, poultry and game, wine, wood, pottery, ironmongery, and old articles. There is even a corner for books. Every merchant has his place, which he reserves by paying a fee; in the shade of an awning or an umbrella he sets out his goods on trestles, near his craft and his resting beasts. Shoppers walk about; traders call to them; porters and messengers offer their services. Shouts, oaths, and quarrels. . . . When the open-air markets are shut the customers make for the covered hall, which is like an Eastern bazaar, with counters occupying the end.[59]

Similar activities would take place at the fairs, which were held in connection with the festivals.

The earliest evidence of coins comes from the Lydian capital of Sardis and dates back to around 650 B.C.[60] The Greeks soon appropriated the idea, and by the fifth century B.C., the use of coins for commercial purposes had become widespread in Greece.[61] The bank soon became "the indispensable organ of trade."[62] The first banks were in fact temples, which would accept individual and state deposits and lend them out at interest; later, banks became private institutions.[63] The earliest considerable evidence of Greek banking is related to the

Athenian grain trade and dates back to the fourth century B.C.[64] With the emergence of banks came, ipso facto, the profession of banking:

> For a long time there had been seen, sitting at a table, at the harbor or on the market, men whose business was to exchange money. . . . As time went on, the money-changers extended their business, investing funds outside the country and lending money for all kinds of undertakings. They needed a large capital, and acted as intermediaries between the sellers and buyers of money. In addition to exchange the *trapezitai* did business in deposits and loans. They were bankers.[65]

Speculation

It was precisely the union of banking and trade that naturally led to speculation,[66] which became so pronounced that it even prompted Aristotle to write about *chrematistichè*, or the art of getting rich.[67] Seemingly everything was used as a pretext for speculation, as Glotz explains:

> Corn and metal especially lent themselves to lucrative manipulation. Information was obtained on the state of the harvest in the producing countries, advantage was taken of political crises which impeded export or the free use of the seas, a storm, a shipwreck, the sudden arrival of a boat, everything was a pretext for rigging the market, and, failing true news, false news was invented. Since there were no time bargains to nullify variations by distributing them over a certain period, the smallest incident produced its effect instantaneously.[68]

Glotz gives the example of a Sicilian banker who cornered the metal market by buying up the iron of all the factories, making a profit of 200 percent in the process, and suggests that Pythocles had done similarly with lead.[69] At the Athenian stock exchanges, which according to Lévy "differed from ours only in the absence of regulations," traders were constantly watching news and prices, which at times fluctuated wildly, and they soon realized how they could manipulate prices to their advantage. In 585, famous mathematician and inventor of meteorology Thales of Miletos cornered the oil market by buying or renting all the oil presses after having forecasted a good harvest of oil crop. And acquiring all the grain and iron prior to wartime was a profitable endeavor, since the demand for these materials would rise sharply during the war.[70] In their price sensitivities, Athenians were not only opportunistic but also prone to panics: When they thought the prices were too high, their hoarding and selling would push the prices into a downward spiral and crisis was imminent. The great orator Lysias referred to such panics in his speeches.[71]

In the fourth and third centuries B.C., Greek culture spread to include southwestern Asia and northeastern Africa, including Mesopotamia, Egypt, and Italy. This expansion was at first peaceful, then characterized by Alexander the Great's conquests. Mediterranean culture became more unified and trade became more open.[72] The new Hellenistic market economy emerged, "[creating] a far larger area of trade in which the market replaced the port of trade and for the first time really integrated the ancient Near East with the Greek world."[73]

During the Hellenistic age, the art of speculation flourished. Speculators would often try to limit production in order to impose their own prices.[74] The most famous example is the wheat corner planned about 330 B.C. by Cleomenes.[75] Furthermore, the first system of insurance ever mentioned in history came into being during this time. Namely, in 324 B.C. Antimenes the Rhodian insured owners against the flight of their slaves for an annual premium of 8 percent.[76]

Technical Analysis

While speculation and technical analysis are different endeavors—in their purest form, the former is akin to gambling and the latter to scientific forecasting—attempting to anticipate future prices is central to both. The very popularity of speculation in ancient Greece naturally led to the development of methods for technical analysis. Athenian merchants knew that information was crucial. They certainly knew the value of geographical and environmental information, such as trading routes, hazards along the way, and winds. For this purpose merchants devised their own manuals, such as the *Periplus Maris Erythraei* (its Roman equivalent is called *Expositio Totius Mundi)*, which provided information about the products sold in countries along the route to India and the attitudes of their rulers.

Adaptive Athenian traders also coveted timely news, and, combining news with data on price fluctuations, would change their strategies rapidly.[77] For example, upon hearing that grain prices had changed in a way he did not anticipate, a merchant might immediately redirect his ships, in effect recognizing persistence in prices and using past prices as an indicator of future ones:

> Some of these men would send off the goods from Egypt, others would travel on board with the shipments, and others would remain here in Athens and dispose of the merchandise. Then those who remained here would send letters to those abroad to inform them of the prevailing prices, so that if grain were expensive in Athens they might bring it here, and if the price should fall they might head to some other port. This was the main reason, men of the jury, why the price of grain rose: it was due to such letters and conspiracies.[78]

Athenian merchants also made inferences about market sentiment to try to predict future prices and decide how much of a given commodity to buy or hold. As Whitby puts it, "What counted overall were impressions, since a belief that grain was in short supply would rapidly escalate into reality as those who could afford to increased their personal stores, while those with substantial reserves held them back from the market in the hope of yet higher prices."[79] To assess changes in sentiment—just as modern technical analysts do—ancient Athenians used prices: "[T]heir best indicator was probably the price level on the markets, which might fluctuate in response to rumors and changes in sentiment."[80]

Ancient Rome

Commerce played an important role in ancient Rome from its earliest days, so much that in early fifth century B.C. a guild of merchants dedicated a temple to Mercury—thought to be Rome's first temple honoring this god.[81] In fact, Mercury's very name is derived from the Latin *merces*, which means "the price paid for something, wages, reward, recompense," which in turn is derived from the Latin *merx* meaning "ware, merchandise."[82] Every year on May 15, Mercury's birthday was commemorated by traders in a lavish ceremony:

> Thus the *Ides* of May became a festival for traders (*mercatores*) and Mercury's temple the center of their guild (*collegium*). Ovid [43 B.C.E.–17 C.E.] . . . refers to an aqua Mercurii . . . a spring or fountain . . . from which a merchant would draw water in fumigated jars; with this water he wetted a laurel bough and then with this he sprinkled the goods he had on sale as well as his own hair.[83]

During the early Roman Empire, particularly the peaceful and prosperous Augustan age (c. 43 B.C.–18 A.D.), Roman commerce was at its height. This period was characterized by market-oriented agricultural production, an increase in the demand for luxuries, more regular issue of Roman coinage, and a free movement of trade both nationally and internationally.[84] Farmers and craftsmen produced for the market; they would sell their produce and buy what they needed at periodic markets, *nundinae*, so called because they were held every ninth day—a different day in different cities to provide for more trading opportunities.

The Romans built permanent market halls, *macella*, where people could buy their foodstuffs. Wholesale customers frequented Forum Boarium for cattle, Forum Holitorium for vegetables, Forum Vinarium for wine, and Forum Cupedinis first for delicacies and later for more general provisions. Monumental market buildings were constructed: the Macellum Liviae by Augustus, the Macellum Magnum by Nero, and the Mercatus Traiani by Trajan.[85] As merchant stalls gave a commercial feel even to regular *fora*—open spaces in Roman towns where various religious or civic activities were conducted—with surrounding streets lined with shops and stalls.[86] Economically, Rome was at a level that was not only unprecedented but also would not be matched until early modern times. As Temin puts it:

> From an economic point of view, the important characteristic of the early Roman Empire was the relatively large role played

by market forces, certainly as compared to the medieval economy that would follow. Large-scale production and movements of resources in the early Roman Empire were dominated by markets. This mode of organization promoted the exploitation of comparative advantage, helped by political stability, personal security, and widespread education. It also promoted a modest rate of economic growth that resulted in the prosperity of the early Roman Empire, which was not to be equaled in the West for almost two millennia thereafter.[87]

It is from this period that much of the market evidence stems.

It may at first seem surprising that evidence of price records from an economy as advanced as ancient Rome is so scarce. But while the Babylonians recorded prices on clay tablets, ancient Romans used wax-covered wooden oblongs—a highly perishable medium. What did survive are occasional inscriptions of important transactions in stone, as well as papyral records from Egypt. However, despite the dearth of direct evidence, researchers generally agree that the Roman Empire was a true market economy.[88] An extensive study by Duncan-Jones on the economy of the Roman Empire finds that capital, labor, and goods all had prices,[89] and referring to commodity prices such as wheat, wine, and donkeys, Rathbone notes that they were "basically formed by the operation of free-market forces, that is, the fundamentals of supply and demand in a monetized economy."[90]

Because free-market prices contained information about the supply of and demand for goods, "it would be strange indeed if farmers and craftsmen operating in this context did not take prices into account when planning their activities," writes Temin.[91] He goes on to elaborate that "Roman prices, in other words, contained information about the availability of goods and even about the advantage to be gained from selling [the] farmer's own produce."[92] This suggests that ancient Romans were making inferences about profit opportunities based on past prices, which is precisely what technical analysts do today.

It is not hard to imagine that prices exhibited a seasonal pattern, since in those days news traveled from Rome to Egypt at different speeds during different seasons: What took weeks in good weather took months in the winter. In fact, Temin points out that the available scattered data are consistent with such a seasonal pattern and notes that due to the seasonality effect, "arbitrage could not have equalized prices in Rome and Egypt in any short period."[93] In other words, arbitrage opportunities could be identified based on seasonality patterns in the price data; with this in mind, it is hardly inconceivable that market participants engaged in a form of cyclic analysis resembling that used by technicians today.

Negative Attitudes toward Traders

In ancient times, traders and bankers—indeed, all who avowed the profit motive—were universally despised. In ancient China merchants were hardly recognized as men, living at the very bottom of the social hierarchy. And as we will see in the next chapter, certain kinds of medieval merchants were routinely suspected of "having killed and skinned any cat that was missing."[94] While the ancient Greeks deemed farmers moral and suitable to be generals, traders were viewed as greedy, dishonest, and unreliable—one source notes that "merchants can pile up money, but that does not qualify them to be generals."[95] Traders were not considered trustworthy, as Xenophon's Socrates explains while offering advice about choosing whom to have as friends:

> "What about a good businessman who is determined to make a great deal of money and so always drives a hard bargain, and who enjoys getting money but is reluctant to hand it over?"
> "In my view he is even less desirable than the last."
> "What about the man who is so dedicated to making money that he has no time for anything that won't be profitable?"
> "He should be avoided, in my opinion; he will be no use to anyone who associated with him."[96]

A passion for making money was considered a deep character flaw that evinced poor control over one's emotions and an amoral willingness to exploit others for one's own profit and to lie freely—"and there is no form of behavior that is less noble than lying."[97]

Wealth should not be seized; the wealth that comes to us from the gods is far better. If a man acquires great wealth through violence or force, or if he steals it through his words, as often happens when a man's mind is clouded by the desire for gain and dishonor tramples down honor, the gods soon deal with him.[98]

Despite their social outcast status, traders themselves were proud of what they did and even celebrated their profession on their tombstones.[99] Although the social criticism presented above was directed at traders in general—referring to technical trading no more than it does to fundamental or speculative kinds—it goes to show how deeply ingrained in the human mind anti-trading attitudes were. In the rest of this volume, we will shed some light on why so many remain attached to technical analysis to this day.

Chapter 2

The Middle Ages and the Renaissance

Between the fifth and the nineteenth centuries technical analysis became a truly global phenomenon. Price charts became widespread in the West; Chinese merchant manuals advised their readers to learn to predict changes in the price and availability of goods based in part on market cyclicality; and Munehisa Homma developed the Japanese version of technical analysis based on candle charts, which remains popular to this day worldwide. Such progress in technical analysis was a result of the rise of exchanges and the maturing of the merchant class. It was also related to softening societal attitudes toward investing and speculation. As modern sensibilities emerged, contempt for traders gradually turned into tolerance and eventually respect. Medieval Italian merchants at first learned to disguise the sinful loan at interest as something permissible, such as a bill of exchange. By the seventeenth century Japanese traders would greet each other with "Are you making a profit?"

And by the mid-nineteenth century in Europe it came to be seen as socially irresponsible *not* to engage in financial markets.

Western Europe

Middle Ages

Medieval Europe made great strides in warfare, but most other fields of science, technology, and learning were stagnant or slow to evolve. Luckily, trade and financial activity did not stagnate; rather, they provided a crucial force of movement, change, cultural flourishing, and economic prosperity. Soon there were two worlds existing side by side, one traditional, the other forward-looking. The traditional world "was the world of masters and apprentices, of innumerable workshops where a humble crowd of artisans, usually unlettered and uncultivated, produced for a market restricted to the limits of one city or one quarter, using as a medium of exchange the coins of the *piccoli*. It [was] a world . . . in which the intimate satisfaction of doing artisan-like work, and sometimes of creating a masterpiece, substituted for the satisfaction of the material well-being."[1]

On the other side of the spectrum was the world of the merchant-bankers, "the world of the avant-garde, consisting of companies dealing with international trade, of rich warehouses piled high with costly goods, where sophisticated and cultured men with long experience, bold views, and unbounded ambition conducted commercial and financial dealings with the main economic centers abroad and handled not only the golden florins but the moneys of all other countries."[2] However, it is important to realize that only a small elite could be properly described as "avant-garde." The commercial world of the Middle Ages was far from monolithic, and in fact the contrast between traveling merchants and their sedentary colleagues was as sharp as the divide between the traditional and the forward-looking forces of medieval society itself.

The least sophisticated among traveling traders were peddlers, who traveled alone, possibly with a horse, and sold a wide variety of commodities on their way. For illustration, a thirteenth-century French peddler declared that, among other things, "he had girdles, gloves, cords for viols, needles, thimbles, purses, veils, arrow points of iron, buckles,

Medieval merchants depicted on a fifteenth-century stained glass window in the cathedral of Tournai.

pins of brass and silver, kerchiefs of linen for young beaux and of hemp for clowns, rolling pins, brooches, cowbells, tablets and pens for clerks. For ladies' toilets he had razors, tweezers, mirrors, toothbrushes, toothpicks, combs, rouge, and powder, . . . and for men he had dice, including two which when thrown fall on the aces."[3] More sophisticated were the traveling merchants, who dealt in raw materials, food, livestock, manufactures, and Eastern imports. Their goods were significantly more valuable than those of a peddler; hence, to protect themselves, when frequenting the fairs they traveled in armed groups rather than individually. More sophisticated still were the sedentary merchants. As the name suggests, sedentary merchants were stationed at a city office or a warehouse—the headquarters of their international businesses—while their partners traveled for business. For example, an Italian sedentary merchant, Dantini of Prato, conducted business with many of the Italian cities, Spain, France, Bruges, London, North Africa, and the Levant, exporting and importing a diverse list of products including spices, arms, armor, cloth, religious ornaments, fruit, wool, and handkerchiefs. Like other sedentary merchants, Dantini of Prato communicated with his agents via the slow and imperfect means of land mail, receiving an average of 2,400 letters per year.[4]

Though markets and fairs became one of the defining characteristics of medieval commerce, they have been a familiar fixture of culture and civilization since the earliest times, as we saw in Chapter 1. Just as in the ancient civilizations, where buyers and sellers gathered outside temples, in early medieval Europe they gathered in churchyards after Sunday services. The church, however, found this practice disrespectful and decreed that markets be held on weekdays at specifically designated places such as town streets or squares.[5] With time, markets became numerous and well established—being held twice or thrice per week with different hours allotted to different articles and moving to protective market halls in bad weather. As Fontana notes, markets grew into "one of the most important elements of the basic urban framework."[6]

While markets served local populations, fairs provided periodic meeting places for distant traders. Fairs could only be founded by a territorial prince, so unsurprisingly they were usually held in small, sleepy towns rather than in densely populated ones. Present in many countries, they dealt in wholesale rather than retail business, lasted several days or even weeks, and were held yearly or half-yearly. With few exceptions, such as the fair of Saint Denis near Paris, which went back to at least 629, fairs broadly emerged in the eleventh century and flourished during the subsequent two centuries.[7] Though never specialized, fairs were often celebrated for a particular article. So by the eighth century the St. Denis fair became known as the wine fair, by the ninth century the Novgorod fair came to be renowned as the fur fair, and the Venice Christmas fair was famous for its variety of exotic spices from India. The fairs' international flavor is well illustrated by Heaton's description of the Sturbridge fair near Cambridge, where "there for three weeks were gathered English wool or cloth merchants, Venetians and Genoese with oriental and Italian wares, Flemings with cloth and metal goods, Spaniards and Frenchmen with wine, Greeks with currants and raisins, and Hansards with fur, amber, and tar."[8]

The most famous fairs were those held in Champagne, their golden age running from 1150 to 1300. Located midway between Europe's two most highly developed economic regions—northern Italy and the Low Countries—the Champagne fairs were held almost continuously, rotating throughout the year among the towns of Provins, Troyes, Lagny, and Bar-sur-Aube.[9] The fairs were highly organized, with the counts of Champagne and the church protecting traders, providing them with guides on the roads, and building cellars to protect their goods.[10] The following quote by Clough and Cole vividly captures the spirit of a typical Champagne fair:

> At the beginning of the fair, eight days were allowed for unpacking. Then in regular order came special *divisions* as they were called. First, for twelve days were sold textiles— linens, woolens, tapestries, carpets from the Levant, cloth from Flanders, silks from Italy, cottons, muslins, velvets. At the end of the period the sergeants went about crying "Hare! Hare!" ("Pack up!") and the cloth fair was closed, only to be followed by eight days for the sale of leather, skins, and furs. During these periods there were also carried on transactions in goods sold by weight—wool, flax, silk, dyes, drugs, spices, sugar, grain, hemp, lard, cheese, salt, fish, meat—and likewise

in cattle, horses, sheep, and swine. Then began the fair of
the money changers and brokers, who sat behind their tables
weighing out gold and silver, examining strange coins, making
loans, and collecting their debts. Meanwhile the local inhabitants were profiting by the sale of food, drink, and lodging,
and enjoying the busy and festive atmosphere. Jugglers, danc-
ers, clowns, minstrels, men with tame bears, swarthy men with
monkeys amused the fair-goers, native and foreign alike.[11]

Merchants would spend the closing days of the fair clearing accounts
and settling debits and credits, which made the fair look very much
like a clearinghouse. Moreover, the Champagne fairs played an important role in the development of credit, with people buying or borrowing at one fair and promising to pay or repay at a later one. Their
promise was guaranteed by a fair letter or *lettre de foire*.[12]

Fairs and the merchants who pumped Europe's wealth through
them were one of the main catalysts for the fading of the medieval
mindset and the emergence of modern perspectives on human life and
activity. Trade and finance required fluency with numbers and knowledge of precise scientific methods, as well as of foreign languages—
particularly French, which, thanks to the popularity of the Champagne
fairs, was the lingua franca of business. Thus the merchant class was vital
in instituting lay education in the Middle Ages, putting an end to solely
monastic education and the use of Latin in business and private life.[13]

Fairs remained a symbol of European commerce for centuries
to come—until the transport and communications advances of the
Industrial Revolution led to their decline and replacement by produce
markets or exchanges, which stayed open year-round on a daily basis.[14]

The Renaissance

By 1660 Europeans had discovered the New World and the route to the
Far East around the Cape of Good Hope. The West was also penetrating
into Russia and other Slavic lands. "To no other society in history had
a whole world been opened for its exploitation," writes Nussbaum.[15]
The exploration and conquest of distant lands not only extended
European markets overseas, but also incited rivalries between the nascent nation states, which were rapidly replacing the myriad medieval

Counting money from behind their counter, these two Tuscan bankers are a reminder that many bankers grew out of simple money changers.

provinces, dukedoms, and city-states. Competition flourished as each state sought to retain revenues from the merchant class and thereby consolidate its position at home and abroad. Economic prosperity and population growth came hand in hand. The old business centers like Venice, Florence, Milan, Lisbon, and Antwerp were soon eclipsed by new, bigger ones—Amsterdam, London, and Paris, and even the colonized cities of Mexico, New York, and Boston. Bustling with activity, the Renaissance urban landscape was soon defined by grand boulevards complete with street lighting, specialized retail shops, opera houses, luxury hotels in major cities, convenience stores even in villages, and a network of roads and highways crisscrossing the continent—thus creating ideal conditions for the efficient conduct of business.[16]

In fact, "growth in trade and urbanization are nearly equivalent expressions," writes Rosenberg, for at a time when communications were slow, gathering in a single urban market was crucial.[17] The existence of a single urban market led, in turn, to the development of trading institutions such as the maritime insurance markets and bourses of Amsterdam, Paris, and London. Meanwhile, the ballooning volume of business contracts and conflicts prompted the development of commercial law. Urbanization put enormous pressure on local markets. Whereas in the Middle Ages peasants would bring their produce to local markets, in the Renaissance middlemen of all sorts would visit peasants at their homes and buy their produce for speculation and consumption.

Bills of exchange came into being in medieval Italy when merchants started writing them to each other instead of dealing in cash to facilitate large transactions. They also became popular in Renaissance Holland. Soon, less-reputable merchants realized that by depositing money with their better-known colleagues they could draw on it when writing bills of exchange. The merchants who accumulated such deposits realized, in turn, that only a fraction of the deposits needed to be available for withdrawals at any given time, while the rest could be lent out at interest.[18] It did not take long for deposit banks to come into being, with the Bank of Amsterdam, founded in 1609, and the Bank of England, founded in 1694, rising as the most prominent examples.[19] Such banks not only encouraged individuals to save and invest, but also increased the supply of capital available to merchants, thereby fueling economic growth. The bourse—the "meeting-place

On March 23, 1575, Lyons-based Lodovico Benedito Bonbisi and Co. sent this letter to Francisco de la Pressa and the heirs of Victor Ruys at Medina del Campo (who received it three weeks later on April 13) to settle their bills of exchange. The settlement calculations (sums), as well as exchange rates in various cities, are shown at the bottom of the letter.

of bankers, merchants and businessmen, exchange currency dealers and
bankers' agents, brokers and other persons"—was another institution
for which Amsterdam was famous.[20] Originating in 1409 in the city
of Bruges, the bourse got its name from the Hotel des Bourses next
to which it was located; the hotel itself was named after the van der
Bourse family and decorated with that family's coat of arms, which
included three purses or *bourses*.[21] Together with the bank, the bourse
became a defining feature of the Renaissance economy.

Frontispiece of *Le Parfait Négociant* by Jacques Savary, 1675.

La Bourse de Londres.

The London Royal Exchange, originally published by Pieter van der Aa, 1707.

The interior court of the Amsterdam Exchange. Painting by Emanuel de Witte, oil on panel, 1653.

Technical Analysis

Middle Ages

The cutthroat, venal, competitive environment of medieval fairs provided a breeding ground for speculative activities.[22] One of the main actors in the medieval money market was the banker. Initially a simple money changer, he frequented the fairs where he used to erect his *banca* (bench or table) and exchange local coins for foreign ones. He later started handling deposits, lending deposited money as well as his own, and allowing depositors to withdraw money with prior notice. Depositors were awarded interest or a share of any profit a banker made on their money. Bankers also began transferring money from one man's account to that of another. Bankers assumed these functions surprisingly early in the development of capitalism; in Genoa, for example, all this was taking place by 1200.[23] While the initial purpose of banking was to facilitate trade, by the fourteenth and fifteenth centuries it was becoming more and more purely financial and speculative. Testimony of this can be found in the accounts of the great merchant bankers of the day, in which the volume of money business greatly exceeds that of trade.[24] By that time, money markets were truly governed by the demand and supply of money and were also subject to seasonal and cyclical fluctuations. For example, the cycle of *strettezza* and *larghezza*—the contraction and expansion of credit—was well established. Exchange rates themselves were governed by these fluctuations, as well as by the rate of concealed interest and speculation, among other things.[25] Given the prevalence of market cyclicality ideas at this time, it would be strange indeed if they had not been used to infer future prices based on patterns and trends in recent price movements.

As business practices grew more complex, business methods had to grow more systematic. The adoption of Arabic numbers in the twelfth century was a big step forward because they tremendously simplified calculation. In the fourteenth century, double-entry bookkeeping was developed in Italy and then spread to northern Europe. Manuals of business instruction were compiled in Italy between the thirteenth and the fifteenth centuries. Like their ancient Greek and Roman counterparts, these manuals instructed merchant-bankers about the locations of markets and fairs, transportation, commodities traded, and customs of local populations. In addition, these new manuals had a significant quantitative component, describing weights, measures, different currencies and exchange rates, business techniques, and accounting methods.[26]

One important such text was *Liber Abaci*, written in 1202 by the famed mathematician Leonardo Fibonacci of Pisa, who as a young boy was introduced to trading by his merchant father. In addition to introducing Arabic numbers to the Western world and developing the numerical sequence that bears his name, Fibonacci described a variety of commercial arithmetic methods such as calculating present value, compounding interest, evaluating geometric series, converting measures and currencies, and pricing goods in complex ways.[27] Among their many applications, Fibonacci numbers—originally developed to solve a problem about the population growth of rabbits—would later become the mathematical basis for the Elliott wave theory, a standard part of a modern technician's toolbox.[28]

Another unique manual of business instruction is *Memoria de tucte le mercantile*, believed to have been compiled by a Pisan merchant or notary in 1278. In addition to a comprehensive collection of weights, measures, and prices, it included an unconventional feature—a lengthy astrological appendix—which Lopez describes as follows:

> Such a close connection of spices and stars does not occur in any other manual, and it certainly gives food for thought. After a strictly businesslike directory of weights, commodities, and tariffs, which *mutatis mutandis* would fit the most rational commercial handbook of our time, we are suddenly thrown deep into the Middle Ages. No doubt it was known that astrology played a great part in the decisions of princes, clergymen, philosophers, and physicians; but it did not readily occur to our mind that it might influence so strongly an ordinary merchant.[29]

Lopez suggests that merchants might have made their purchasing decisions according to forecasts of the following nature: "If the calends of January fall on a Sunday . . . grain will be neither cheap nor expensive. If they fall on a Monday . . . there will be plenty of grain. If they fall on a Tuesday . . . grain will be dear. . . . Libra: it is good . . . to buy and to sell, for this is a token of air. Virgo: . . . buy, sell, begin anything, for this is a token of land."[30] This was hardly typical; the trove of documents left by the great families of merchant-bankers such as Datini and Medici do not include astronomical references. The *Memoria* manual seems like a throwback to ancient Babylon, when, as mentioned in the Introduction and elaborated on in Chapter 1, commodities were assigned to the astrological regions of Pisces and Taurus depending on whether they were bullish or bearish. But given that this was only an appendix of an otherwise modern and quantitative manual, it is doubtful that medieval merchants based their decisions to buy or sell on astrology alone. Like the ancient Babylonians, they probably used astrology as just one input for their decision making alongside past price data, current news, and market sentiment.

The Renaissance

As early as the mid-sixteenth century there had been speculation in grain futures in Amsterdam. The earliest list of price quotations from the Bourse dates back to 1585; later, shares of great companies—the East India Company, founded in 1602, and the West India Company, founded in 1621—were traded on the exchange. In the early seventeenth century herring, spices, and whale oil, as well as grain, were objects of speculative trading.[31] This period also saw the advent of purely financial speculation in company shares, which included transactions in options and in futures: "One sees that without possessing actions or even a desire to acquire any, one can carry on a big business in them. . . . The seller, so to speak, sells nothing but wind and the buyer receives only wind."[32]

Manipulation was rampant from the start: "We hear of a ring of Amsterdammers who bought up whale products and forced up prices, of an attempted corner in Italian silks, one in sugar, another in perfume ingredients, another in saltpeter, another in copper."[33] Associations of bearish investors such as the one led by Isaac Le Maire, made scandalous, if not criminal, efforts to depress the prices of shares. The striking volume of speculation at the Bourse of Amsterdam was due to the participation of numerous small speculators, rather than just big capitalists. The following quote by Joseph de la Vega describes how they functioned:

> Our speculators frequent certain places which are called *coffy-huysen* or coffee-houses because a certain beverage is served there called *coffy* by the Dutch and *caffé* by the Levantines. The well-heated rooms offer in winter a comfortable place to stay, and there is no lack of manifold entertainment. You will find books and board games, and you will meet there with visitors with whom you can discuss affairs. One person takes chocolate, the others coffee, milk, and tea; and nearly everybody smokes

while conversing. None of this occasions very great expense; and while one learns the news, he negotiates and closes transactions. . . .

When a bull enters such a coffee-house during the Exchange hours, he is asked the price of the shares by the people present. He adds one to two percent to the price of the day and he produces a notebook in which he pretends to put down orders. The desire to buy shares increases; and this enhances also the apprehension that there may be a further rise (for on this point we are all alike; when the prices rise, we think that they fly up high and, when they have risen high, that they will run away from us).[34]

De la Vega's bull, who pretends to write down the orders, is not only all too well aware that the fear and greed of market participants determine the price level, but also that it is a natural part of human psychology to use past prices as an indicator of future ones.

It is not only the sheer volume of speculation, but also its sophistication, that stands out about the Bourse of Amsterdam. Speculative techniques were abstract, ingenious, and distinctly modern; a spectacular description is provided by Joseph de la Vega's 1688 text entitled *Confusion de Confusiones.* One of the most interesting examples of speculation is the famous tulip-mania that occurred in 1633–1637 in Amsterdam. Imported into Western Europe from Turkey, tulip bulbs were traded in flower beds if they were common and individually if they were rare. Later they were also traded in the form of future bulbs or outgrowths still attached to the mother bulb, which were particularly risky because it was uncertain that they would develop properly when planted.

Because of their scarcity and beautiful colors, tulips were valuable from the start; for example, in 1624 a single Semper Augustus bulb cost $480, or 1,200 florins.[35] Until 1634 trade was limited to professional bulb growers, but thereafter the market attracted people from all walks of life—Posthumus cites weavers, spinners, cobblers, bakers, and other small tradespeople.[36] Novice speculators became members of organizations called *colleges.* They met in public houses where they ate, drank, and made deals. One could soon trade not only by the piece or the pound, by also "in the wind" and "on the grow," thus rendering speculative possibilities virtually unbounded. Differences in buy and sell prices were astounding. For example, a pound of the Witte Croonen tulip bulbs, which cost $50, was sold for $1,440 about a month later.[37] Close to the boom of 1636 most transactions had no basis in goods— "the seller selling bulbs he did not have against a counter value, mostly money at this period, which the buyer did not possess"—and by the autumn of 1636 the market collapsed.[38]

Just like investors today, seventeenth-century investors were at the mercy of their own irrationality. The tulip bulb mania has become a textbook case of how forces of irrationality can drown out those of rationality over extended periods of time. Moreover, it shows that history matters and that the particular path that market prices have taken over the past few years influences current aggregate risk preferences— in other words, the investors caught in the bubble were experiencing, if not consciously applying, the basic belief of technical analysis that past market action carries predictive value.[39]

With the emergence of bourses, the possibility of making and losing large amounts of money in an instant became a reality for many. As a result, it became more urgent than ever to develop methods for measuring and predicting market action. For example, "dealing in commodities in Antwerp [was] a risky business for anyone not able to follow the market from hour to hour and even for those who did so," notes Ehrenberg.[40] It was under such conditions that around 1540 Christopher Kurz, an Antwerp commodity trader, developed a technical trading system based on astrology. Though himself an astrologer by background, Kurz was critical of the profession and tried to distinguish himself from it by backtesting his signals using historical data: "For our astrologers aforetime have written much, but with little reason: wherefore I trust not their doctrines, and when I have them, I search in the histories whether it hath fallen out right or wrong."[41]

Irrespective of how diligent Kurz's backtesting may have been, the idea of basing price forecasts on astrology, or calling Kurz a technical analyst for that matter, may sound absurd to modern ears. However, in the sixteenth century, astrology was a way of life. Ehrenberg notes that in Kurz's time "astrological prognostication flourished in the Netherlands; there were prophecies of every kind which were reproduced in print"—and, in fact, Kurz counted Lienhard Tucher of the highly influential Tucher merchant family as his client.[42] Describing Kurz's system and the seriousness with which he was taken by his most important client, Ehrenberg writes:

> Christopher Kurz had puzzled out an astrological system by which he could foretell prices. He praised his invention to the Tuchers, mixing sober business statements with fantastic combinations in a way that seems absurd to us, but which probably at the time gave quite a different impression. . . . Lienhard Tucher made marginal notes on the reports Kurz sent which prove that he read them carefully and did not fail to observe the prognostications.[43]

Kurz engaged in price forecasting of commodities, such as cinnamon, nutmegs and cloves, and bills, which he claimed to be able to forecast up to twenty days in advance:

> In the same manner, I have known how to show for the matter as touching cinnamon, nutmegs and cloves . . . likewise with bills can one hap on many a good chance. As ye have often noted in my writings to you how great an alteration is there here day by day in bills on Germany, Venice, or Lyons, so that in the space of eight, ten, fourteen or twenty days with other folks' money, a man may make a profit of 1, 2, 3, 4, 5, or more percent, with such there is here each day great business on the Bourse. On these also have I my experiment so that I may foretell not only from week to week the Strettezza and Largezza (tightness or ease in money), but also for each day and whether it shall be before midday. I have, however, nigh forgot this again, since I have found you so reluctant.[44]

As Poitras points out, Kurz's claims not only have the same imprecise flavor of present-day technical statements but also refer to the same technical principles—for example, Kurz's cycle of Strettezza and Largezza echoes the technical tenets that history repeats itself and that prices often move in long-persisting trends.[45] Moreover, Kurz was combining his technical insights with fundamental information—recall his use of what Ehrenberg describes as "sober business statements"—as many technical analysts do today.

Bourses stimulated another important development related to technical analysis: the emergence of price charts for visualizing the market. In the 1830s, price lists became regular parts of newspapers and price charts of stocks, commodities, and interest rates came into existence, mainly in France and England, but also in Bavaria. Their purpose then, as now, was to capture the "abstract entity called 'the financial market,' 'the stock exchange,' or 'la bourse,'" which is "disentangled from its anecdotal ties to the particularities of the marketplace"—in other words, to analyze the stock and not the company.[46] Charts took a variety of forms: portable foldout charts, extra-large charts to be hung on walls, black-and-white charts, or color charts. Charting was so prevalent that some people—including William Stanley Jevons, James Vansommer, James Wyld, and Hamer Stansfield—went into the business of producing sophisticated price charts and selling them to various offices.

Charting was also advanced: Rather than plotting a single asset at a time, chartists would often engage in what modern technicians would call intermarket analysis; for example, Wyld would superimpose corn, money, and bonds on his charts for over half a century. As Preda explains, charts "were at once a representation of (financial) markets as dynamic entities, an instrument for analyzing them, and a tool used in market operations," and it was through them that "the market had developed a history, from which its future could be inferred: it could be decomposed into movements that could be compared."[47]

Societal Attitudes

Middle Ages

Religion was a dominant force at all levels of medieval society, including the economic ones. The Catholic Church taught that the purpose of life was to secure a place in Heaven by following church teachings; all other areas of life were subordinate to earning salvation. Unfortunately for traders, the church frowned on the making of money: According to the just-price doctrine, it was wrong to sell a thing for more than it was worth, and according to the usury doctrine, charging interest on loans was a mortal sin.[48] In fact, Dante Alighieri placed the usurers of Cahors in the inner ring of the seventh circle of hell in Canto XVII of his *La Divina Commedia*—lower than murderers.

Nevertheless, conniving traders found ways to circumvent the doctrines of the church—for example, a bill of exchange purchased at a price lower than its face value was said to reflect the counterparty risk rather than interest.[49] Despite the threat of damnation, traders were constantly tempted to speculate; even when they shared the church's views intellectually, being merely human they faced temptation with every operation they undertook. For example, they would often buy up the peasants' grain and other produce or intercept goods on their way to the market, only to resell them at a higher price or hold them to limit the supply, thereby cornering the market. Such speculative activities were especially condemned when they involved food, for in those days famine was a real and constant threat. In fact, *forestalling* or buying up goods before they got to the market, *engrossing* or cornering the market, and *regrating* or buying goods with the purpose of reselling them at a profit were considered cardinal business sins not only by the church, but also by the guild of merchants, since they were disadvantageous not only for consumers, but also for other merchants.[50]

With time, however, the church began to recognize that prices were governed by the laws of supply and demand, and that the costs associated with missing a profit opportunity and bearing risk justified the practice of usury.[51] A striking illustration of the changing attitudes of the church is found as early as the thirteenth century, when Pope Nicholas III threatened Archbishop Peckham of England with excommunication unless he paid the interest he owed to some Italian bankers.[52] By the fifteenth century, the very word *usury* changed its meaning from "interest charged for loans" to "*excessive* interest charged for loans," as can be seen in Saint Antoninus's (1389–1459) proclamation that "it was sometimes permissible for a seller to charge as much as 50 percent more than the fixed price."[53]

Renaissance

"In 1660 Europe was in revolution. At no time in its brief history as a society had any generation stood to the future with an orientation so distinct from that of its ancestors," begins Nussbaum in his book *The Triumph of Science and Reason*.[54] For two thousand years before the purpose of natural science had been to serve religion; in the seventeenth century its purpose became to master the material world, which was now assumed to be rational and distinct from the world of God. It was during this period, often called the Age of Reason, that Descartes declared that man, not Earth, was at the center of the universe, and Newton explained the world with a set of mathematical principles.[55]

Just as the scientific revolution of the Renaissance emphasized the individual, so the Protestant Reformation of the sixteenth century put moral responsibility on the individual. It reduced the authority of the church, and provided a moral system based on thrift, hard work, and promise keeping, ushering in an ethos that was better suited to the rise of capitalism than that of Catholicism.[56] As Rosenberg and Birdzell put it, "religion was gradually transformed from a restraining influence upon capitalist development to a force that both sanctioned and supported mercantile capitalism by precisely the moral teachings required for the smooth running of the rising commercial system."[57] In fact, the Grain Act of 1663 legalized forestalling and regrating, two of three cardinal sins of the Middle Ages (engrossing remained illegal), thereby encouraging speculative activities and free trade.[58] A century later, a visionary by the name of Adam Smith would set the competitive spirit completely free to thrive.[59]

Social attitudes toward trading continued to soften to the point where by the mid-nineteenth century it became not only socially acceptable to invest but also desirable. One reason for this change in attitude was the general belief that financial markets promoted national wealth; for example, media in France would encourage citizens to participate in financial markets by suggesting that the British had a more advanced economy because their financial markets were better developed.[60]

Another reason was that financial markets were viewed as a mechanism capable of uniting the bourgeoisie and working classes into a single "investing class," thus promoting social harmony. In this respect, Preda quotes Lefevre as having said in 1870 that "when all citizens learn to invest, everyone will benefit; stocks and stock trading are in fact answers to serious social problems, since they create common property."[61] He further notes that the 1863 edition of *Shareholder's Circular and Guardian* advocated that participating in financial markets was in one's personal and reproductive self-interest, for one's long-term well-being depends on his wealth.[62] In fact, the relationship between trading and morality became redefined at this time: "It was morally questionable *not* to engage in these activities."[63]

By the mid-nineteenth century financial speculation was thought of as "one of the great four principles of wealth production, along with work, capital, and trade; moreover, it is situated above the other three and unifies them."[64] The market was now seen as a living, breathing being that could be visualized, understood, dissected, and analyzed; as Preda eloquently explains: "Stock price lists and charts provided an overview of the market, in the most concrete sense. Financial markets were not difficult to grasp, made of a myriad of gossips; they could be pointed at and were entities with a history and their own life but were also related to external events. It is not by mere chance that investor manuals abounded in biological metaphors when describing financial markets."[65]

Chapter 3

Asia

As we saw in the previous chapter, during the Middle Ages and the Renaissance, "survival of the richest" became a dogma of the nascent European capitalism. Trading was considered a wealth machine that improved longevity and reproduction rates, and, in cutting across class lines, promoted social harmony. The societal embrace of trading did not materialize in medieval and renaissance Asia to the same extent, despite its technological superiority (for example, the Chinese invented the printing press and used it to print money at least three centuries before Europeans). Some reasons for this divergence are cultural. For example, in Japan the progressive culture of idea sharing was lacking, and trading know-how was tightly guarded within families. Other reasons are political—Asian merchants had to work against governments that were far more oppressive than those in Europe.

More often than not, when faced with counterproductive government policies, merchants found a way to circumvent them. When, in the sixteenth century, Hideyoshi Toyotomi came to power in Japan and put an end to the currency economy introduced by his predecessor, merchants resolved not to let it cripple commercial activity. They devised sophisticated methods, such as technical analysis, to trade and analyze markets; as a result, markets became more vibrant than ever before. And despite the fact that medieval Chinese merchants acted more as government representatives than their own independent agents, their activities brought splendor to Chinese cities that awed Marco Polo, who immortalized it in his travelogues. It is this "can-do" attitude of merchants that gave rise to the commercial revolution and technical analysis in medieval and renaissance China and Japan.

Japan

The development of technical analysis in Japan was closely related to the emergence of the country's rice exchanges, which in turn were shaped by the country's political unification in the late sixteenth and early seventeenth centuries. The sixteenth century in Japan is known as *Sengoku Jidai*, meaning "age of country at war"—a reference to the virtually continuous period of warfare between feudal lords that racked the country for almost 150 years.[1] Beginning in the late 1500s the country was at last unified under a centralized feudal system by generals Nobunaga Oda, Hideyoshi Toyotomi, and Ieyasu Tokugawa.

Nobunaga, the first of the three generals to take charge, is credited with abolishing the monopolies of guild-like organizations known as the *za* in order to liberalize commerce.[2] He is also credited with having tried to establish a currency economy in Japan. To this end he imported Eiraku coins from Ming China; however, the currency economy did not last long.

In his quest to replace the money market with a rice market, Nobunaga's successor, Hideyoshi, invited merchants to Osaka—a new castle town he considered the geographical center of Japan—causing Osaka's population to grow from 70,000 to 170,000.[3] This increase in population brought on an unexpected rice shortage, and at Hideyoshi's request, local lords from many different parts of Japan sent rice to Osaka. The incoming rice first had to be graded based on its quality, and then distributed.[4] This gave rise to a rice market, which was set up in the yard of Hideyoshi's "war merchant" Yodoya Keian.[5] The demand and supply of rice at Yodoya's yard rice exchange largely depended on weather, which was often unpredictable; as a result, speculation became more and more refined.[6]

During the subsequent long reign of the Tokugawa family (1615–1867), Osaka developed into a great commercial center. It grew into the national storehouse and a distributor of supplies and became known as the "kitchen of Japan." While merchants continued to belong to the lowest social class in other parts of Japan, in Osaka they came to dominate the social scene. Commercial activity was so destigmatized that people began greeting each other with *mokarimakka*, meaning "are you making a profit?"[7] By the late seventeenth century Yodoya's front yard exchange was institutionalized to become the Dojima Rice Exchange, which was located in downtown Osaka. The exchange soon counted 1,300 rice dealers. Until 1710, trading was done in actual rice. The year 1710 saw the introduction of rice coupons or futures contracts, which became a huge part of the national economy. For example: "In 1749, there were a total of 110,000 bales . . . of empty rice coupons traded in Osaka. Yet, throughout all of Japan there were only 30,000 bales of rice."[8]

Technical Analysis

One of the greatest speculators from this time, also considered the father of Japanese technical analysis, was Munehisa Homma. Known as the "god of the markets," Homma was born in the port city of Shonai-Sakata in 1724 to an extremely wealthy family. In 1750 he gained control of the family business and began trading in rice futures at the Sakata rice exchange. Later in life Homma worked as a financial consultant to the government and was made a samurai. He died in 1803.[9] Homma's writings are treasured by traders and historians alike, not only for their wisdom, but also because they represent rare documentation of early Japanese technical analysis; as Okamoto points out, Japanese technicians of Homma's time seldom publicly disclosed their knowledge, preferring to keep it a family secret.[10]

Market Psychology

Homma's writings bear a close resemblance to those of Charles H. Dow and his successors. For example, Homma noticed that traders' emotions significantly influenced the price of rice, and he concluded that "the psychological aspect of the market was critical to his trading success."[11] Thus he began "studying the emotions of the market," which he believed "could help in predicting prices."[12] Similarly, as Russell points out, Dow's "observations concerning the emotions of the crowd and the movements of stocks form an intricate part of [Dow] Theory."[13]

Dow's is not the only present-day theory that stands on the shoulders of Homma. In his 1755 book *The Fountain of Gold—The Three Monkey Record of Money*, Homma also wrote, "When all are bearish, there is cause for prices to rise. When everyone is bullish, there is cause for the price to fall." As Nison suggests, these ideas closely echo the commonly used Neill theory of contrary opinion, rediscovered by Humphrey B. Neill two centuries after Homma in his 1954 book *The Art of Contrary Thinking*.[14] Moreover, Homma understood the importance of market information and its effect on crowd psychology, and hence on prices. A communication network he developed stands as testimony to this. Homma would post men on rooftops four kilometers apart, forming a chain between Sakata and Osaka, and the men would exchange signals by waving flags.[15]

Trends

The accord between the technical wisdom of today and that of Homma's time is astounding. In *The Fountain of Gold*, Homma advised speculators to "buy when the share price declines and [to] sell when it rises,"[16] which is equivalent to Hamilton's advice that "speculators should learn to take losses quickly and let their profits run."[17] It not only embodies the idea that prices move in trends, but also implicitly assumes that a trend, once established, tends to remain in force. Both of these ideas are important tenets of the Dow theory. Homma also wrote, "to learn about the market *ask the market*—only then can you become a detestable market demon,"[18] which is essentially the "market discounts everything" principle of Dow theory.

Homma went on to describe the rotation of Yang, or bullishness, and Yin, or bearishness. As Nison clarifies, "this [rotation] means that within each bull market, there is a bear market, and within each bear market, there is a bull market,"[19] which is strikingly similar to the ideas Dow presented in his famous editorial "Swings within Swings" almost a century and a half later. Moreover, comments such as "volume has declined considerably" show that Homma paid attention not only to price, but also to volume, further revealing the sophistication of his technique.[20] Later, Dow considered the relationship between volume and price in his editorial that appeared in the March 7, 1902, edition of *The Wall Street Journal*.[21]

Candle (Candlestick) Charts

The earliest predecessor of the candle chart was the stopping chart, also known as a point, line, or star chart. The name derives from the fact that it only plotted closing prices, which were connected with a straight line. Next came the pole chart, which was essentially a series of vertical poles, each pole representing the period's high-low range. A bit more advanced was the bar chart, which plotted a vertical line representing the high-low range for each period under consideration and then, to the right of that vertical line, added a short horizontal line to indicate the closing price.

More advanced yet was the anchor chart, so named for its resemblance to a ship's anchor. According to legend it was invented by rice traders who used to gather in port cities during the Kyoho era. As in a bar chart, an anchor chart plotted a vertical line depicting the high-low range of each period under consideration; in addition, for each high-low range it indicated the opening price with a short horizontal line and the closing price with an arrow. The arrow would point upward when the open was below the close and downward in the opposite case.

The candle chart was an improved version of the anchor chart. Just like the anchor chart, the candle chart plotted the vertical high-low range as well as opening and closing prices. While an anchor chart indicated the inequality between opening and closing prices with an arrow, a candle chart indicated this through color: The real body of the candle was white when the open was below the close, and black otherwise.[22] Many candle chart patterns are named after military terms—such as "night and morning attacks," "advancing three soldiers pattern," "counter attack lines," and the "gravestone," to name a few. Given the pervasive martial character of the society, the prevalence of such metaphors is not at all surprising.[23]

It is natural to wonder why such advances in technical analysis were developed in feudal, agrarian Japan over a century before they were re-discovered in the scientific, industrializing West. What was the key to the innovativeness of early Japanese technicians? Part of the answer can be gleaned from Hiroshi Okamoto's description of *The Fountain of Gold*—namely, the analytical method of technicians like Homma must have had a strong ring of normal discourse. Their method boiled down to "Buy when the share price declines and sell when it rises." The low price was judged not by some index or indicator but by certain cir-cumstantial evidence. This is where normal discourse steps in. The key was how to assess the "bearish atmosphere all around." It is remarkable that Homma was able to make a comment like "Volume had declined considerably," because volume is a modern-day analytical judgment, and in Homma's day there were no statistics available.[24]

This implies that the early Japanese technicians possessed great skill because of their connection with the reality of the markets, and not because of their statistical expertise. As Rhea noted, "statistics are, of course, valuable, but they must always be subordinated to a view of the market . . . as those who confine themselves to statistics as market guides have never proved to be true prophets. . . . Mark Twain is once supposed to have said, 'There are three kinds of prevari-cation: lies, damn lies, and statistics.'"[25] Perhaps early technicians were so innovative precisely because they were not hindered by statistics.

In view of the striking similarities between the Japanese and the American versions of technical analysis, another natural question is whether the American version developed independently or was some-how borrowed from its Japanese predecessor. Okamoto believes that the latter is true, and adds that the rice market in Osaka opened many years before the United States even won its independence in 1776.[26] Nison further suggests that Western charting methods, where bar charts are prominently featured, are less evolved than their Japanese counterparts, for the bar charts in Japan were the precursors of candle charts.[27]

China

The origins of Chinese markets can be traced back millennia to the "Commentaries" of the ancient *Book of Changes*, also known as the *I Ching* or *Yijing*:

> When the sun stood at midday, the Divine Husbandman held a market. He caused the people of the world to come together and assembled the riches of all under Heaven. These they exchanged with one another and then returned home, each thing having found its appropriate place.[28]

However, it should be noted that before the foundation of the Ch'in Empire in the third century B.C., commerce was somewhat less important in China than in other ancient civilizations.[29] It was only around the third century B.C. that trade began to flourish and a merchant class appeared in China.

The merchant class matured between the eighth and the thirteenth centuries (late T'ang and Sung). During this period China's economy experienced unprecedented growth and established socioeconomic patterns that would remain largely unchanged until the nineteenth century. China's spectacular economic expansion can be chalked up to several factors, including rapid population growth and a variety of technological advances. Innovations especially relevant for merchants were the abacus—which came into use during the late Sung—and printing. Printing was initially used to produce important books, such as a whole Buddhist sutra in 868 and all of the classics by the mid-tenth century, and later to make the world's first paper money.[30]

But the most obvious reason for China's medieval economic boom was the expansion of trade, which promoted greater local specialization and led to increased production. Even the traditional Chinese contempt for trade softened during this time.[31] While during the early T'ang the government still tried to control commerce and restrict it to designated government marketplaces, by the late T'ang such restrictions had been loosened.[32] It was at this time that village markets and fairs arose. Since the official government markets were few and largely inaccessible to peasants, it is not surprising that unofficial markets were set up in the villages to cater to the peasant population. Known as empty markets, periodic markets, mountain markets, rural markets, small markets, morning markets, early markets, village markets, and hay markets, these markets were held every few days for a few hours early in the morning.[33]

In contrast to the local orientation of village markets, fairs were typically associated with long-distance trade and specialized items from faraway places.[34] Also known as temple markets, fairs were frequently held near religious objects and in conjunction with religious ceremonies. Altars of the local spirits, where people would not only pray and make sacrifices but also set up plays and other entertainment, and the gatherings of Buddhists and Taoists are but a few examples of the types of events around which the fairs would be set up to sell candles and other ceremonial and ordinary items.[35]

Some of the most famous fairs of the Sung were the celebration of Buddha's birthday, the festival for the deliverance of hungry ghosts, the birthday of the Hill-god, the Buddhist festival of the five intelligent beings, the Peak fair (the Southern Peak was one of the five sacred mountains of China), the lantern fair, and the medicine and silkworm fairs.[36] In connection with the lantern fair, *The Gazetteer for Kuei-chi* reported at the turn of the thirteenth century:

> Merchants come from more than ten nearby prefectures and from beyond the seas. Jades, white silks, pearls, rhinoceros horns, renowned perfumes and precious medicines, silk damasks, and goods made of lacquer and of cane pile up like mountains or clouds, dazzling the eyes of the onlookers. Buddhist books, famous paintings, bells and tripods, ritual vessels, and amusing rarities also make their appearance here.[37]

From very early times, at least since the time of the Chin dynasty (265–419 A.D.), there were brokers. Brokers would compose a contract between the buyers and sellers involved in a transaction, collect taxes and commissions, and report transactions to the government.[38] There were brokers for all sorts of goods "from curios and perfumes to charcoal and sites for burial."[39] In addition to their brokerage businesses, they also frequently owned inns, stores, and warehouses, and would often buy up goods as they came into the market and engage in speculation.[40]

Merchants and brokers had their own esoteric argot and specialists' jargon. In *A Further Collection of Miscellaneous Items* (*Tsa-tsuan hsu*),
written in the twelfth century, Wang Chih highlighted this issue with
the following humorous lines:

> Without guarantee: the solemn assertions of brokers
> Hard to understand: the market talk of agents
> Impossible to fool: someone who really knows how to bargain
> Incomprehensible: the jargon of the various trades
> Not to be trusted: a seller's assertion when he asks the price
> Unable to tell good from evil: a man watching a beheading
> who says brokers are fine fellows[41]

Inevitably, the economic revolution led to the urban revolution
and the growth of large cities.[42] Chinese cities of the thirteenth century
amazed foreigners who came in contact with them, to say the least. Upon
encountering the city of Su-chou, Marco Polo wrote: "[Su-chou] is so

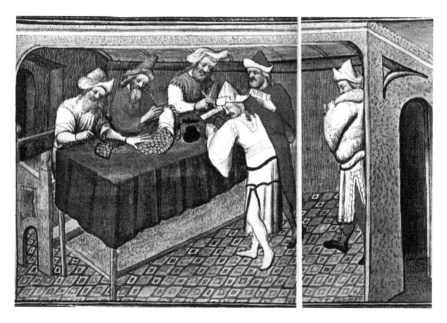

This picture from *The Book of Marvels*, a thirteenth-century French travelogue
commonly known as *The Travels of Marco Polo*, illustrates the delivery of gold to Kublai
Khan's countinghouse in Hang-chou.

large that it measures about forty miles in circumference. It has so many inhabitants that no one could reckon their number." And the former southern Sung capital at Hang-chou Marco Polo described as "without doubt the finest and most splendid city in the world."[43] Curiously, despite the fact that medieval China was, as Elvin puts it, "the most urbanized society in the world," Chinese cities were not centers of personal and political freedom. And in contrast to the merchants of medieval Europe—who were the main drivers of social and political progress— Chinese merchants operated in concert with the government, not against it. This is one of the important ways in which China diverged from the West during the Middle Ages.[44]

The merchant class reached its peak during the seventeenth and eighteenth centuries, a period when the number of market towns was increasing at a rate greater than that of the ever-expanding population. As the late Ming work *A Record of the Customs of Wu* describes:

> The large villages and famous towns all developed shops, which sold every kind of commodity, so as to monopolize the profits; and those who carried goods on their backs between towns and villages were all in distress.[45]

Market towns were formed around temples, manors of great landlords, houses of great merchants, pottery shops, customs houses, salt stores, and military stations. Not surprisingly, they were also found at fords and bridges and along major water and land routes. Many markets were founded intentionally, but markets were often set up spontaneously, too, such as in the wake of a bad harvest or plundering by rebels.[46] Although generally markets were held daily in urban centers and once or twice every 10 days in villages, the most advanced rural regions already had permanent markets at this time.[47] In any case, the extent of trade was truly astounding, as the following early seventeenth-century passage conveys:

> Throughout the prefectures, the departments and the counties of Kiangnan there are waterways everywhere. Everywhere there are local specialties. Everywhere there is trading. At the present time there are controls on all this. At the river ports of every county and prefecture even such commonplace arti-

Residents gather in the crowded streets and outdoor shops of the northern Sung capital to do business and socialize.

cles as rice, salt, chickens and pigs, and even such coarse ones as firewood, coals, vegetables and fruits are all affected. Every commodity is subject to a tax. Every person is subject to a tax. In no county is there one village at peace, and in no village is there one family at peace. People are being interfered with everywhere. Rich and poor alike are being molested.[48]

Precisely because the market mechanism was so good, merchants were generally not directly involved in the production process. For example, cotton cloth merchants would not invest in the cotton industry and tie up their capital, but would prefer to hold it in a liquid form such as cash. Consequently, they had no personal appreciation for how the products they were selling were produced and no interest in the innovation of the production process; in times of boom they would not benefit, nor would they be penalized in times of slump.[49] The fact that commerce and production were separated meant that the pressure toward technological innovation was extremely weak. As Elvin remarks, "there was less technological progress during this time than at almost any other previous moment in two thousand years of Chinese history," which he argues is at least part of the reason as to why China's dynamic and healthy economy did not produce a homespun version of the industrial revolution that emerged in Europe.[50]

Technical Analysis

The advanced state of the Chinese market system of the late imperial period (1550–1930) set the stage for the emergence of a well-defined merchant culture. Chinese merchants operated on the belief that the market "was not a mysterious force beyond control" but one that could be "understood, mastered, and manipulated."[51] Merchants placed great faith in the "free operation" of the market and in the "inevitability of favorable market conditions."[52] At the same time, educational manuals for tradesmen flourished, providing instruction not only on technical matters, but also on Confucian character training and personality cultivation. Indeed, technical and social skills were deemed closely intertwined, and aspiring merchants had to train both their mind and their spirit to "achieve 'inner mental attentiveness,' subdue selfish desires, distinguish good from evil, and practice reciprocity."[53] Benevolence, righteousness, propriety, moral knowledge, sincerity, caution, moderation, diligence, loyalty, courage, cultivating one's nature, *xing*, and nourishing one's vital spirit, *qi*, were all promoted in merchant education.[54]

Among the widely used manuals were *The Merchant's Guide* (*Shanggu bianlan*)—compiled by Wu Zhongfu in 1792 mainly from the earlier two manuals, *Essentials for Travelers* (*Fianghu bidu*) and *Essentials for Tradesmen* (*Gongshang qieyao*)—and *Encyclopedia for Gentry and Merchants* (*Xin'an yuanban shishang leiyao*), dating back to the late Ming.[55] In what follows we will consider some of them and highlight the similarities between the methods of late imperial Chinese merchant culture and present-day technical analysis.

Like technical analysis, the merchant manuals emphasized the cyclicality of markets and its role in accurate market timing. For example, *Essential Business* argues: "When goods become extremely expensive, then they must become inexpensive again. When they become extremely inexpensive, then they must become expensive again. This is the ultimate principle."[56] The same manual asserts that "no item will remain expensive for over one hundred days and no item will remain cheap for one hundred days," and that "when things reach an extreme, they will return the other way."[57] Similarly, *Encyclopedia for Gentry and Merchants* explains:

> Goods have their flourishing and waning and prices are not set. You must recognize that in the depressed market, upswings will also occur. When market prices are high, downturns are concealed. When prices begin to rise, anticipate a good time for selling.[58]

Yet another example is found in *The Golden Lotus*: "When the river is frozen, nobody buys rice. The price will go down again as soon as the ice melts."[59] As Lufrano suggests, this emphasis on market timing comes as no surprise if one remembers that ever since ancient times the Chinese have held the concept of timeliness as a central tenet.[60] In particular, the belief that time is cyclical, and that periods of order and economic growth alternate with periods of disorder and decline, can be traced as far back as *The Book of Changes*.

Another parallel with technical analysis is the importance the manuals attached to market information. *The Merchant's Guide* advises its readers to write letters so that they can know the "flow of goods everywhere" and thereby "know the information and opportunities in time and know what to do and what not to do."[61] Similarly, the author of *Essential Business* urges tradesmen to leave their shops from time to time and visit other tradesmen in order to acquire current information regarding prices, demand, and supply of goods on the local market, and also to seek news about the regions where goods are produced. The manual then cautions readers that not all market changes are genuine and advises them to analyze their information carefully. In particular, in order to determine whether the market change is genuine, one must weigh all the factors that caused the change. The degree of change is crucial as well: According to *Essential Business*, a large fall or rise in prices suggests that someone is manipulating the market and causing a false change. Market manipulation is further discussed in *Encyclopedia for Gentry and Merchants*, where tradesmen are warned to beware of gossip-mongering when acquiring information.[62] Yet more advice on the subject is provided in *Shishang yaolan*, which explains: "Whatever is priced low can be bought and hoarded. If you want to do this, you must have a lot of money; as soon as prices rise, you can gain a profit that will not be small."[63]

Just as some technical gurus teach their students that technical analysis is a tool for measuring supply and demand, late imperial Chinese merchants were given detailed instructions on how to watch supply and demand and use the imbalances to their advantage. The following quote from Lufrano illustrates this point well:

> When buying and selling goods, the experienced tradesman must pay attention to supply and demand. When few customers come to his shop and goods begin to accumulate, he is advised in one essay to stop buying and to wait for the market to bottom out. When many customers demand a certain product and his stock begins to dwindle, he is advised to buy. However, if goods are too expensive, the author explains in another essay, then the tradesman must wait until prices go down again to purchase them. If he anticipates a rise in prices, the manual counsels in a later essay, then he must buy large quantities of wholesale goods while they are still cheap. The author also encourages the reader to store his goods rather than sell them when their price is at their lowest and no profit can be earned. In yet another essay, the reader is urged to be sensitive to even small price changes, for eventually small increases will lead to large accumulations of money.[64]

Finally, some of the manuals emphasize proper execution of trading. According to *Shishang yaolan*, in the face of constantly changing prices, tradesmen must remain patient and self-controlled, and at the same time make decisions quickly, before it becomes too late.[65] Furthermore, an essay in *Essentials for Travelers* advises merchants to learn to predict changes in the price and availability of goods, though it does not develop the idea further.[66]

Chapter 4

The New World

I n late-nineteenth-century America a technological revolution swept over financial markets. Three innovations stand out in particular: the stock ticker, the telegraph, and the telephone. These three break-throughs in communications made time shrink, transforming the way business was conducted on Wall Street and solidifying an ethos of impartial, numerical representation of financial reality.

It was at this time that Charles Dow, the father of modern technical analysis, started publishing his so-called Dow Jones Industrial Average—the average price of the eleven most active stocks on the New York Stock Exchange—as an objective barometer of the stock market and the economy. Thanks to the contributions of Dow and his successors, technical analysis evolved into a scientific endeavor—complete with data gathering, hypothesis testing, and mathematical rigor. It emerged, moreover, as a respectable, bona fide profession, distinct from gambling. The technologically transformed market reality required permanent presence in the marketplace and constant vigilance, long study, and careful scrutiny of the stock price movements; in other words, market analysis became a full-time, skill-based occupation.

Inevitably, an esoteric form of market analysis based on astrology quickly sprang up in the shadow of the new economic science. Of course, this new pseudo-science was no more a part of true technical analysis than an amateur inventor's quest to design a perpetual motion device in his garage is part of serious physics research. Such odd hybrids of rationalism and mysticism will always be with us, so it is important to keep the crackpot theories separate from the legitimate ones.

Despite society's growing orientation toward science and the future, the scientific stance assumed by technical analysis did not immunize it from skepticism and mistrust; curiously enough, technical analysis remained associated with the very market-manipulative operations it aimed to detect and protect against. We suggest that technicians were the victims, not perpetrators of pool operations, and their tools were not only honorable but also forward-looking, socially responsible, and ahead of their time.

Wall Street

The first European settlement of New York dates back to 1621, when Dutch colonists established the colony of New Netherlands with New Amsterdam as its capital.[1] It was the Dutch who first laid out Wall Street. The municipal boundary where Wall Street would soon run was initially hedged by a brush fence whose purpose was to keep hogs and goats in the city and Native Americans out.[2] The "practical and unpretentious" town of New Amsterdam was blessed with "the largest and finest harbor of [the] North Atlantic."[3] Thanks to the Dutch emphasis on fair trade, New Amsterdam became the crossroads of commercial routes connecting Europe with the riches of the New World. Truly it was "the perfect spot for traders and merchants."[4]

In contrast, England's North American colonies were mainly agricultural. The early colonists were predominantly farmers who were attracted by the New World's abundance of good, cheap land; for most, manufacturing, mining, and entrepreneurship were nothing more than side interests. The English colonists tended to reinvest most of their surplus earnings into family enterprises and leave just a little for speculation in land or English bonds. New Englanders soon began to envy their Dutch counterparts. Now the citizens of New Amsterdam had two hostile groups to worry about: Native American tribes and their own British neighbors. Peter Stuyvesant, the governor of New Netherlands, decided that the brush barrier was no longer adequate, and in 1653 had the former replaced with a 1,340-foot-long and 12-foot-high wooden stockade. For obvious reasons, it soon became known as Wall Street.

In 1664 the British did indeed invade—although not by land as the Dutch had anticipated, but by sea. Taken by surprise, the Dutch surrendered peacefully under favorable surrender terms that allowed New Netherlands to continue doing business as usual. In particular, the British agreed that "all differences of contracts and bargains made before this day by any in this country, shall be determined according to the manner of the Dutch."[5] The *Articles of Capitulation* also stated that "any people may freely come from the Netherlands and plant in this country, and that Dutch vessels may freely come hither, and any of the Dutch may freely return home, or send any sort of merchandize home in vessels of their own country."[6] Elected Dutch officials were even permitted to remain in office. These gentle terms of conquest proved to be a highly intelligent move on the part of the British, because it allowed them to benefit from "the strong currency, secure banks, reasonable interest rates, and fluid markets of the Netherlands, one of the most advanced economies in the world."[7] However, to honor the duke who had financed their invasion, the British did require that the city be renamed New York immediately.[8]

As New York expanded, the wooden wall became useless and was torn down in 1698. In that same year the first Trinity Church appeared at the western part of Wall Street, and two years later a new city hall was erected close by. Wall Street's western end, flanked by Trinity Church and City Hall, became one of the city's most fashionable residential areas.[9] During the eighteenth century the Street grew into a colorful place. Among other things, it became a gathering place of pirates, with Captain Kidd himself residing at 56 Wall Street.[10] Merchants moved to the Street in the early eighteenth century. Slaves, "those staples of seventeenth- and eighteenth-century commerce," were the main commodity of interest at this early time.[11]

Later, in 1752, New York's first formal market came into existence when a group of merchants organized a meeting place for dealings in slaves and cornmeal. Held irregularly, it was located at the foot of Broad Street and later in Fraunces Tavern.[12] The Street was at first quiet, but later, as markets increased in number and coffee houses proliferated, it became the bustling center of the city. However, it should be emphasized that doing business in colonial America of the middle and late eighteenth century was not easy, as the country was highly heterogeneous. In particular, each colony had its own currency. Business between merchant traders could be conducted in British pounds, French francs, Spanish doubloons, or the new American dollars. Risky transactions required payment in gold or silver bullion. Colonial markets were not nearly as efficient as those of the mother countries, Britain and Holland, and many of the basic institutions were still lacking. Notably, the idea of an exchange "was slow in crossing the Atlantic."[13]

Until the establishment of a strong federal government in the 1780s following the American Revolution, there were no full-time financial markets in North America. The reason is simple: There were few, if any, financial instruments to be traded. Then, in 1789, the Constitution came into effect, George Washington was inaugurated at New York City Hall, and Alexander Hamilton was appointed the first secretary of the treasury. Hamilton would emerge as one of most important figures on the fledgling nation's financial scene.

Hamilton argued that "one of the primary purposes in establishing a strong central government was to give people faith in the financial structure of the country and in the soundness of the currency and financial instruments of the government."[14] He managed to convince Congress that the first natural step toward realizing this aim was to refund the debts it had incurred during the Revolutionary War; new federal bonds were soon issued for that very purpose. As Gordon explains, the significance of these new issues was twofold: First, they constituted a body of "rock-solid" securities that could be traded, and second, they greatly diminished the cloud of uncertainty in which the country had been enveloped, and "it is uncertainty—far more than disaster—that unnerves and weakens markets."[15] Hamilton's efforts also established "a vital precedent for the future of Wall Street: that the United States Government would stand behind its financial instruments and not repudiate them for political reasons."[16]

This precedent played a critical role in the establishment and growth of the country's financial markets. Philadelphia, then the country's largest city, became the nation's capital in 1790. It was in Philadelphia that Hamilton established the first United States Bank, which he modeled after the Bank of England. Even after the federal government moved to Washington, the bank stayed behind. Philadelphia became the banking center of the nation, and in 1800 became the home of its first real stock exchange.[17]

Soon after the new federal bonds (or "stock" as they were then called) and state bonds came into existence, they began to be traded.[18] Initially the trade was handled by commodity brokers who would meet on Wall Street or an adjacent street, such as Pearl; later, these brokers

Under the buttonwood tree. Museum of the City of New York, Buttonwood diorama.

began to specialize in trading securities. When the weather was nice, their favorite meeting place was the shade of an old buttonwood tree at 68 Wall Street; in bad weather, they sought refuge in nearby coffee houses. "And thus, for all its present marble magnificence, the New York securities market began very humbly indeed in the heat and rain and dust of a village street," writes Meeker.[19]

At the same time, capital accumulation was taking place throughout the nation. Merchants and farmers continued to prefer to put their funds back into their shops and farms, rather than invest in companies. Given their "better a new piece of land and new tools than questionable pieces of paper" mentality, it is not surprising that both exchanges and brokers were widely deemed unimportant in those early days of the nation.[20] In fact, a trader who dealt only in securities was considered "either an idler or a fool."[21]

But fortunately for the nation, traders were not deterred by the low esteem in which they were held. In addition to being involved with bonds, these early brokers were heavily engaged in a variety of other activities, such as insurance, banking, and the sale of lottery tickets. They competed with each other fiercely, displaying a notable lack of business ethics. Early in May 1792 a group of prominent securities traders decided to put an end to their rivalry, organize their operations, and also unite against the auctioneers, whom they felt had too much control over the market. So on the 17th of May they gathered at Corre's Hotel and signed the agreement that among other things stated:

> We, the subscribers, brokers for the purchase and sale of public stocks, do hereby solemnly promise and pledge ourselves to each other that we will not buy or sell from this date, for any person whatsoever, any kind of public stock at a less rate than one-quarter of one per cent commission on the special value, and that we will give preference to each other in our negotiations.[22]

The Stock Market

The Corre's Hotel pact, better known as the Buttonwood Agreement, in effect established a guild of brokers. The first stock exchange agreement of any kind in this country, the Corre's pact is taken to have "inaugurated" the New York stock market.[23] The first meeting of the new market was held in the old Merchant's Coffee House. In the winter of 1792 the founding brokers decided it was time to construct a building of their own, so they erected the Tontine Coffee House at the corner of Wall and Water Streets.[24]

Despite New York's efforts to improve its commercial clout, Philadelphia was still the financial capital of the country. Philadelphia had supreme and more prestigious banks and got most of the European business. Rivalry between the two cities was fierce, with the Chestnut Streeters viewing the Wall Streeters' actions "with suspicion and distrust."[25] Convinced that Philadelphia's financial supremacy stemmed from its better-organized auctions, twenty-eight prominent brokers formed the new Board of Brokers (later renamed New York Stock and Exchange Board) with a constitution that was almost an exact copy of the Philadelphia charter.[26] This first constitution dates back to March 8, 1817.[27]

The New York Stock and Exchange Board was located at 40 Wall Street. There the board rented a meeting hall from George Vaupell, who furnished it with chairs, kept it clean, and provided heat in the winter for $200 a year.[28] The board was a "high-powered version of the Tontine," where "the easy informality of the coffee-house era" was gone.[29] New members were admitted to the board by vote. Applicants were viewed as potential competition, and three nays were sufficient to reject one. Also rejected were those who had been in the brokerage business for less than a year. Brokers were required to be present at each session—if they missed or interrupted a session, they were fined.[30] Some business ethics were enforced as well. Specifically, the constitution provided that "any member making a fictitious sale or contract shall, upon conviction thereof, be expelled from the board."[31] "Wash sales"—the sale of securities by one broker to another who acted for him or his client— were strictly forbidden. These had been used to give the impression that transactions had taken place when in reality none had occurred, the aim being to artificially simulate a bull or a bear market.[32]

The list of securities traded on the board was short and dominated by government bonds. Two formal trading sessions were held per day. The morning session, which was the more important of the two, would start at 10:00 a.m., with the presiding officer reading out the names of securities listed on the board.[33] Writing in 1870, James K. Medbery described the happenings of a typical session as follows:

> The assembled brokers with their budget of orders, wait expectant; and the instant a stock is reached that is in their day's book, they spring into the arena with a bid or an offer. When a "speculative" or favorite stock is called, the excitement deepens, and the air is rent with rival cries. The presiding officer repeats the transactions to the Assistant Secretary at his side, who at once records them, while the "marker," or blackboard clerk, writes off the prices upon the tablet at the head of the room.[34]

It is from this blackboard that the stock board derives its name. In fact, the past names of the New York Stock Exchange include the Regular Board and the Big Board.[35] In 1863 the New York Stock and Exchange Board changed its name to the New York Stock Exchange. At that time it was decided that the exchange needed to be housed in its own building, rather than in a rented one, and it had one erected at 10-12 Broad Street. The building's lavish style was a means by which the new Wall Street elite "displayed its material achievement" and "aligned itself with the new investment banker aristocracy in its competition for financial hegemony on the Street," Wachtel explains.[36]

Given the exclusivity first of the board and then of the exchange, it is not surprising that much of the business took place outside, and not only among the nonmembers. The members themselves traded there after hours and in securities that were not listed on the board. This outdoor exchange, also known as the curb market, was an "odd confabulation, whose roof was the sky, whose offices were in [brokers'] pockets, whose aspirations were boundless."[37] Some of these outdoor exchanges survived, others were absorbed by the board, but most of them "just withered away when the financial climate, or even the weather, turned colder."[38]

Though curbside brokers did their business outside, they would have a small rented office nearby. There, their recording clerks stood perched on windowsills, one foot inside the office, the other outside in good weather. Since brokers transmitted information to their clerks by hand signals, it was important for them to stand out in the crowd and be easy to recognize. They hence wore brightly colored hats and scarves. Oftentimes the curb would become so crowded that brokers would spill out into the streets and interfere with traffic. Conflicts with the police were not uncommon either. In 1872 *The Times* of London wrote about this "web of human life . . . woven in colors so glaring and diversified as to strike with painful effect upon eyes accustomed to the more subdued tints and graduated shades of European existence."[39]

In the 1860s, curbstone brokers, such as the ones depicted here, handled at least as many—and often vastly more—trades as their New York Stock Exchange counterparts.

In 1864 some of the curbers formed the Open Board of Brokers at 16-18 Broad Street. They became more organized and introduced rules for their innovative practices, which included admitting the public to the trading room as well as continuous and specialist trading. The curb and the Open Board became serious rivals to the New York Stock Exchange. In fact, the volume traded on the curb market would often greatly exceed the volume traded on the floor of the Exchange. On July 29, 1869, a mutually beneficial merger took place between the New York Stock Exchange, the Open Board, and the Government Bond Department (a specialized government bond exchange). By 1873 the merged entity had adopted many of the Open Board's innovative practices.[40] Despite this consolidation, new curb markets continued to spring up from time to time. As Wachtel explains, this was due to the conservative attitude of the New York Stock Exchange toward new companies, which consequently could be traded only on the curb.[41] The last surviving outdoor exchange, which at the time was known as "the Curb" and now is called the American Stock Exchange, was established in the 1920s.[42]

Floor of the New York Stock Exchange in 1894.

Merchants were drawn into the financial-services business from very early on. Many merchant bankers began their careers traveling in horse-drawn carriages and selling hardware and household goods. They would borrow money from individuals or small banks to pay for the goods and would repay the loans upon returning from their trips. However, it did not take long for these road roamers to realize that those loaning them money worked less hard and earned more. Hence, as soon as they had enough capital they would set up their own shops and become merchant bankers.[43] These new bankers were the early, primitive form of investment bankers and their shops the most primitive form of investment houses. By the 1830s, many new investment houses emerged to help investors trade shares and raise capital for new companies and entrepreneurs. For example, Nathaniel Prime, one of the early members of the New York Stock Exchange, established Prime, Ward and King in 1826 as a private bank. John Eliot Thayer established a similar institution in Boston around the same time, which later became Kidder, Peabody and Company. There were also Thomas Biddle and Company of Philadelphia, and Alexander Brown and Company of Baltimore. The new bankers would buy bonds from a company when they were first issued and either hold them as investments or arrange to sell them to other financial institutions for a small fee.[44] By the second half of the nineteenth century the investment banker in the true sense of the word had come onto the scene.

"The reigning monarch of Wall Street in the last quarter of the nineteenth century" was an investment banker by the name of J.P. Morgan.[45] In 1861 he formed J.P. Morgan and Company, which in 1871 merged with Drexel to become Morgan, Drexel, and Company. His favorite sectors were railroads, gold, oil, and steel. His business was based in a grand building he erected in 1873 on the corner of Wall and Broad Streets, which, incidentally, was one of the first in New York to have an elevator. Sometimes his actions were influenced by astrology, as was the case with many of his Wall Street predecessors. As Wachtel points out, "when not ruling over a financial world largely of his own creation, Morgan dabbled in the occult during his frequent consultations with the astrologer, Evangeline Adams."[46]

Though J.P. Morgan did not invent the concept of the trust form of organization—Wall Street lawyer Samuel C.T. Dodd is conventionally credited with its design—he is credited with establishing and popularizing it in the nation's railroad industry.[47] In an effort to eliminate the disputes among competing railroad owners, Morgan converted stock owners to owners of trust certificates, which he issued to them. In particular, stockholders gave up their control of the company, such as voting power, but retained their right to earnings from the ownership of the trust certificate; Morgan, for his part, would help the underlying companies when they were in trouble. This novel arrangement supported the growth of the American railroad industry, and in the late 1800s ultimately inspired Charles Dow to compute a separate market index for railroad stock—the so-called Dow Jones Transportation Average, often referred to as the "rails" in the early financial literature.

Impact of Technology

In 1866 the first permanent transatlantic telegraph cable was laid, connecting London and Wall Street. The following year a telegraph operator, Edward A. Calahan, an engineer of the American Telegraph Company, invented the stock ticker—a printing device for stock prices that could be transmitted via telegraph. The stock ticker connected the brokerage office directly to the floor of the exchange and provided data about prices in real time.

Before the invention of the stock ticker, keeping track of prices was a real problem for stockbrokers. Prices and transactions realized on the floor of the stock exchange had to be inscribed on little slips of paper, which were given to messengers or "pad shovers," who would literally run the slips from the exchange to the brokerage houses and back.[48] Among other drawbacks of this system, these courier-borne slips of paper were easy to lose and even forge. The first ticker, installed in the brokerage office of David Groesbeck in December 1867, "consisted of a stiletto, placed under a glass jar bell and powered by a battery, which recorded prices and company names on a narrow paper strip. . . . The ticker tape was divided in two stripes: the security's name was printed on the upper stripe, and the price quote on the lower one, beneath the name."[49] The stock ticker rapidly gained in popularity. The 1927 edition of *The Magazine of Wall Street* estimated that in the United States there were 400 tickers in 1890, 900 in 1900, and 1,200 in 1902,[50] while another publication estimated the existence of a striking 23,000 tickers in the United States in 1905.[51] The ticker was soon embraced by other markets and exchanges, too: The Gold Exchange placed on the front of the exchange building the so-called "gold indicator," a clock-like device displaying prices in real time,[52] and the bond market followed its lead by introducing the bond ticker in 1919.[53] Some New York City restaurants even had tickers in their dining rooms so their customers could follow the market and trade while they ate.[54]

Delmonico's restaurant, which counted brokers and speculators among its loyal customers, prominently displayed the stock ticker in its dining area.

In 1878—about ten years after the ticker came to the scene—the first telephone was installed at the New York Stock Exchange. The telegraph, the stock ticker, and the telephone "[pushed] the human brain's capacity to move information more quickly over space and to handle more of it," thereby revolutionizing the way business was conducted on Wall Street.[55] As Preda points out, these three inventions made time shrink, necessitating that orders be placed faster than ever before. As a result, brokers instructed their clients to communicate with them using special telegraphic code language; for example, the manual of the Haight & Freese brokerage house in Boston noted that the code words "army event bandit calmly" should be used to mean "Cannot buy Canada Southern at your limit. Please reduce limit to 23."[56]

Guglielmo Marconi, was a winner of the 1909 Nobel Prize in physics (shared with Karl Ferdinand Braun) for his contributions to the development of wireless telegraph. Marconi is pictured here with the radio telegraph system he invented for "telegraphy without wires," 1896.

"A major cognitive effect of the ticker was that it gave a decisive impetus to cognitive instruments and procedures like the chart analysis," explains Preda.[57] Charts had been commonly used in England and France since the 1830s, but the data charted were of very low frequency. With the advent of the ticker, monthly, daily, and even hourly charts became not only possible, but the norm. This gave rise to "tape readers"—clerks or brokers who would stand next to the ticker and record prices on a chart as they came out—and spurred the late-nineteenth-century financial magazines to regularly provide detailed hourly charts in their publications.[58] The ticker reinforced the scientific view of financial markets, so popular in the late nineteenth century, by bringing on what Preda calls "cognitive standardization"—everyone could see the same prices at the same time. This in turn led to the development of standardized analytical instruments (charts), standardized analytical language (technical analysis jargon), and standardized trading language (the broker's telegraphic code).[59] The scientific view of the financial markets encompassed brokerage business operations, as the advertising manual of one such firm illustrates:

A passenger standing on the observation platform in the engine-room of a modern ocean-liner will observe great masses of steel, some stationary, some whirling at terrific speed; he may go down into the boiler-room where is generated the power with which the great ship is driven, but all this will give him only a crude idea of the actual workings of the machinery of propulsion. He must know and be able to grasp all the component parts of that machinery, and their relation to each other, in order to appreciate what a tremendous undertaking it is to move this gigantic mass of men and materials over the watery miles separating two continents.

So it is with the machinery of a large banking and brokerage house. A client may spend many days in the customers' room, from which vantage point he will observe much, but his knowledge of the inner workings of the machine, built to handle orders in the various markets, must still be superficial. . . . Everything is run with clock-like precision. No matter how large a business is being done, there is no confusion, the plant being designed to handle the maximum volume of orders.[60]

Societal Attitudes

By the 1820s New York had become "the greatest boom town the world had ever known,"[61] the center of North American exports and imports, or, as Oliver W. Holmes puts it, "the tip of the tongue that laps up the cream of the commerce of a continent."[62] Application of the steam engine to the printing press made newspapers accessible to the masses. "It was the newspapers that unified the Victorian age," much as the Internet unifies ours.[63] More and more people from the nearby states as well as from Europe were lured to New York by the economic opportunities it promised, causing the city's population to rise by a factor of 20 between 1800 and 1860.[64]

The *nouveau riche*, or the newly affluent, came to dominate the Victorian age, to which they gave the character of "prosperity, social conformity, piety, hypocrisy, and a profound sense of progress in human endeavor."[65] Indeed, the culture of this new class left an indelible mark on both the appearance and the spirit of mid-nineteenth-century New York, much as corporate culture would in the twentieth century.[66] It was a culture that was conservative and socially insecure, which

George Stephenson's "Rocket," an 1829 locomotive with the steam engine, the epitome of nineteenth-century technological progress.

explains the preference of the nouveau riche for the "formidably uniform" row houses that came to dominate New York's streetscapes.[67] Gordon writes that "by the 1850s the Italianate style, with its brownstone front, elaborate bracketed cornice, carved lintels, high stoop, and double front door beneath a small but ornate portico was virtually the only style of row house being built."[68] It was also a culture that unreservedly embraced the gospel of wealth and considered striking a fortune a "sign of God's grace."[69]

The nouveau riche truly were obsessed with business. Crowds would gather for 10 hours a day on Wall Street, Broadway, and other downtown areas. "Neither the boulevards, the Strand, nor the Corso of Rome in carnival time can give an idea of this tumultuous movement," a French visitor noted at the time, pointing out that "our Parisian strollers hardly resemble this unpleasant, preoccupied, hurried throng which elbows its way among the trucks and carts."[70] Similarly, during his tour of North America in 1862 Anthony Trollope observed that "every man worships the dollar, and is down before his shrine from morning to night."[71]

Wall Street in 1866.

Customers from a variety of socioeconomic backgrounds visit a broker's office in the 1860s.

American writers, too, commented on their countrymen's grand obsession with money. For example, in 1872 American James D. McCabe wrote: "Here, [in New York], as in no other place in the country, men struggle for wealth. They toil, they suffer privations, they plan and scheme, and execute with persistency that often wins the success they covet."[72] In addition to money making, money gossip was of intense interest to the nouveau riche. The cost of everything, including people's houses, their net worths, and their taxable incomes, was published in newspapers, pamphlets, and guidebooks of New York.[73]

Around the same time, societal attitudes toward statistics and numerical representation of reality were changing. In eighteenth-century Europe and America many considered the census sinful, for it had been the devil's idea to count God's people in the Bible. It was also thought then that measuring a child's height would stunt his growth, and that taking medicine in measured dosages would nullify its healing ability. By the mid-nineteenth century, in contrast, "the economy became conceived as an enormous mechanism, operating with measurable and predictable regularity and expressible in various economic laws."[74] One of the main developments that contributed to this mental shift was the colonial expansion, which in the minds of European Christians juxtaposed the doubt of God's authority and the assertion of God's will, and brought to the fore "man's awesome powers of self-assertion."[75] The Europeans found relief and a way of "managing" their doubts (and ruling their colonies) in the physical sciences. Naturally they strived to represent economic reality in similar terms, but with experimental discovery replaced by empirical studies and statistics.[76]

In his 1862 address to the Statistical Society, British economist William Stanley Jevons argued that "all commercial fluctuations should be investigated according to the same scientific methods with which we are familiar in other complicated sciences, such especially as meteorology and terrestrial magnetism. Every kind of periodic fluctuation, whether daily, weekly, monthly, quarterly, or yearly, must be detected and exhibited."[77] Writing in 1871, he emphasized the importance of accurate data in this endeavor: "I do not hesitate to say, too, that Economics might be gradually erected into an exact science, if only commercial statistics were far more complete and accurate than they are at present, so that the formulae could be endowed with exact meaning by the aid of numerical data."[78] In his striving for impartial representation of economic reality, Jevons started collecting, tabulating, and graphically representing economic and financial data himself; he wrote that his purpose was "to ascertain and measure these great changes with some approach to certainty and accuracy, and to establish them as facts of observation. To explain or account for them is a matter which I do not undertake."[79]

The striving for impartial representation of reality meant that the financial news was to be supported by facts and numbers to the extent possible; after all, statistics were viewed as less biased than words and less prone to distortions. So in the first edition of *The Wall Street Journal* in 1889, Dow announced that the paper's mission was "to give fully and fairly the daily news attending the fluctuations in prices of stocks, bonds and some classes of commodities. It will aim steadily at being a paper of news and not a paper of opinions. It will give a good deal of news not found in other publications, and will present in its market article, its tables, and its advertisements a faithful picture of the rapidly shifting panorama of the Street."[80] That same edition was the first to publish the Dow Jones Industrial Average.[81]

The trend toward objectivity led the late-nineteenth-century financial newsletters to emphasize the distinction between gambling and speculation: The first edition of the *Financial Times* (1888) made it clear to its readers that it was "the friend of the honest financier, the bona fide investor [and] . . . the legitimate speculator" and the enemy of "the gambling operator."[82]

It was at that time that technical or stock analysis emerged as a respectable, bona fide profession; as de Goede explains, "the professional practice of the stock analyst and investor consisted of prediction and constant scrutiny of both the movement of stock prices and his own actions, which discursively protected him from accusations of gambling and idleness."[83] Technical analysis manuals, such as that by Schabacker, stressed that technical analysis and stock trading required "time, study, thought and planning . . . just as one would expect to do in any other type of business, and thus to make eventual and consistent profit a logical reward rather than an unmoral gift or luck," and that it was "the long study, careful analysis, the systemic planning that account for Mr. So-and-So's success."[84]

Moral responsibility, impartiality, and discipline were deemed necessary qualities in a technical or stock analyst; as a journal article of that time stated, a stock analyst "would have to stand on a plane with George Washington and Caesar's wife. He must have no connection with any bond house or brokerage establishment, and must permit nothing whatever to, in any way, warp his judgment. He must know all securities and keep actual records of earnings and statistics which show not only whether a security is safe, but whether it is advancing or declining in point of safety."[85] It is no coincidence that the emergence of technical analysis as a distinct profession coincided with the emergence of the stock ticker; now it was essential for a trader to have a permanent presence in the marketplace and pay constant attention to market events. As Preda sums it up, "the ticker durably bound investors and brokers to its ticks"—which could be accomplished only via a full-time occupation.[86]

Despite a growing scientific orientation in the conduct of business, early Wall Street operated almost entirely without regulation or oversight, and was a breeding ground for predatory practices. As Geisst explains, "without constraints, it was only natural that trading would become more predatory while American industry grew larger by the year."[87] Newspapers were often used as instruments for influencing public opinion. For example, manipulators would place unfavorable news in the press to help them corner shares cheaply as the price fell, then sell the shares later at a higher price.[88] Furthermore, traders would engage in "forward trading," whereby they would buy a stock at an arranged price and deliver cash for the transaction in a month or two, hoping that in the meantime the price would rise. When the time to finish the deal came, they would quickly sell at a higher price and make instant profit. Such contracts were quite common during the stock exchange's early years, despite the fact that they were not legally binding.[89] As previously mentioned, there were also "wash sales": Traders would conspire to buy and then immediately sell stock to each other at above or below market prices, thus manipulating prices to their own advantage.[90]

The abundance of predatory practices emphasized that the market was still immature, but fortunately the world did not lose faith. The major factor influencing American business expansion in the 1840s, as in the colonial period, was foreign capital, which "[continued] to flow into the country despite the shoddy treatment that some foreign investors received from the brokerage community and bankers."[91]

In the later nineteenth century, Darwinistic metaphors became deeply rooted in the zeitgeist, as did personal ruin and bankruptcy. The New York Stock Exchange and other regional exchanges became personal battlegrounds of the robber barons. The notion of survival of the fittest was reinforced by the role of war, particularly the Civil War, in American society.[92] Though the robber barons came from a variety of socioeconomic backgrounds, they had two things in common: a lack of formal education and a gift for exploiting the structural deficiencies of the financial system. Cornelius Vanderbilt, Fisk, Gould, Drew, and Russell Sage are but a few prominent examples.

The barons accumulated vast fortunes at the expense of others by the means of bear raids and corners and were considered social outcasts in their own time.[93] The state of affairs was worrisome to many, and in 1912 prompted the convention of the Committee for Banking and Currency in Washington—also known as the Pujo Committee— whose task was to establish whether the management of U.S. corporations and financial institutions was concentrated in the hands of a few financiers who had power to set prices and "to control the security and commodity markets; to regulate the interest rates for money; to create, avert and compose panics."[94]

Samuel Untermyer, the committee chairman, viewed speculation and price manipulation as one and the same, and opined that the problem they were facing could be traced to the advent of the exchange, which made it easy for brokers to execute their speculative orders and influence market prices. As he wrote in his 1915 paper presented at the *American Economic Review* conference, "the dealings on the Exchange have become mainly speculative and . . . prices are regulated, not by intrinsic values, but by the technical phase of the market created by the manipulation of the particular security by the big interests."[95]

The connection between technical analysis and price manipulation to which Untermyer alludes is legitimate in the sense that in its early stages the former was used as a tool for detecting evidence of the latter in the data. For example, Dow's theory of responses clearly delineates the progression of events by which the market is manipulated: A large operator who wants to advance the market first buys two or three leading stocks, then examines the effect this has on other stocks, in effect, seeking to determine whether the public is bullish or bearish, and whether the general market will follow the leading stocks. But to suggest that technical analysis was a tool for executing criminal pool operations is as absurd as the idea that the goal of software development is to perpetrate virus attacks. Technicians were as exposed as anybody else to the dangers posed by manipulative activities, and they learned to use their tools in defense. So Samuel A. Nelson, Dow's contemporary and follower, emphasized that "an operator should always keep in mind that big traders and bankers seek to manipulate the price by buying below value and selling above value," and hence "pay more attention to the value of the stock in which he is dealing, than to prices" in order to protect himself.[96]

What seems to have been lost in the annals of history is that technicians were the casualities, not the villains of pool operations, and their tools were honest means of detecting the danger in order to survive. And survive they did, growing in numbers and sophistication despite the skepticism and, in some cases, animosity of fundamental analysts, quants, and economists.

Chapter 5

A New Age for Technical Analysis

As we saw in the last chapter, at the turn of the nineteenth century the field of technical analysis was made concrete, formal, and even scientific. It was also made popular; Thomas notes that at that time "quite a cult of chartists mushroomed up who based their trading along technical lines."[1] (Technical analysts are sometimes called "chartists" due to their fondness for charts, plots, and diagrams.) The leading figure in this development was Wall Street legend Charles H. Dow. Dow got his start as a financial reporter for the *New York Mail* and *Express*, and then for the Kieran News Agency. He also worked as a broker and a floor trader on Wall Street. With Edward D. Jones he cofounded the Dow Jones and Company news service, and on July 8, 1889, Dow Jones and Company first published *The Wall Street Journal* with Dow as the editor.[2]

Known as the "father of technical analysis," in his editorials in the early 1900s Dow communicated his ideas about stock market dynamics and methods of stock speculation. After his death in 1902 Dow's ideas and observations became known as Dow theory thanks to the writings of Samuel A. Nelson. Dow argued that stock speculation is far removed from gambling, for it is based on the perception of a stock's value and of the underlying market movements.[3] "The market is not like a balloon plunging hither and thither in the wind," Dow used to say.[4] Rather, "it represents a serious, well-considered effort on the part of farsighted and well-informed men to adjust prices to such values as exist or which are expected to exist in the not too remote future."[5]

In this chapter we delve deeper into some of the specifics of Dow theory. We also introduce important theoretical and methodological innovations in market analysis that evolved around the same time as Dow theory and helped establish the full modern tool kit of technical analysis.

Dow Theory

At the core of Dow's theories is an understanding of human psychology and the effect it has on market prices. This may seem unremarkable nowadays, but in early twentieth-century America such thinking was well ahead of its time. "There is always a disposition in people's minds to think the existing conditions will be permanent," Dow wrote, and went on to say: "When the market is down and dull, it is hard to make people believe that this is the prelude to a period of activity and advance. When the prices are up and the country is prosperous, it is always said that while preceding booms have not lasted, there are circumstances connected with this one, which make it unlike its predecessors and give assurance of permanency. The fact pertaining to all conditions is that they will change."[6]

A defining element of Dow theory is the idea of a trend. In the January 4, 1902, edition of *The Wall Street Journal*, Dow communicated his famous principle of successive highs and lows as indicators of a trend: "It is a bull period as long as the average of one high point exceeds that of previous high points. It is a bear period when the low point becomes lower than the previous low points."[7] He further elaborated on the idea of trends in his editorial *Swings within Swings*:

Nothing is more certain than that the market has three well-defined movements which fit into each other. The first is the daily variation due to local causes and the balance of buying and selling at that particular time. The secondary movement covers a period ranging from ten days to sixty days, averaging probably between thirty and forty days. The third move is the great swing covering from four to six years.[8]

According to Hamilton, this observation *is* Dow theory; while other formulations of the theory may be broader, they all have this idea at their core.[9]

Dow implemented his ideas by computing the Dow Jones Industrial Average, which he published to enable traders to visualize basic market trends. The first averages appeared in the Dow Jones market letters in the early 1880s. As described in the previous chapter, they were made up of eleven stocks that were considered to be the most active and representative of the market as a whole; not surprisingly, nine of them were railroad stocks. According to Gartley's research, Dow began computing his industrial average in 1881, first mentioned it in his writings in 1887, and began publishing it regularly after January 1, 1897. At one point he began constructing a separate average specifically for railroad stocks (see Chapter 4); between 1884 and 1896 he would occasionally mention his railroad average, and he began publishing it regularly after November 2, 1896. Dow argued that the railroad and the industrial averages had to confirm each other for a signal to be conclusive in judging future trends. Later still, in 1929, an average for utilities came into use as well.[10]

Dow viewed the stock market as a natural system and likened the averages to a measuring instrument:

A person watching the tide coming in and who wishes to know the exact spot which marks the high tide, sets a stick in the sand at the points reached by the incoming waves until the stick reaches a position where the waves do not come up to it, and finally recede enough to show that the tide has turned.

This method holds good in watching and determining the flood tide of the stock market. The average of twenty stocks is the peg which marks the height of the waves. The price-waves, like those of the sea, do not recede at once from the top. The force which moves them checks the inflow gradually and time elapses before it can be told with certainty whether the tide has been seen or not.[11]

The averages were meant not only as a measurement of present conditions, but also as an indication of the future ones: "Within limitations, the future can be foreseen. The present is always tending toward the future and there are always in existing conditions signals of danger or encouragement for those who read with care."[12]

According to the theory of averages, in the long run, the number of advancing days for a stock approximately equals the number of declining days. In Dow's words, "if there comes a series of days of advance, there will almost surely come the balancing days of decline."[13]

The extent to which Dow's methods were precisely quantified is illustrated by his law of action and reaction, which establishes that after a primary market move there is generally a secondary move that retraces by a specific amount—at least three-eighths—of the primary move; the longer the primary (or action) move, the greater the secondary (or reaction) move.

The theory of responses demonstrates powerfully that Dow's methods were not short-lived, data-driven rules, but were instead measures of the fundamental reality of market dynamics. According to this theory, the market is always subject to manipulation in the following way: A large operator who wants to advance the market first buys two or three leading stocks, then examines the effect this has on other stocks. Based on the market's response the operator can determine whether the public is bullish or bearish and whether the general market will follow the leading stocks.

With "the intuitiveness of an artist" and "the analytical power of a mathematician," as Rhea would later write, Dow dissected the market organism and wrote about concrete methods for analyzing and forecasting its dynamics. He discussed these "methods of reading the stock market" in his editorials.[14] For example, in his July 20, 1901, editorial he provided one of the earliest descriptions of the so-called book method, which became known as figure charting in the 1920s and acquired its current name—point and figure—in the 1930s. On a point-and-figure chart, price changes are recorded in a succession of columns—ascending columns of x's when prices are rising and descending columns of o's when prices are falling—the column being changed when the price changes direction. If a stock stays within a narrow range (known as the trading range)—that is, after trending downwards (or upwards) it shows little to no price movement—it forms a long horizontal line, which indicates that the stock has been accumulated (or distributed) and that a reversal on the upside (or downside) is likely.

Credited with shaping the point-and-figure charts into what they are today, and using them in ingenious ways to apply and extend the Dow theory, is legendary trader and financial magazine publisher Richard D. Wyckoff. Wyckoff entered the business in 1888 as a 15-year-old "pad shover," but soon became a broker in his own right and a partner in numerous enterprises. By 1907 he was a publisher of the *Ticker Magazine*, later known as the *Magazine of Wall Street*. After his second wife Cecilia—dubbed by the media the "Prima Donna of Wall Street"—seized control of the magazine after he divorced her, he went on to found the Richard D. Wyckoff Analytical Staff, an investment advisory firm. Based on his own experience and conversations with the great speculators of his time, including Jesse Livermore, E.H. Harriman, James R. Keene, Otto Kahn, and J.P. Morgan, Wyckoff formulated the so-called Wyckoff method, for which he is now famous.

In a nutshell, the Wyckoff method is a use of bar charts and point-and-figure charts to study the supply/demand imbalances with the purpose of determining future price trends, and has the following three fundamental laws at its core. The first is the law of supply and demand: When demand exceeds supply, prices will rise, and vice versa, and the relationship between supply and demand can be gauged using bar charts that plot price and volume over time. The second is the law of effort versus results: When volume and price diverge, the price trend is likely to change direction; to measure the relationship between price and volume, Wyckoff developed his "optimism vs. pessimism" index, an on-balance-volume type of indicator (see Chapter 6). Finally, there is the law of cause and effect: The extent of the accumulation or distribution during the trading range (the cause) is directly proportional to the extent of the subsequent price move (the effect); point-and-figure charts are used to count horizontally the units of the cause, and project them into vertical units of effect. This method is used in virtually the same form by traders today, and since 1990 it has been a central part of the Graduate Certificate in Technical Market Analysis at Golden Gate University in San Francisco under the leadership of Henry Pruden, a contemporary expert of the method.[15]

Having amassed a vast fortune in the early 1900s, including a nine-and-a-half-acre Great Neck estate neighboring that of the General Motors boss Alfred P. Sloan, Wyckoff turned his attention to philanthropic and educational endeavors. So in 1931, he formed Richard D. Wyckoff Associates, which became the Stock Market Institute, one of the first institutions to rigorously teach technical analysis.

The ideas from Dow's editorials were compiled and organized by his publisher colleague and admirer Samuel Armstrong Nelson in his 1903 book *The ABC of Stock Speculation*. (Nelson had actually tried to persuade Dow to write such a book himself, but, as he used to say, his attempts were unavailing.[16]) It was in this book that Nelson first referred to Dow's work as Dow theory and elaborated on Dow's idea that market averages and stock prices in general serve as probes and metrics of the stock market and the broader economy: "Stock Exchange prices register values and the state of trade, precisely as a thermometer registers heat or cold."[17]

More generally, in his other two books, *The ABC of Wall Street* and *The Consolidated Stock Exchange of New York*, Nelson strived to represent market activity as emerging from a set of laws. Speculation, in his view, was governed by universal laws such as "never overtrade," meaning you should take a large interest if and only if you have large capital; "never double up," that is, always change your position cautiously and gradually; "run quick or not at all," in other words, take action at the first signs of danger, but otherwise hold onto at least a part of your position; and "sell down to the sleeping point," namely, when worried or in doubt, you should reduce the amount of interest.[18]

Despite his penchant for systematizing, Nelson never lost sight of the fact that human psychology played a big role in investing: While he considered the preceding laws absolute, he also recognized conditional laws, so called because they should be modified to suit a speculator's individual level of greed and fear, as well as his temperament.[19] Indeed, Nelson strongly emphasized that an operator's personality played a big role in his success. A successful operator must possess "the temperament and accurate and swift reasoning powers necessary to cope with the ablest money getters in the world."[20] He must be calm by nature and always seek to preserve "the balance of mind," since when "a fluctuation in the market unnerves the operator," then "his judgment becomes worthless."[21]

Dow theory was further championed by William P. Hamilton, a journalist who immigrated from England and joined *The Wall Street Journal* in 1899. As is evident from his writing, Hamilton enthusiastically embraced Dow's tenet that markets discount everything:

> The farmers say . . . "what does Wall Street know about farm-ing?" Wall Street knows more than all the farmers put together ever knew, with all that the farmers have forgotten. It can, moreover, refresh its memory instantly at any moment. It employs the ablest of farmers, and its experts are better even than those of our admirable and little appreciated Department of Agriculture, whose publications Wall Street reads even if the farmer neglects them.[22]

Moreover, Hamilton believed that the theory was universal and the principles underlying it were so sound that they held true for any market.

Hamilton not only organized but also expanded Dow's ideas. As Gartley pointed out, "the Dow Theory as generally understood was almost entirely the joint work of Dow and Hamilton."[23] In 1922 Hamilton published a book called *The Stock Market Barometer* in which he combined Dow's ideas with his own and put forth a method of predicting a stock market. In particular, Hamilton regarded the stock market as "the barometer of the country's and the world's business."[24] As he put it, "the sum and the tendency of the transactions in the Stock Exchange represent the sum of all Wall Street's knowledge of the past, immediate and remote, applied to discounting of the future."[25]

Hamilton argued that market crises were caused by "too much imagination" and underscored the need for "soulless barometers, price indexes and averages to tell us where we are going and what we may expect."[26] Essential to the predictive power of the barometer is the idea that speculation is based on expectations, rather than on com-mon knowledge: A bear market *anticipates* a contraction, whereas a bull market *anticipates* an expansion in business activities. As a Wall Street maxim puts it, "a movement is over when the news is out."[27] And it is precisely in the objectivity of the barometer where the key to its usefulness lies: "A barometer predicts bad weather, without a present cloud in the sky. It is useless to take an axe to it merely because a flood of rain will destroy a crop of cabbages in poor Mrs. Brown's backyard."[28]

In this light, Hamilton went on to praise Dow's stock market averages: "The best, because the most impartial, the most remorseless of these barometers is the recorded average of prices in the stock exchange."[29] Moreover, he noted that Dow theory is the best tool for reading this barometer. Hamilton is also known for his editorial, "The Turn of the Tide," published in the October 29, 1929, edition of *The Wall Street Journal* (shortly before his death) in which he correctly predicted the end of the great bull market of the 1920s.

Robert Rhea further systematized the theories of Dow and Hamilton. The son of a stock market speculator, Rhea was exposed to Dow's writings from a young age. Plagued by health problems since youth—first tuberculosis, then a plane accident that further damaged his lungs—Rhea spent the latter part of his life bedridden, where he continued to chart the stock market and study Dow theory. He was a Dow historian rather than an innovator. It was Rhea's understanding that "the element of independent judgment or 'art' . . . must accompany all Dow Theory interpretations."[30] Rhea published three books: *Dow's Theory Applied to Business and Banking* (1938), *The Dow Theory* (1932), and *The Story of the Averages* (1932). He also published a complete historical collection of daily charts of the Dow Jones averages.

One of Rhea's signal contributions was to reduce Dow theory (as interpreted by Hamilton) to a set of definite theorems and axioms. These axioms include the "manipulation" axiom, according to which day-to-day movement of the averages can be manipulated, the secondary reaction can be manipulated to a limited degree, but the main movement can never be manipulated; the "averages discount everything" axiom, which says that Dow Jones rail and industrial averages capture the fears, hopes, and knowledge of all market participants, and hence are able to anticipate future events; and the axiom that the "Dow Theory is not infallible," in other words, the market cannot be beaten.

Among the theorems, a special place belongs to the theorem of Dow's three movements. According to this theorem, there exist three distinct and simultaneous movements of the averages: a primary, a secondary, and a day-to-day movement. Primary movements, which refer to major bull and bear markets, are direct reflections of human psychology. For example, the primary bull market evolves in three phases: It starts when people become confident about a bright business future, becomes more pronounced when earnings indeed rise, and finally the top is reached as the stock prices continue to rise. But this rise is founded on hopes and expectations, rather than on value; as Rhea put it, "This is the phase where worthless stocks are bought for no other reason than because they look cheap and because gamblers hope they will double in price."[31] A secondary reaction, or retracement, refers to a significant decline in a bull market or to a significant advance in a bear market, lasting from three weeks to three months. Finally, Rhea advises that day-to-day movements should be charted because they usually develop into a pattern of forecasting value.

Other notable theorems include the "determining a trend" theorem, which says that highs terminating above preceding highs and lows terminating above preceding lows indicate a bull market, while the inverse is bearish; the "relation of volume to price movements" theorem, according to which an overbought market sees light volume on rallies and heavier volume on declines, while the reverse is true for an oversold market; and a theorem about individual stocks, which says that active and well-distributed stocks of great American corporations generally move in tune with the averages.[32]

Dow theory was subjected to a good deal of empirical testing and validation both by academics, such as Brown, Goetzmann, and Kumar (1998) (see Chapter 8), and practitioners, such as Richard Russell, a prominent contemporary Dow theorist. In his work *The Dow Theory Today*, a collection of twelve articles between December 1958 and December 1960, Russell examined market developments by applying Dow theory to current and historical data.[33]

For example, Dow had discussed the particular behavior of low-priced stocks—the so-called "cats-and-dogs" or "fancy stocks"—during a bull market. In 1899, near the peak of the 1896–1899 bull market, Dow wrote about "a perceptible increase in trading in fancy stocks" and noted that "this has not always been the best sign of a continued general upward movement for any great length of time, although it is certainly an accompanying feature of a bull market."[34] Seeking to generalize Dow's remarks, Russell studied the market action data from the 1900s to 1960s. He concluded that, in general, low-priced stocks often undergo significant advances during the third, final phase of a major bull market. Moreover, Russell used the market history to check the validity of Dow's 1902 statement that "when a stock sells at a price which returns 3.5 percent on the investment, it is obviously dear, except there be some special reason for the established price" and that "in the long run, the prices of stocks adjust themselves to the return on investment, and while this is not a safe guide at all times, it is a guide that should never be laid aside or overlooked."[35]

Russell observed that at the top of the 1929, 1937, and 1946 bull markets, the average yield of the Dow Jones industrials was 3.1 percent, 3.7 percent, and 3.3 percent respectively. He concluded that indeed, as Dow had established, the bull markets ended when the average yield on the Dow Jones industrials entered a zone of about 3.5 percent or less.[36] Russell further used historical market data to study the relationship of the Dow Jones Industrial Average to its own 30-week moving average. He concluded that, historically, the industrial average was always above its 30-week moving average in a major bull market and that the industrial average moving below its 30-week moving average for the second time was a sure bearish indication.

Many others have contributed to the Dow theory literature over the years. C.J. Collins, a Dow theorist of the 1930s, helped popularize the theory in his weekly market letter, *Investment Letters*, in which he regularly published his discussions of the technical aspects of the market interpreted in the light of Dow theory. His interpretations of Dow theory also appeared in *The Wall Street Journal*. Gartley recommended Collins's work to technical students, praising it as "clean-cut and dependable."[37] Also worthy of mention is Samuel Moment, who sought to reduce Dow theory to a set of precise and mechanically applicable rules and to thereby eliminate the subjectivity or "art" from technical thinking. In the process he greatly modified the theory, at one point even eliminating the premise that the averages must confirm. In fact, as Gartley suggested, "many followers of Dow feel that Moment has varied the Theory until the founder would no longer recognize it."[38] His most important reports are "The Dow Theory—A Test of Its Value and a Suggested Improvement" and "The Secondary Trend Barometer," both of which were published by Dunnigan's *Forecast Reports*.

Relative Strength

Although Dow theory is largely considered the foundation of the technical approach, other methods for reading and interpreting the market emerged around the same time and evolved in parallel with Dow theory. One of these is the notion of relative strength—a measure of how a stock is performing relative to other stocks in its industry. Though veiled, one of the first references to this concept is due to Nelson, who combined Dow's theory of responses with Dow's proposition that "value has little to do with temporary fluctuations in stock prices, but is the determining factor in the long run," to conclude the following:

> An operator should always keep in mind that big traders and bankers seek to manipulate the price by buying below value and selling above value. If the public follows the lead, temporary movements in the price of a stock occur. However, in the long run, it is the investor who establishes the price of a stock based on its value. An intelligent operator should pay more attention to the value of the stock in which he is dealing, than to prices. He should first study the general market conditions, and then examine the role his stock plays in the improvement or deterioration of those conditions. In this way he can determine whether the value of his stock is rising or falling.[39]

Nelson did not label his idea as relative strength; that distinction belongs to Rhea. In his article "Stock Habits," which appeared in the May 8, 1933, issue of *Barron's*, Rhea gave the first explicit discussion of relative strength in stock market speculation and explained how to compute and interpret the relative-strength ratio. In particular, he described it as the ratio of the price of a stock to the price of the market average; if this ratio is rising over time, then the stock is outperforming the market, and if a given stock consistently outperforms the market over a period spanning several market swings, then it is safe to assume that the stock will continue to outperform.[40]

Russell fully endorsed Rhea's conception of relative strength. He believed that technical analysis of individual stock charts had to be accompanied by relative strength analysis. He proposed the following relative-strength-based stock selection strategy:

> First examine the relative strength for different groups of stocks. Select the groups with best RS, preferably those characterized by a RS that is turning up after a long decline. From the groups selected in step 1, pick the stocks with the best RS. From the group selected in step 2, pick the stocks that exhibit best technical patterns and buy them. Constantly watch the RS ratio of the stocks you bought. Sell a stock when its RS line reverses.[41]

Market Cycles and Waves

Another development that evolved apart from Dow theory is the theory of market cycles. Seminal research in this direction was conducted by British economist William Stanley Jevons, who proposed his sun-spot theory in a series of papers published in the journal *Nature* between 1878 and 1882. Jevons's thesis was that economic cycles occur as a result of "the varying power and the character of the sun's rays."[42] Specifically, in his paper "Commercial Crises and Sun-Spots," Jevons analyzed two hundred years of English price data on corn, wheat, and other commodities, and documented a market cycle lasting on average 10.466 years. He wrote: "I am perfectly convinced that these decennial crises do depend upon meteorological variations of like period, which again depend, in all probability, upon cosmological variations of which we have evidence in the frequency of sun-spots, auroras, and magnetic perturbations."[43]

Charles Dow was a disciple of Jevons's work. "This ten-year movement is given in detail by Professor Jevons in his attempt to show that sun-spots have some bearing upon commercial affairs," he wrote. And later: "Without going into the matter of sun-spots and their bearing upon crops, commerce, or states of minds, it may be assumed that Professor Jevons has stated correctly the periods of depression as they have occurred in England during the last two centuries."[44] Dow extended Jevons's work by arguing that the 10-year cycle consisted of five to six years of boom or confidence followed by a period of bust or depression of about the same duration. Furthermore, he documented the same cycle in the United States that Jevons had documented in England.

Dow used the sun-spot theory to correctly predict the 1907 financial crisis in the United States, according to Hamilton in his 1922 book *The Stock Market Barometer*.[45] Market participants as a whole have "a tendency to go from one extreme to another,"[46] and the reason it takes time to go from one extreme to the next lies in the fact that "the stock market reflects general conditions and it takes several years for such a change for better or for the worse to work its way through the community,"[47] postulated Dow. Thus, as with his other theories, Dow found a basis for the sun-spot theory in the very nature of crowd psychology.

Another landmark in the theory of market waves and cycles is the wave principle. It was developed by Ralph Nelson Elliott, an accountant who started studying the stock market relatively late in his life—in 1932, at the age of 61. The wave principle postulates that the stock market follows a basic cyclical pattern, where each cycle consists of eight waves (five waves in one direction, followed by three waves in the opposite direction). Elliott's thinking was influenced by Rhea's book, *The Dow Theory*, as well as by Rhea's market letter, *Dow Theory Comment*; however, as Robert Prechter, an authority on the Elliott wave principle, points out, while Elliott "was undoubtedly directed initially by exposure to the tenets of Dow theory," his "ultimate discovery was all his own."[48] Elliott himself considered his wave principle "a much needed complement to the Dow Theory."[49]

Similarities between Elliott and financial astrologer William D. Gann, Elliott's contemporary, are often raised. Gann, for example, believed in a universal natural order that ruled everything, including the stock market. As he reflected while describing his road to discovery:

I soon began to note the periodical recurrence of the rise and fall in stocks and commodities. This led me to conclude that natural law was the basis of market movements. After exhaustive researches and investigations of the known sciences, I discovered that the Law of Vibration enables me to accurately determine the exact points to which stocks or commodities should rise and fall within a given time.[50]

Likewise, Elliott believed that "no truth meets more general acceptance than that the universe is ruled by law," and furthermore that "all life and movement consists of vibrations, and the stock market is no exception."[51] For this reason Elliott has often been classified together with Gann and astrology, and denounced as one of those "trader/fanatics who operate mostly on faith and can offer little evidence or logic to support their beliefs."[52] However, Prechter suggests that, except for occasional Gann-like comments, Elliott "stayed focused on his empirical observations," and hence should be given credibility.[53]

Chart Patterns

Technical analysis today is often identified with the subjective practice of detecting with the naked eye certain weird patterns with weird names in past price data—think "head and shoulders" or "ascending triangle." Because it is based on human pattern recognition, rather than on rigorous, fine-grained statistical analysis, it is often disparaged as "voodoo finance." However, in the precomputer age, patterns were a way of processing the data and detecting supply/demand imbalances; furthermore, each pattern had an underlying explanation, a story based on market psychology and crowd action and reaction.

For example, the head-and-shoulders pattern, observed on a price chart in the final stages of market rallies, captures the tug of war between buyers and sellers. As the sellers come in and test the downside market potential, the prices are brought down, leaving behind a peak corresponding to the "left shoulder" in the pattern; as buyers respond in panic, they take the market to a new high—the "head" of the pattern. However, their efforts are only temporary as sellers reemerge and test the downside again; the buyers make another tentative effort leading to another, lower peak—the "right shoulder"—until they are finally overtaken by new sellers who join in at the market top. Similarly, a sequence of successively higher highs and lower lows, which traces the so-called "triangle bottom" pattern in price data, was interpreted as the embodiment of strengthening confidence punctuated by subsiding terror, and hence as the presage of an uptrend.

Chart patterns were pioneered by Richard W. Schabacker—*Forbes Magazine*'s financial editor with previous stints at the Federal Reserve Bank of New York and the Standard Statistics Company (which later became Standard & Poor's)—in his three highly influential books, *Stock Market Theory and Practice* (1930), *Technical Analysis and Market Profits* (1932), and *Stock Market Profits* (1934). Edwards and Magee used Schabacker's writings and theories as a primary source in writing their book *Technical Analysis of Stock Trends*, widely regarded today as a primer of technical analysis instruction. Most prominent among Schabacker's patterns are the common basic formations indicating a major accumulation (distribution). These include head-and-shoulders bottom (top), common upward (downward) turn, triangular bottom (top), ascending bottom (descending top), double bottom (top), complex bottom (top), and broadening bottom (top). There are also types of continuation triangles, such as symmetrical, ascending, and descending triangle, and other types of continuation formations, such as ascending peak and descending bottom. Minor editions of the basic formations indicating a major accumulation (distribution), or a growing irregularity on high volume in a bull move, are examples of reverse formations. In addition, Schabacker identified a number of miscellaneous formations. These include false moves and shake-outs, support points and resistance levels, and gaps. Gaps are observed if today's low is higher than yesterday's high, or if today's high is lower than yesterday's low.[54]

Schabacker recognized that the public tends to judge the day as a whole based on the closing prices they read in the evening paper. Thus, he emphasized that closing prices are largely what govern the public's predictions of the future, and that this insight should be used in charting. However, he was well aware of the limitations of the available price data—"stock price lists had a very bad reputation in the United States (and not only), as being unreliable and manipulated," notes Preda.[55] Hence, Schabacker advised his readers to keep in mind that the closing prices are not always genuine due to the practice of "window dressing"—portfolio managers are known to spruce up the performance of their funds by increasing significantly, through price manipulation, the prices of securities to which they have high exposure—at the close of a day's trading.[56]

Like his patterns, Schabacker's practical advice was deeply rooted in his understanding of the reality of the markets. For example, he observed that stop-loss orders—a popular strategy for cutting losses short—were undermined by bear traders: As the demand of bear traders for such stocks increases, the price of those stocks decreases; this triggers the automatic selling of those stocks and causes prices to decline even further, which allows the bear traders to cover their short positions and make a profit. However, since this collapse in prices is artificial and temporary and prices rebound, stop-loss traders often lose positions in very good stocks. Schabacker therefore advised traders to combine their practice of placing stop-loss orders with the practice of buying at support levels in order to minimize the potential loss and maximize the potential profit.[57]

Volume of Trading

After the 1929 stock market crash, speculative techniques received their fair share of criticism. There was a clear and urgent need for more accurate and objective market statistics. The general view was that detachment and objectivity in financial dealings were not only in the investors' interests, but also in the nation's. This sentiment prompted the New York Stock Exchange (NYSE) economist J. Edward Meeker to proclaim:

> There is today a particular need of statistical yardsticks with which to measure its activities. For only by recourse to definite figures can a basis be provided for a serious and unprejudiced study of the activities and functions of the Stock Exchange. The need of adequate statistics is all the more important because mass psychology is regularly so considerable a cause of most stock market phenomena.[58]

Meeker announced that monthly statistics concerning trading activity on the NYSE and monthly indexes and averages would be made "as promptly and as generally available to the public as possible," and stressed that the statistics would be "entirely without comment, for while the Stock Exchange wishes to make every effort to discover and make public factual evidence concerning stock market conditions, it leaves it to others to interpret and comment upon this material."[59] He went on to say: "It is the beginning of wisdom to recognize quite clearly and frankly the defects of the statistical record we already have, and to purify these necessary economic agents of ours as far as possible by painstaking care in collection and compilation, patient experimentation and critical impersonal analysis. These, after all, are the methods of true science."[60]

As stock market statistics became more readily available, it was only natural to incorporate the new resources into technical reasoning. One such statistic is trading volume—the number of shares involved in a stock sale or purchase. Volume can be decomposed into demand volume, which occurs during advances, and supply volume, which occurs during declines. Hence, volume can be used as a measure of supply and demand for shares. A pioneer in this area was Harold M. Gartley—one of the founders of the New York Society of Security Analysts and later a director of the National Securities and Research Corporation, one of the 10 largest mutual funds at the time. In his 1935 book *Profits in the Stock Market*, Gartley formalized Wall Street's ideas about the volume of trading. Writing in 1966, Schulz noted that Gartley's "famous chapter on Trading Volume . . . [was] a real landmark in technical theory and one of the very few extensive studies on the subject of volume ever published."[61]

Gartley himself acknowledged that the available published information concerning volume was indeed small at the time he undertook his endeavor:

> Many financial writers have, more or less vaguely, referred to the activity on the Stock Exchange (which we call volume), but detailed analyses are, for the most part, lacking. Perhaps the reason is that a detailed study of volume of trading is a tedious and laborious task, the results of which frequently do not seem worth the effort.[62]

Although technical notions of volume had not been standardized before Gartley's seminal work, volume has been part of Dow theory from the start. Charles Dow introduced his ideas concerning the relationship between volume and trend in the March 7, 1902, edition of

The Wall Street Journal, where he wrote that "in a bull market, dullness is generally followed by an advance," while "in a bear market by a decline."[63] Furthermore, in the May 29, 1901, edition, Dow observed: "There is a relation between the volume of business and the movement of prices. Great activity means great movements whenever the normal balance between buyers and sellers is violently disturbed."[64] Hamilton continued Dow's studies on volume, but his views on the subject were inconsistent. Until 1910 he clove to the old Wall Street maxim that volume follows a trend—in other words, that volume on rallies indicates strength, while on declines it indicates weakness. As he wrote in the May 21, 1909 edition of *The Wall Street Journal*:

> One of the platitudes most constantly quoted in Wall Street is to the effect that one should never sell a dull market short. That advice is probably right oftener than it is wrong, but it is always wrong in an extended bear swing. In such a swing, the tendency is to become dull on rallies and active on declines.[65]

But in 1910 Hamilton changed his mind, arguing that averages discount everything, including volume. From that point onward he seemed confused on the subject of volume, sometimes saying that he "[preferred] to neglect volume," other times returning to the old maxim he once endorsed.[66]

In his interpretation of Dow theory, Rhea incorporated volume in the discussions of trends, turns, and penetrations. For example, he would say that dullness on declines and activity on rallies indicate strength, while the reverse indicates weakness; that bull markets usually terminate in heavy volume and bear markets terminate in light volume; and that when a critical point is penetrated on high volume, the signal such penetration produces is more valid.[67] C.J. Collins, the author of the *Investment Letters*, also believed in the old volume-follows-a-trend maxim. He discussed volume in virtually every market letter he wrote; on the other hand, Samuel Moment ignored volume altogether in his discussion of Dow theory.[68] Gartley for his part believed that trend analysis cannot be complete without consideration of volume: "It is probably no exaggeration to say that volume is one of the best single indicators of trend," he wrote.[69]

Market Breadth

Gartley is also known as the man who empirically tested and set down in writing Wall Street's wisdom concerning market breadth, or the number of stocks advancing or declining for the day. In fact, when he was writing the famous "Breadth-of-the-Market" chapter of his book *Profits in the Stock Market*, he used no references. This was the case because, as he himself acknowledged, "although this subject has been studied by many market students, with the exceptions of the author's work, [he knew] of no published references."[70]

It was the increased availability of market statistics following the crash of 1929 that allowed Gartley to start his market-breadth research. In 1931 he began collecting data on the number of issues traded, number of advances, declines, and prices unchanged, number of new high and lows, total volume, and the ratio of trading in the 15 most active stocks to total volume, with the objective of determining whether these statistics could be used as means of judging intermediate price reversals. He made the following three observations. First, he found that whenever the seven-day moving averages of the ratio of advances to declines exceeds 60 percent of the total issues traded, it is likely to be the signal of a turning point. Second, he saw that the ratios of advances and declines appear to be more accurate in suggesting buying signals than selling signals. And third, he observed that market-breadth statistics appear to be very useful in judging final phases of major bear markets but not so useful in the bull markets.[71]

Nontechnical Analysis

Financial astrology is often categorized with technical analysis. This is entirely unjustified, of course: It is the use of past market—not cosmic—data that defines technical analysis. Nevertheless, no history of technical analysis would be complete without a survey of this perennial phenomenon. As we saw in the first three chapters, the temptation to invoke mystical aid for predicting the future is strong and deeply rooted in the human psyche.

Starting from the belief that the planets' orbits, the sun, and the moon have an effect on the minds and actions of people, and therefore on the stock market, financial astrologers study the natal horoscopes of markets and companies, as well as the positions of planets in the sky at any given time, and use them to astrologically chart and forecast the cycles and prices of stocks and commodities.[72] A company's natal horoscope (or birth chart) is a map of the heavens that corresponds to its birth data—that is, to the time, place, and date of its incorporation. Just as a personal horoscope describes one's character, talent, and ability, a company's horoscope is a measure of its market potential.[73] The positions of planets in the sky at any given time, also known as the transits, are the main indicators of the likely course of events.[74] More precisely, "it is [the planets'] constantly changing relationship to the natal horoscope chart that is the basis of almost all astrological prediction."[75] Financial astrologers might also consult their own horoscopes, those of their clients and advisors, the first-trade horoscope of a company, and the horoscopes of various countries, stock markets, and central banks.[76]

Financial astrologers generally believe that their craft should be used in conjunction with conventional techniques, rather than in isolation. In fact, "very few financial astrologers use *only* astrological tools to forecast markets, and most likely these are the beginners," suggests Weingarten.[77] Astrology is just one of the three "screens" or "layers" necessary for a successful investment strategy, the other two being fundamental analysis and technical analysis.[78] Along the same lines, Hyerczyk explains that the "knowledge of astrology is necessary to interpret and convert the degrees of the planets, but knowledge of technical analysis techniques is still needed to build charts, interpret tops and bottoms, find support and resistance, and place stop orders."[79]

One legend of the early twentieth-century financial astrology was William D. Gann (mentioned earlier), whose 80 to 90 percent success rate on trades earned him the moniker "master trader."[80] Combining astrology and market data, he predicted several months in advance that September 1909 wheat would sell at $1.20 by the end of the month, which is indeed what happened on the very last trading day and in the very last trading hour of September. Gann wrote eight books, the best known of which are *Wall Street Selector* (1930), *45 Years in Wall Street* (1949), and *Truth of the Stock Tape* (1923).

As Marisch points out, "Gann's trading methods are based on his personal beliefs of a natural order existing for everything in the universe."[81] Or, in Gann's own words: "Everything in existence is based on exact proportion and perfect relationship. There is no chance in nature, because mathematical principles of the highest order lie at the foundation of all things."[82]

Turning to ancient esoteric pseudoscience for direction, he became a student of numerology, astronomical cycles, astrological interpretations, time cycles, Biblical symbology, and sacred geometry.[83] In addition, Gann researched early Egyptian writings and even traveled to India to gain access to the ancient pre-Hindu literature.[84] Moreover, Gann's religious beliefs profoundly influenced his trading. For example, in the book entitled *Tunnel Thru the Air*, Gann advised his readers to "read the Bible to learn about cycles and about the manner in which the Creator reveals nature's universal laws."[85] To explain his general market philosophy, he would often quote Ecclesiastes 1:9–10 from the Bible: "What has been, that will be; what has been done, that will be done. Nothing is new under the sun. Even the thing of which we say, 'See, this is new!' has already existed in the ages that preceded us."[86]

Gann researched the 3½-day, -week, -month, and -year cycle in the market data. As Hyerczyk explains, the number 3½ fascinated Gann because it occurs several times in the Bible—"for example, in the Book of Revelation, where the woman was sent into the wilderness for three and one-half years; during Daniel's vision of 42 months (3½ years); when the Christ child was hidden in Egypt for three and one-half years; and during Christ's public ministry, which lasted for exactly three and one-half years."[87]

The flavor of Gann's theories is captured by his law of vibration, which he said enabled him "to accurately determine the exact points to which stocks and commodities should rise and fall within a given time," and to "[determine] the cause and [predict] the effect long before the Street is aware of either."[88] Gann used physics as motivation for his law: Stocks were analogous to "electrons, atoms, and molecules, which hold persistently to their own individuality in response to the fundamental Law of Vibration." Science teaches "that an original impulse of any kind finally resolves itself into periodic or rhythmical motion," wrote Gann, and that "just as the pendulum returns again in its swing, just as the moon returns in its orbit, just as the advancing year ever brings the rose to spring, so do the properties of the elements periodically recur as the weight of the atoms rises."[89]

Physics was not only a way of thinking about the stocks; in Gann's mind, the speculative endeavor itself was rendered scientific under his law:

> Through the Law of Vibration, every stock in the market moves in its own distinctive sphere of activities, as to intensity, volume and direction; all the essential qualities of its evolution are characterized in its own rate of vibration. Stocks, like atoms, are really centers of energies, therefore they are controlled mathematically. Stocks create their own field of action and power; power to attract and repel, which in principle explains why certain stocks at times lead the market and "turn dead" at other times. Thus to speculate scientifically it is absolutely necessary to follow natural law.[90]

Gann was one of the first to convert astrological signals into price and incorporate them into a trading system. As he described in his article "Soy Beans: Price Resistance Levels," which appeared in the early versions of the W.D. Gann Commodities Course:

> . . . 67 (cents), add 90 gives 157 or 7 degrees Virgo. Add 135 gives 202 or 22 degrees Libra. Add 120 gives 127 or 7 degrees Leo. Add 180 gives 247 or 7 degrees Sagittarius. Add 225 gives 292 or 22 degrees Capricorn. Add 240 gives 307 or 7 degrees Aquarius. Add 270 gives 337 or 7 degrees Pisces. Add 315 gives 382 or 22 degrees Aries. Add 360 gives 427 or 7 degrees Gemini. Add 271¼ gives 438¼. High on May Beans was 436¾. After that high the next extreme low was 201½. Note that 67 plus 125 gives 202, and that one-half of 405 is 202½, and 180 plus 22½ is 202½, which are the mathematical reasons why May Soy Beans made bottom at 201½. All of the above price levels can be measured in Time Periods of days, weeks and months, and when the time periods come out at these prices, it is important for a change in trend, especially if confirmed by the geometrical angles from highs and lows.[91]

Unfortunately, rather than disclosing his ideas in a systematic way, Gann preferred to make statements such as: "It is impossible here to give an adequate idea of the Law of Vibration as I apply it to the markets."[92] According to Plummer, "it seems that there was a central body of theory underlying Gann's analysis which he was either unable, or unwilling, to reveal."[93] Whether Gann chose to be so obscure because he "simply did not know why his techniques worked" or because "he considered that the underlying theories were too esoteric for general consumption" is an open question.[94] However, one thing for certain is that Gann himself did not lack confidence. This was clearly reflected in his writings; for example, he wrote: "After years of patient study I have proven to my entire satisfaction as well as demonstrated to others that vibration explains every possible phase and condition of the market."[95]

Astrology remains part of unconventional trading systems to this day. Notable contemporary market technicians who openly use astrology in their work include Arch Crawford and Bill Meridian. *Barron's* financial weekly has named Arch Crawford "Wall Street's best known astrologer." Moreover, as Colby points out, "Crawford's combination of astronomical cycles and technical analysis to make market calls has earned him top ratings in market timing in the Hulbert and *Timer Digest* surveys." He is known for having predicted the crash of 1987, the bear markets of July 1990 and March 2000, as well as many minor trend changes. Perhaps the most remarkable of Meridian's findings is his 1994 study of the effect of the lunar cycle on the Dow Jones Industrial Average, which, according to Colby, was confirmed by an analysis at the University of Michigan in 2001. A designer of analytical software, Meridian has developed a program for computing correlations between time series data and planetary cycles.[96]

Proponents of financial astrology argue that it should not be ignored, if for no other reason than for its prevalence. Writing in 1996 Weingarten noted that "currently, over $14,000,000,000 in the United States and Europe follow the stars," and warned his readers that "someday soon astrology was going to become a factor in the market, simply because so many people believe in it, and inevitably that would influence money flows."[97] This is certainly true—as far as it goes. But this is merely the argument that astrology might introduce exploitable inefficiencies into the market simply by dint of rendering predictable the decision-making behavior of some people; it says nothing in favor of astrology's inherent predictive value.

For our predecessors of precomputer eras it may have seemed justifiable to use astrology as an input in their price-based forecasting models. In fact, astrological inputs may have been genuinely useful to prediction insofar as they played the same role that random-number generators play in today's forecasting models. As interesting as this is from a historical perspective, to classify astrology with technical analysis in this day and age is a fallacy. Financial astrology should be called what it is, a distinct branch of esoteric financial decision making with tools and a cult following that are all its own.

Chapter 6

Technical Analysis Today

The world has grown relentlessly more complex over the past several decades, and many fields of science and thought have had to evolve to keep pace. For its part, technical analysis is a far more intricate field than it was a century ago. Nevertheless, the principles on which it is built have remained unchanged since the time of Charles Dow and his immediate successors in the first half of the twentieth century. Then, as now, markets moved in trends and cycles. Now, as then, technical analysts pore over their famous panoply of assorted charts in search of clues, trends, patterns, strength, and cycles in market data. This is not because technical analysis is an anachronism, frozen by traditionalist sensibilities in Edwardian-era amber. Quite the contrary: Technical analysis has had to undergo so little change precisely because it is so robust and so deeply relevant to how markets operate.

We begin this chapter by reviewing some of the main tools technicians use to recognize market developments. The intention of this part
is to give unfamiliar readers a flavor of the craft rather than provide an
in-depth survey. We then go on to describe how the changes on Wall
Street in the second half of the twentieth century have led technicians
to reinterpret their craft.

Trends

Price trends are the main tool of technical analysis; indeed, "trend is
your friend" is the technician's mantra. An essential trend-following
device is the moving average, which is computed by averaging prices
over a moving time window in an equally weighted or exponentially
weighted manner. Moving averages smooth out the spiky, jittery fluctuations of fine-grained market data to reveal overarching trends or
other patterns over various time scales. Moving averages detect trends
that are already in place—rather than anticipate them—and are useful
to help traders let their profits run and cut their losses short in trending
markets. Of course, the shorter the time window over which the average is computed, the faster the recognition of the trend's reversal, but
the more likely there will be false signals.

To manage this inherent trade-off between early signal detection
and sensitivity to random noise, Perry Kaufman, highly regarded for
his work on technical trading systems, developed the "adaptive" moving average. Depending on the relationship between price direction
and volatility, this metric allows one to use a faster or a slower moving average depending on the relationship between price direction
and volatility. Moving averages are also used in crossover methods—
superimposing averages from different time scales to spot tell-tale
patterns based on intersections and divergences between each other.
For example, the shorter average crossing above the longer indicates
a downtrend and produces a sell signal, and vice versa. Furthermore,
percentage envelopes—such as 3 percent envelopes around a 21-day
moving average for short-term traders, or 5 percent envelopes around
a 10-week average for long-term ones—are often placed at fixed per-
centages above and below a moving average to help identify market

extremes. To account for the dynamic nature of volatility, in the early 1980s John Bollinger proposed plotting the market-extreme lines approximately two standard deviations (rather than some fixed percentage) above and below a moving average, a technique known as the Bollinger bands.

More generally, trends are analyzed using indicators, which measure trend momentum and market extremes. We will mention four of them here. First is the momentum line, which is simply a continuously computed difference between the current price and the price a desired number of periods ago. Second is the relative strength index (RSI), developed by J. Welles Wilder and introduced in his 1978 book, *New Concepts in Technical Trading Systems*. RSI is a function of the ratio of the average prices when the market closed up to the average prices when the market closed down during some prespecified period. Third is the rate of change line (ROC), which is a ratio of the current price to the price a desired number of periods ago. Finally, there is the moving average convergence/divergence (MACD), developed by Gerald Appel in the late 1970s and presented in his 1980 book, *Stock Market Trading Systems: A Guide to Investment Strategy for the 1980s*. MACD is modeled through the interaction of a faster signal—which is computed as the difference between two exponential moving averages—and a slower signal, obtained by smoothing the faster signal line with an exponential moving average. When the faster line crosses above the slower one, a buy signal is generated, and vice versa.

The price of a security is not the only quantity technical analysts chart. Volume—the number of shares being traded—is typically tracked alongside price and serves as a confirming indicator of a price trend. Volume tends to expand in an uptrend and contract in a downtrend, and when price and volume diverge it may indicate a coming trend reversal. Technicians have devised a number of heuristics to help them gauge volume trends. One such heuristic is the on-balance volume, which was popularized in the 1963 book *Granville's New Key to Stock Market Profits* by Joseph Granville—who is known as much for his writings on technical analysis as for his extravagant investment seminars, where he would dress up as Moses or appear to walk on the surface of water. On-balance volume is computed as a cumulative total of volume, where volume is added when the price closes higher on a particular day and otherwise is subtracted. Volume is sometimes thought to precede price—that is, the weakening of the buying pressure in an uptrend and of the selling pressure in a downtrend becomes apparent in volume before it shows up as a price trend.

Trends are also frequently studied using point-and-figure charts. The most popular form of point and figure in use today—the three-box reversal—is an extension of the work of Richard D. Wyckoff (see Chapter 5) and is due to Abraham W. Cohen. Cohen, the founder in 1947 and first editor of *Chartcraft* (later known as *Investors Intelligence*), a technical analysis research service, formulated this method in his 1968 book, *How to Use the Three-Point Reversal Method of Point and Figure Stock Market Trading*. As we saw in Chapter 5, on a point-and-figure chart price changes are recorded in a succession of ascending columns of x's (for positive price changes) and descending columns of o's (for negative price changes). Traditionally, all price changes are plotted as they occur (including the intraday ones), and a new column starts forming as soon as the price changes direction—this is called the "one-box reversal" method. However, in the second half of the twentieth century, the ever-increasing speed of the market action and the growing number of stocks to be charted rendered the one-box reversal charts noisy and the manual charting process unsustainable. To solve this problem, Cohen proposed plotting only the high and low prices (readily available in newspapers) and using the "three-box reversal" method, where a new column is started only when the price changes direction by the value of at least three x's or three o's. On the three-box reversal charts, trends are gauged using 45-degree trendlines, drawn by connecting the diagonals of the adjacent x- or o-filled boxes. An upward (downward) sloping trendline being penetrated by a column of o's (x's) is an indication of imminent trend reversal.[1]

Another way to gauge price trends is through the theory of contrary opinion, which says that whatever the majority thinks is likely to be wrong. More precisely, if the majority of traders are on one side of the market, it means that not enough buying or selling pressure is left to continue the present trend. Indicators that assess the bullishness/bearishness of market participants are one vehicle through which technicians apply this theory. Two popular such indicators are the NYSE

Bullish Percent and the Advisors Sentiment, created by Abraham W. Cohen in 1955 and 1963, respectively. The NYSE Bullish Percent index is simply the percentage of stocks traded on the New York Stock Exchange (NYSE) that exhibit buy signals on point-and-figure charts, and the Advisors Sentiment is a survey of over a hundred independent investment advisors, summarized as the percentage of those who are bullish, bearish, or expect a market correction.

Patterns

Technicians rely on certain patterns in price and volume to study the behavior of ongoing trends. Traditionally, as cemented in *Technical Analysis of Stock Trends*, the influential 1948 work by Edwards and McGee, patterns have been classified into two main types: reversal patterns, which signal a trend reversal, and continuation patterns, which signal a pause in a prevailing trend. Although widely regarded as misleading by today's technicians, as most patterns occur at both continuation and reversal points without preference, this classification persists as a hangover from the past. Longer patterns have higher failure rates, but if they do materialize, they tend to yield greater subsequent moves than shorter patterns.

Among reversal patterns, "head and shoulders," which we described in the previous chapter, is the most famous. This pattern occurs at market tops and provides a great example of how technicians use volume in conjunction with price to analyze market movements. It starts with the formation of the left shoulder, which is a price peak that is higher than the previous peak and is accompanied at first by expanding volume, and then by contracting volume at the subsequent reaction low. After the left shoulder comes the head, a peak that is even higher than the left shoulder and is accompanied by lighter volume. This lighter volume is the first warning of an approaching trend reversal. The head is then followed by a second reaction low that is lower than the left shoulder, and then by a subsequent rally to a third peak called the right shoulder, which is lower than the previous peak (at the head) while volume continues to contract. After observing the right shoulder, a flat line called the neckline is drawn under the last two reaction lows. The breaking of this neckline completes the price pattern and is accompanied by a burst in volume. After the breaking of the neckline, prices may bounce back to it but typically will not recross it—this is called "a retracement." Often, though not necessarily, the retracement is accompanied by a contraction in volume; after it is over, the volume significantly expands and the downtrend is resumed.

There are variations of head and shoulders. Complex head and shoulders are patterns with double tops or double shoulders. Failed head and shoulders is a pattern that starts out looking like a head and shoulders but then, after breaking the neckline, prices bounce back and recross the neckline.

Other reversal patterns that occur at market tops include "triple tops," "double tops," and "spike tops." Triple tops consist of three peaks at about the same level and two troughs in between them, which are also at about the same level. The patterns are complete when the troughs have been broken with an accompanying burst of volume. Double tops, which are characterized by two peaks that are at about the same level, are complete when a reaction low following the first peak has been broken on a burst of volume. Spike tops are seen when market action suddenly changes direction. This can happen when some unexpected news suddenly becomes available or when markets become extremely overextended.

Each of the foregoing patterns has a mirror-image form: inverse head and shoulders, and triple, double, and spike bottoms, all of which occur at market bottoms.

Among continuation patterns, a prominent place belongs to so-called triangles. The "symmetrical triangle," or "coil," has a declining upper trendline and a rising lower trendline that approach each other as we move from left to right and finally meet at the apex. The "ascending triangle" has a flat upper trendline and a rising lower trendline and most commonly appears in an uptrend. In the "descending triangle," the situation is reversed. The "broadening formation" or "megaphone top" looks like a triangle rotated by 180 degrees (that is, the apex is at the far left of the formation and the trendlines diverge from that point rightwards); this pattern is often seen at the end of major bull markets that are driven by a high degree of public participation, which causes significant volume expansion during the pattern's formation. "Flags" and "pennants" refer to pauses in extremely sharp and almost vertical market moves known as "flagpoles." The "wedge" formation looks like a small symmetrical triangle that slopes against the prevailing trend and is most important as a reversal pattern after a speculative peak or panic bottom. The "rectangle" or "trading range" looks like a rectangle within which the prices move in broad swings.

Strength

The assessment of the continuation or reversal of market trends is aided by the assessment of market strength. The overall health of the marketplace is measured by the so-called advance-decline line, computed as a cumulative total of a normalized difference between the number of stocks that advanced and the number of stocks that declined. As long as this measure is advancing with the major market averages such as the Dow Jones Industrial Average, the market is considered strong, or in technicians' lingo, "the troops are keeping up with the generals."

Other ways of measuring market strength include comparing the number of stocks reaching new highs to the number reaching new lows, or comparing the level of volume in the advancing issues to that in the declining issues—in both cases, the greater the volume on the upside, the stronger the market. Perhaps the best known strength metric is the relative strength ratio (RS ratio), which is obtained by dividing the close of a stock (or a group of stocks) by the S&P 500 or another market index, then plotting this ratio as a line; if the relative strength line is rising, a stock or group is deemed to be acting better than a market as a whole. Robert Levy, a pioneer in the study of relative strength, documented statistical evidence for the validity of the RS ratio as a criterion for stock selection in his 1968 book, *The Relative Strength Concept of Common Stock Price Forecasting.* As with most elements of technicians' craft, the RS ratio is not an innovation of the second half of the twentieth century. George Chestnutt—a prominent technician who in the 1950s not only wrote about this concept but also for nearly 30 years managed the highly successful American Investors Fund, based on this idea—put it this way: "The principle of measuring the strength of a stock in relation to a market average . . . has been in use for many years. I began experimenting with relative performance ratios in the early thirties. The best stock market technicians of that era had been using them for at least a generation before."[2] His adherence to the principle was based not only on statistical evidence but also on intuition:

> Which is the best policy? To buy a strong stock that is leading the advance or to "shop around" for a "sleeper" or "behind-the-market stock" in the hope that it will catch up? . . . On the basis of statistics covering thousands of individual examples, the answer is very clear as to where the best probabilities lie. Many more times than not, it is better to buy the leaders and leave the laggards alone. This is often difficult from a psychological standpoint. You always want to buy the stock that looks cheap in relation to recent prices. The leader, which will already have advanced, will never look cheap in relation to its price before the advance began. However, too many laggard stocks never do come to life because there is a good reason why they are laggards. The reason may be obscure but your buying will not eliminate the reason. In the market, as in many other phases of life, "the strong get stronger, and the weak get weaker."[3]

Cycles

Some technicians take a philosophical stand, arguing that technical analysis is not only a reflection of human psychology but also directly shaped by the forces of nature. For example, Robert Colby, the author of *The Encyclopedia of Technical Market Indicators*, writes: "Western culture prefers the illusion that each individual can completely control his life. Yet our lives are inevitably shaped, even predetermined, by cycles. Every living being's life is prescheduled and prescripted within actuarially predictable ranges of time."[4]

Market cycles, defined as regularly occurring sequences of events, are influenced by numerous naturally cyclical forces. For example, annual seasonal cycles are reflected in virtually all markets. Seasonality is most obvious in agricultural markets, where, around harvest time, supply increases and prices fall. A well-known phenomenon in the grains market is the "February break": Farmers, who cannot work their fields because of the bad weather, use this time to convert their inventories into the cash they need to prepare for the coming crop season, and consequently, supply increases and prices fall.

Cycles have been a subject of systematic investigations through history. In 1860 the French statistician Clemant Juglar described a 9.25-year cycle in stock prices, now known as the Juglar wave. In 1923 Harvard professor Joseph Kitchin found a four-year cycle, known as the Kitchin wave, in bank clearings, wholesale prices, and interest rates in Great Britain and in the United States for the period 1890 to 1922. The Kondratieff wave, first identified in 1926, refers to a 49- to 58-year cycle of economic activity that is made up of approximately 13 four-year cycles. More recently, in his 1993 Charles H. Dow Award–winning paper, "Charles Dow Looks at the Long Wave," Charles Kirkpatrick, the author of *Technical Analysis: The Complete Resource for Financial Market Technicians*, a standard textbook in the field, observed that from 1700 to 1994, every period that saw both a decline in long-term interest rates and a rise in the stock market has been followed by a major stock market collapse.[5]

Related to the study of cycles in technical analysis is the study of Fibonacci numbers—a sequence constructed such that each successive number is the sum of the two previous numbers (1, 1, 2, 3, 5, 8, . . .)—and their ratios. With the exception of the first four numbers in the sequence, the ratio of any number to its next higher number approaches 0.618—an important mathematical constant, the so-called "golden ratio," which appears in many natural and biological systems (it has also been a favorite of numerologists, mystics, and artists since ancient times). Fibonacci circles, arcs, fans, pentagons, stars, and time zones are but a few visual representations of the Fibonacci ratios that technicians chart. In addition to being useful in and of themselves in gauging price levels, Fibonacci numbers underlie the Elliott wave principle (see Chapter 5). According to this principle, the stock market follows a cyclical pattern consisting of a five-wave stretch in one direction and a subsequent three-wave stretch in the opposite direction; each wave is further subdivided into smaller five- and three-stretch waves.

Wall Street's Reinterpretation of Technical Analysis

A common criticism of technical analysis is that it has not kept up with the changing times. It is true that its tools have remained virtually unaltered for several decades. However, technicians are quick to point out that keeping up with the times does not necessarily require new tools. "[T]echnical analysis has seen a proliferation of a lot more junk out there. What can you say about technical analysis? There's nothing new to say about it. You're testing a previous high or a low, you're buying a retracement and a trend, or you're following a breakout strategy. It's really simple." These words were spoken by Linda Raschke, a highly successful technical trader and one of the interviewees in our book, *The Heretics of Finance*, describing the recent evolution of technical analysis.[6]

What technicians will more readily acknowledge is that changing times call for a *reinterpretation* of some of their tools. The 1950s ushered in an unprecedented transformation of the investing practices on Wall Street, brought on by the rise of institutional trading in large blocks of shares, integration of domestic and worldwide markets, and, most significantly, the widespread use of computers. In this section we survey some of the main developments in these areas and point out how they have prompted leading technical analysts to refine and adapt their craft.

Small Investors

The catalyst of the events of the post–World War II era was the increasing prominence of small investors on the investment scene. During the bull market of the 1950s, the investing business prospered and flourished—so much that its appeal widened beyond its traditional (realms) of institutions and floor traders and began to lure small investors and day traders. The growing popularity of investing came hand-in-hand with the betterment of the social status of its practitioners: While the profession of stockbroker was still considered slightly disreputable through the first half of the twentieth century, by the end of the 1950s its status had risen to the echelon of doctors, lawyers, and CEOs.[7] The same could be said for the reputation of technical analysis.

In their 1964 *Financial Analysts Journal* article, a father-and-son team, Edmund and Anthony Tabell, who between them had been doing technical research and consulting with institutions since the early 1930s, wrote: "It was barely a decade ago that the average portfolio manager, if he was aware of technical analysis at all, regarded it as some sort of black magic. Today, almost all professionals have at least a familiarity with the terminology and a good many make such analysis a major part of their decision-making process."[8]

The integration of small investors into the marketplace would continue throughout the decades, aided by technological advances such as the Internet and automated trading platforms. Many of them used technical trading strategies, and their presence waxed and waned with the bull and bear market cycles. John Murphy, author of *Technical Analysis of the Financial Markets*, a standard reference in the field, sums it up with an anecdote:

> Until 2000, we had a lot of people who were day-trading. They were making a fortune. I remember giving a lot of seminars to these people. Then we went into a big downtrend in stocks, and they all went broke. I remember a lot of them saying to me, "Mr. Murphy, these signals did not work anymore." Of course, they didn't work. All they were doing was buying. The short-term buy signals that you get are legitimate if the market is going up. If the market is going down, those little buy signals don't work. You have to look at the environment! So it's not so much the signal; it's the environment.[9]

Seasoned technical analysts such as Laszlo Birinyi, president of Birinyi Associates and a leading authority in the field, argue that the presence of small investors calls for a reinterpretation of their craft. "We should recognize that what worked in an environment in which we had a historical classical long-term investor is totally different from what works in an environment where people are day-trading," says Birinyi, adding, "We still think that charts and indicators work in the same way, when in fact they work differently now."[10]

Institutional Trading

The desire of small investors to take part in the bull markets of the 1950s and 1960s led to a proliferation of mutual funds, specializing not only in the U.S. stock market but also in international investments. Examples of the latter include the Canadian fund, the Japan Fund and ASA (American South Africa) Ltd., the Mexico fund, and the Korea fund.[11]

Boston-based mutual fund management companies Fidelity Investments and Wellington Management maintained (and still do to this day) elaborate chart rooms and based their operations in part on technical analysis. For example, in 1957 the legendary investor Gerald Tsai, then at Fidelity, started managing a hugely successful mutual fund, called the Fidelity Capital Fund, based on broker information and technical analysis (the fund was operated by Tsai but actually run by his boss, Fidelity chairman Ned Johnson). Less than a decade later, after Fidelity refused to give him stock and make him the future chairman, Tsai struck off on his own to launch another mutual fund, the Manhattan Fund, in the same style. Often described as the Pentagon war room for its plethora of sliding and rotating charts, the Manhattan Fund's chart room required "three men to work full time maintaining literally hundreds of averages, ratios, oscillators, and indices, ranging from a 'ten-day oscillator of differences in advances and declines' to charts of several Treasury issues, to 25-, 65-, and 150-day moving averages for the Dow."[12] While serving as a powerful publicity tool, the chart room, however, had little use in the fund's day-to-day operations, causing Chester Pado, a technician who followed Tsai from Fidelity, to quit in frustration. In the market declines in the 1970s, the fund's performance was so dismal that it was ridiculed in the financial press and among professionals. The fund was finally liquidated when Tsai sold it to an insurance company to pay for an expensive divorce.

Another type of mutual funds that were popular with small investors are index funds. These passively managed portfolios mimicking various market indexes captured public attention after "A Study of Mutual Funds"—prepared for the Securities and Exchange Commission (SEC) by the Wharton School of the University of Pennsylvania in 1962—found that average mutual funds do not perform better than an unmanaged portfolio consisting of the same types of securities.[13]

By the mid-1960s the institutional (mutual fund) trading of equities in large blocks of 10,000 shares or more had become commonplace—a far cry from the time when New York Stock Exchange (NYSE) specialists traded round lots of 100 shares of a stock. And the trend continued: While these so-called block trades accounted for 3 percent of the NYSE's volume in 1965, in 1972 they accounted for 19 percent and in 1987 for 50 percent.[14] For example, Walston and Co., Merrill Lynch, and Solomon Brothers had block desks in the late 1960s and early 1970s. Charles Kirkpatrick recounts how while working on the Walston block desk in the late 1960s, at one time he crossed the then largest block ever to be crossed on the American Stock Exchange—276,000 shares of Research Cottrell (no longer an operating company). In fact, in the late 1960s, block trades were so prevalent that some service providers, such as that run by Don Worden, calculated and provided tick and block volume for all stocks. The strong market and the rise of the dollar in the second half of the 1990s led to a renewed explosion of the mutual fund industry, and by the end of 1996 the three largest funds—Fidelity, Vanguard, and Capital Research—controlled $850 billion in assets. This contributed to a surge in trading volume from the beginning to the end of the 1990s, from low hundreds of millions of shares per day to over a billion.[15] Block trading led technical analysts to conceive new ways of measuring market action data, as Laszlo Birinyi recounts:

> In 1979 I introduced into our work the idea of ticker tape analysis. When we first started doing that, it was a very useful indicator. In the first version of it, we would look only at block trading. We would look at every single block trade to see if it was in an uptick or in a downtick, and that proved very helpful. Then we thought that since we were interrogating every single trade to see if it was a block, why not analyze every single trade further, and therefore we developed the idea called "money flows."
>
> Money flows proved to be very useful until 1982, when they did not have quite the predictability that they had previously. We had to recognize that starting in the early 1980s the dynamics of the trading desk had changed. Before then, when volume was much lower, the specialist on the floor of

the New York Stock Exchange controlled the marketplace. You did not really want to antagonize the specialist. He was a partner in what you did. I remember trading Motorola in the early 1970s and putting on a small trade without really checking with the specialist to see if he wanted to participate. The order came from the floor, from John Coleman, who was one of the great powers on Wall Street: "That young man will not trade Motorola again without my permission!"

In the 1980s, institutions grew, commissions were still very significant, and liquidity increased, so upstairs block trading became a bigger and more important force in the marketplace, and the control of the marketplace went from the specialist to the trading desk. Firms like Salomon Brothers, where I worked, would put on large prints—which in those days were twenty thousand to thirty thousand shares—tell the specialists that this was what they were going to do and to move out of the way. Our money flow concept was not as useful as it had been, because with block trading, gradually the information did not seep into the marketplace. More and more prices were being set too often; prices were being set by retail investors. It was a unique circumstance because the NYSE was at that time, and to some degree still is, the only market in the world where retail sets wholesale prices. A hundred shares of Ford up a dime was a new price. Even though there were many millions of shares outstanding, that was the price that showed up on your screen. So we recognized that we had to differentiate between the retail and the wholesale markets, and we started doing money flows on block and nonblock trades, and we looked at them in different marketplaces.[16]

Negotiated Commissions

As pledged in the Buttonwood Agreement of 1792, which founded the exchange (see Chapter 4), the brokers of the 1950s charged fixed commission rates of no less than one-quarter of 1 percent. This was a great deal for them, especially given the prominence of block trades, and when it came under threat they fought hard to preserve it.[17] In 1969 NYSE chairman and Goldman Sachs CEO Gus Levy went so far as to argue that fixed commissions were "at the very heart" of the financial system. But despite the opposition of Wall Street's elite, the replacement of fixed commissions with flexible ones, which would give the customers power to negotiate the rates and get a discount on large orders, was inevitable.[18]

In 1971 the SEC called for a gradual transition from fixed to negotiated rates—first on trades over $500,000, then over $300,000, until finally on May 1, 1975, so-called "May-day," all commissions were to become fully negotiated. The over-the-counter market NASD (National Association of Securities Dealers) led the way by adopting the automated quotations system known as the Nasdaq, where the prices of various market makers were quoted on a computer and made easily accessible to brokers.[19] (Market makers are specialists on the stock exchange who take the other side of customer orders when there are buy- and sell-side imbalances.) The NYSE had no choice but to follow in Nasdaq's footsteps.[20] This development has had a profound effect on the practice of technical analysis, as Laszlo Birinyi explains:

> There is a cliché, "It's not your grandfather's market anymore." When you have a market that's dominated by traders, when your commissions are one or two cents a share or less, the dynamics are totally different from when you're paying a commission of fifty to sixty cents a share, as people were paying in 1976. In all investing, you look for these wonderful underlying truths, and the more statistically valid they are and the longer they persist, the more confidence you have in them, whereas actually it should be the other way around.[21]

In other words, during the last three decades the market has been evolving so rapidly that the very intuition on which developing technical or quantitative trading strategies is based—the stronger the historical backtest results, the more promising the strategy—got turned on its head. The rate of change has been such that historical viability has become hardly indicative of present success, challenging today's portfolio managers to develop adaptive strategies capable of detecting shifts in the market environment.

Market Integration

The early 1970s saw high inflation and the consequent devaluation of the dollar. Around the same time, markets around the world were becoming highly integrated. In 1971 these two facts came into potent interaction. In August of that year President Nixon took the United States off the gold standard in order to make imports more expensive and exports less expensive; foreign investors, fearing that the dollar was debased, began selling dollars frantically and markets became upset.[22] The lesson was clear: We had entered an era in which investors needed to think about the strength of the dollar. "No longer was talk of currencies a peripheral issue," writes Charles Geisst in *Wall Street*, a popular history of the Street.[23]

The new market environment called for new financial instruments—foreign currency derivatives—that would allow investors to hedge the movements in the dollar; in fact, shortly after President Nixon's announcement, the International Monetary Market (IMM) introduced and started trading currency futures. A few years later, in 1975, futures on Treasury bills, the so-called interest rate futures, emerged.[24] Another major event of that period was the decision of the Organization of Petroleum Exporting Countries (OPEC) to double the price of oil in 1973. This brought Arab and other oil-exporting countries to the forefront of the financial scene and led to a redistribution of wealth from primarily the United States to Europe and later Japan. John Murphy explains the effects these developments have had on the practice of technical analysis:

> I wrote a book on it back in 1991 called *Intermarket Technical Analysis*, and I wrote another one in 2004. This was an outgrowth of my having worked in the futures markets, where we were trading bonds, stocks, commodities, and the dollar, and where I started to notice all kinds of correlations. The whole idea of the book is that all these markets are related. For example, if you're trading the stock market, you also have to follow bonds, since what happens in the bond market has an impact on stocks. And bonds are very much affected by commodity prices. For example, when commodities turn up, that's an early sign of inflation. Commodities' turning up pushes interest rates higher,

and, in time, that becomes bearish for stocks. Now what pushes commodity prices higher is the falling dollar. You can't look at any one of these markets all by itself—you have to understand the impact they have on one another. Also, global markets are very important. Then there are sector rotations; depending on where you are in the business cycle, you need to understand which sectors of the stock market you should be emphasizing. That comes out of the whole body of intermarket analysis.[25]

Technicians have practiced their craft in conjunction with economic analysis since at least the time of Charles Dow. For example, Dow's emphasis on the importance of confirmation between industrial and rail-road averages stemmed from his economic intuition that if the expansion in industrial production were genuine, then the produced goods would start being shipped to customers in greater volume via the railroads. The developments of the second half of the twentieth century underscored the necessity of such an integrated approach, as Murphy suggests:

When I wrote my book fifteen years ago on the intermarket, most stock market analysts did not pay much attention to the price of gold or the price of oil. Whenever the price of oil moves up close to $40 a barrel, the stock market always goes down. That has happened every time over the last thirty years. So, oil becomes a tremendous factor. Every recession we've had has been caused by a rise in oil prices. Fifteen years ago nobody paid any attention to that, but now you turn on CNBC, and they talk about the impact of the dollar on interest rates, and technical analysts talk about these things. . . . Technical analysis is being recognized as a much broader field. . . . Very often, I write pieces on where the economy is. By knowing where we are in stocks, bonds, and commodities, we are actually doing economic analysis. These markets are leading indicators. The stock market is the leading indicator of the economy. So, technical analysts are actually moving into economic analysis.[26]

The integration of markets leaped forward again in June 1975 with the introduction of the so-called consolidated tape—a system for showing all trades as soon as they are executed regardless of whether they are traded on big exchanges such as the NYSE or small, regional ones. The degree of complex interconnectivity the world's markets had achieved was underscored in October 1987, when the Dow Jones Industrial Average abruptly collapsed by over 500 points and other markets worldwide suffered even more.[27]

Decimalization

From the eighteenth century through the end of the twentieth, stock prices were quoted in fractions of a point. This practice became problematic because it increasingly caused the bid/ask spreads on the exchanges to be artificially high, and in an era when volume could readily exceed 400 million shares per day, it allowed the market maker to profit substantially. The problem was especially acute for Nasdaq, where the average spread was 1/4 of a point, or 25 cents per share, whereas the spread on the NYSE was 1/8 of a point, or 12.5 cents per share. In 1994, in a *Journal of Finance* paper, William Christie and Paul Schultz argued that wide spreads on Nasdaq were artificially inflated by market makers who avoided the "odd–eight quotes" and changed bids and offers by 1/4 of a point even if such an amount was not justified.[28] The article spurred the Justice Department and the SEC to conduct an investigation, which confirmed the allegation that spreads were artificially inflated. At the end of 1997, 30 market makers settled a class action antitrust civil lawsuit. This spurred Wall Street to start quoting prices in decimals, rather than in fractions, and by 2001 both the NYSE and Nasdaq followed suit.[29] Together with lower commissions, decimalization has driven out of business a number of market makers and may well have reduced market liquidity. The effect of decimalization on the practice of technical analysis is pointed out by Alan Shaw, whose luminous career in the technical research departments of Wall Street's elite firms throughout the second half of the twentieth century has established him as one of the technical gurus of that time:

> Decimalization has not only affected the advance/decline line; it has affected the high/low statistics as well. Nowadays it's possible for a stock to go up one cent and make a twelve-month

high. Decimalization has distorted these statistics somewhat, but we still keep them on the wall. However, whereas in the past we used to give them the strength of 10, we now give them the strength of 6. We may not pay as much attention to these high/low statistics as we used to, but they're still worth doing.[30]

Electronic Markets

In the early 1990s, the reputations of both Nasdaq and the NYSE were tainted—Nasdaq's by the artificial inflation of the bid-ask spreads described in the previous section, and the NYSE's by a widespread front-running scandal. Front running is an illegal practice by which a floor trader trades his own accounts before customer orders and thereby makes a profit since he knew how the customer's order would affect the price once executed. As a result, investors became disgruntled with traditional exchanges and turned to more transparent electronic communications networks (ECNs) to trade with a measure of assurance.[31]

ECNs, which came about in the 1990s, are stock markets where buyers and sellers get matched up to transact their orders without a market maker or a specialist. They would soon capture one-third of the Nasdaq trading volume.[32] Providing streamlined procedures, fast execution, reduced commissions, and the convenience of after-hours trading, the ECNs quickly became favorites among institutional investors and large block traders, and gained some popularity among day traders, too.[33] Gail Dudack, a long-time leader in technical analysis, points out that ECNs have had a major effect on measurements of volume, a crucial ingredient in the practice of the craft:

> As technicians, we have to be alert to the fact that the actual execution of a trade has changed. Trading used to be done either on the New York and American stock exchanges or on the over-the-counter market. Today, volume is found on the Nasdaq Composite Index, on multiple electronic communication networks, in global twenty-four-hour trading, and on upstairs desks that never hit the system. This change means we

can *no longer* define volume. If we're talking about an NYSE stock, volume could be defined as exchange-only volume or exchange plus after-hours volume, or it could be composite volume. If I'm trying to get one consistent series of volumes on five hundred stocks, it can be a nightmare. For each individual stock, I have three different sets of volumes and three different sets of numbers. Why? The trading structure has changed. Trading no longer starts at 9:30 a.m. on the New York Stock Exchange and ends at 4:00 p.m. Volume is a very important ingredient since it is a measure of conviction.

Thirty years ago the market structure was simple, and we did not have these questions. When I'm buying a volume series, I have too many choices to make. I have to ask myself if after-hours trading is relevant to my project because a different kind of trader is involved there. Is using only the NYSE volume good enough, or do I really want composite volume? How about ECN volume? Some trading takes place today that is not measured, and we never see or hear about it. Since the charts are looking at price and volume, these choices are important. You can come to a wrong conclusion if you inadvertently chose the volume series that doesn't relate to your study. You *must* understand your data to make good decisions. It's better to use a smaller number of indicators, use them really well, and really understand them.[34]

Dudack's point should be understood in the context of volume analysis as confirmation of chart patterns and trends. In effect, it is no longer useful because it is unreliable and in the case of large cap stocks overly influenced by their inclusion in so many exchange-traded funds (ETFs) baskets, and hedge trades.

The Use of Computers

If one development of the second half of the twentieth century had to be singled out for its transformational effect on the practice of technical analysis, that would be the rise of the computer. Its revolutionary potential was apparent from the beginning. In 1965 *Barron's* wrote that "the age of the computer unmistakably is dawning on Wall Street" and that "the potential rewards of the computer, properly used, promise to be immeasurable."[35] "Because it can perform millions of statistical calculations in seconds and recall almost instantaneously hundreds of thousands of details stored for years on its magnetic tapes, the giant brain can relieve an analyst of all such dreary labor, freeing him for more creative activity," the article continued.[36]

Similarly, *The Wall Street Journal* articles at that time emphasized the power of the computer to rank and filter a large number of stocks. "There are more than 6,700 corporations with 300 or more sharehold-ers each, whose shares are traded on one or more exchanges, or are otherwise available to the public. Using human analysts, not even the biggest brokerage house can hope to do a comprehensive job of analy-sis on more than a small fraction of these," one such article wrote.[37]

The adoption of computers in the years to come and the ensu-ing Internet age allowed for automated data collection. "When I first started in business on my own in 1980, my main data source was a VCR hooked to a television set that recorded the stock market chan-nel. . . . Now, with the Internet, all the information is available for free and instantaneously," recounts Walter Deemer, a highly regarded technical analyst with almost half a century of experience in financial industry.[38]

Computers provided automatic ranking and filtering from a large universe of securities. As John Murphy sums it up, "with two clicks the computer will show me a chart of the strongest sector of that day, as well as a chart of the strongest stock, [and] within twenty seconds, I can be looking at the five best-performing stocks in the best sector."[39]

Computers meant instantaneous communication. In Alan Shaw's words, "When I was starting out in the business, it used to take me twenty minutes to get a quote. . . . [Now] we send out a 'tech fax,' and all the brokers and all the clients see it immediately; it goes right to their computers."[40]

One of the first computers on Wall Street devoted solely to techni-cal analysis was at Walston and Co., led by Anthony Tabell, where in the late 1960s Charles Kirkpatrick began the data accumulation that would be used for technical research later on. In those days, the usual programming language was Basic, and the computer was an IBM typewriter terminal

linked to a remote computer service provider through a dial-up telephone connection. Anthony Tabell remembers how his interest in applying computers to technical analysis originated:

> In the late '50s, early '60s, one of the things that moved me
> personally was the use of the computer. I liked computers. I
> liked sitting down and writing computer programs in assembly
> language. But it was a natural marriage with what I was doing
> with technical analysis, because technical analysis is analysis of
> data. I can tell many stories about fighting my way through
> Wall Street in my efforts to merge computers with the prac-
> tice of technical analysis. The whole idea of doing research on
> them was foreign to everyone involved with technical analy-
> sis. I'm probably one of the first people who tried to evaluate
> stock price returns on a computer, necessarily a mainframe.
> The PC was still twenty-five years in the future. This was an
> interest I pursued when my father was still alive, but I got
> involved in it more deeply when we started our own firm in
> 1970. I went out and bought a Digital Equipment PDP-11.
> This was to my knowledge the first computer to be 100 per-
> cent devoted to doing technical research. I regard the compu-
> ter as a watershed in technical analysis.[41]

It was around the same time that computers gave rise to quantitative hedge funds, blurring the lines between technical and quantitative
analysis (which would soon become a force to be reckoned with in
its own right). In his 1967 book, *The Money Game*, Goodman, under
the pseudonym Adam Smith, provides an entertaining account of the
emergence of highly quantitative and aggressive trading on the Wall
Street scene:

> I have a friend called Irwin the professor at one of our nation's
> leading universities who must rank as one of the top architects
> of computer-based technical analysis. . . . Irwin's computer sys-
> tem . . . is on line, real time, and all that. It is hooked up to
> the tickers of the New York and American stock exchanges,
> and it doesn't even have to read the tapes optically; it picks
> up the original electrical impulse which drives the stock

tickers and whisks it right into the memory. . . . I wanted to know how Irwin's computer worked on the Technical side of the market. "The first thing it does is to monitor every stock transaction, the price, the volume, and the percentage move," Irwin said. "We have a Behavior Pattern for every stock. When a stock is behaving out of its pattern, the monitor flashes on."[42]

"Most buying and selling is still done by individuals and institutions," Irwin said, "just as it was in the old days." (The old days to Irwin are 1962 or so, when computers were still doing only clerical chores.) "But," Irwin went on, "there are a couple of sophisticated funds that have computers like ours on the air. Then it really gets to be fun. Our computer scans the pattern of the other computer on the air, what its buying and selling programs seem to be. Once we get its pattern, we can have all kinds of fun. We can chase the stock away from it. Or even better, we can determine where the other computer wants to buy."[43]

Although in principle well developed, as late as the 1980s computer technology did not exist in a format that would make it accessible to the investment masses. Michael Bloomberg, the originator of the Bloomberg terminals, recalls how systems that would let users do even simple statistical analysis were lacking in those days. "A few large underwriting firms had internal systems that tried to fill this need, but each required a PhD to use and weren't available off the shelf to the little guy," he reminisces, and further elaborates:[44]

Merrill wanted its traders to be able to enter a transaction and automatically update the firm's positions themselves. That wasn't a big deal, you would think. But the only systems Merrill had for trade entry used massive, unreliable, and complex terminals that wouldn't fit on regular-size desks, much less in the typical sales-person/trader's small cubicle. They connected these terminals to a single, large mainframe without backup. This wasn't what the market needed.[45]

No one has left a bigger mark in the drive toward computerization on Wall Street than Bloomberg. In his irreverent autobiography,

Michael Bloomberg describes how the situation in the 1980s led him to conceive his product:

> When it came to knowing the relative value of one security versus another, most of Wall Street in 1981 had pretty much remained where it was when I began as a clerk back in the mid-1960s: a bunch of guys using No. 2 pencils, chronicling the seat-of-the-pants guesses of too many bored traders. Something that could show instantly whether government bonds were appreciating at a faster rate than corporate bonds would make smart investors out of mediocre ones, and would create enormous competitive advantage over anyone lacking these capabilities. At a time when the U.S. budget deficit (financed by billions of dollars of new Treasury bonds and notes) was poised to explode, such a device would appeal to everyone working in finance, securities, and investments—combined, a very big potential market for my proposed product.[46]

Bloomberg not only filled that need but also exploited the computer's capabilities in other ways, such as providing integrated charting, system testing, and trading platforms, as well as making news reporting almost instantaneous. In the process he set industry-wide standards.

Although computers have become standard tools of technical analysts, they have not yet replaced them—on that, the leading practitioners of technical analysis interviewed in our book *The Heretics of Finance* unanimously agree. For example, Robert Farrell, a founder and the first president of the Market Technicians Association, who enjoyed an illustrious career at Merrill Lynch spanning the entire second half of the twentieth century, notes that technical analysis is "still a human game."[47] The Elliott wave expert Robert Prechter further elaborates: "The best thing a computer does is save plotting time. I don't think much of the analytical software programs I've seen. The market is so complex to model that you can't use equations and statistics to do it. You can only model aspects of it. I think the future will be in getting computers to recognize patterns and forms despite quantitative variation."[48]

The human eye may have a crucial advantage over computer algorithms in this endeavor. It is well known that computers still struggle with many image-recognition and classification tasks that are trivial for humans. The same may be true for the task of analyzing financial markets, something that would explain the gulf separating technical analysis—still a largely human endeavor—and quantitative financial analysis, a more analytical and algorithmic approach, and why the former practice persists despite the lack of support from the latter. If the human eye does have an advantage over computers in analyzing financial markets, the possibility is raised of using human-computer interfaces to *systematically* harness human skills for financial trading, while avoiding subjective inconsistency and emotional biases to which traditional chart reading is prone. Such an interface—think of it as a starship video game in which trajectories of the starships are given by market prices—would not necessitate the human participant to be aware of the financial context behind the patterns he or she is implicitly recognizing, or to have any financial background, for that matter.

Some of our own work, co-authored with Emanuele Viola and discussed in more detail in Chapter 7, may pave the way toward making this possibility a reality. We conducted an experiment, implemented as an online video game, in which players were challenged to distinguish actual financial market returns from random temporal permutations of those returns.[49] We found very strong statistical evidence that subjects could consistently distinguish between the two types of time series.[50] These results demonstrate that human beings can distinguish market returns from their randomized counterpart—in other words, that market returns carry a unique signature that human beings are able to detect.

Such results, coupled with the fact that human pattern recognition skills outstrip those of any known algorithm, open the door to the development of human-computer interfaces that allow us to translate certain human abilities into other domains and functional specifications. For example, with the proper interface, it may be possible to translate the hand-eye coordination of highly skilled video-gamers to completely unrelated pattern-recognition and prediction problems such as weather forecasting or financial trading. Laszlo Birinyi has warned that "more and more, because the market has changed so much, because we have hedge funds, exchange-traded funds, electronic communication networks, we find that there is no precedent" for current market conditions.[51] Interfaces, such as video games, that allow human subjects to systematically harness their own abilities to recognize, and even predict, market changes better than any computer is currently capable of doing, may prove useful in the face of the fast-evolving market environment.

Chapter 7

A Brief History of Randomness and Efficient Markets

E ver since the emergence of modern finance theory in the mid-twentieth century, the followers of technical analysis have found themselves marginalized by the financial establishment. This ostracism is partly based on misunderstanding, since the technical jargon of head-and-shoulders, wedges, and pennants sounds odd to minds steeped in physics and statistics. It is also based on great faith in the efficient markets hypothesis (EMH), an academic theory which states that in a properly functioning market, changes in market prices are fundamentally unpredictable—in a word, random—if markets are operating as they should. The EMH is based on the idea that in a frictionless competitive market with many self-interested participants, current stock market activity will reflect *all relevant factors* determining value; thus, no factors can possibly be left over that might create useful (exploitable) patterns or trends in market data, otherwise they would have been exploited already. Consequently, even though stock market activity is not *generated* randomly, to an outside observer it is *indistinguishable* from what mathematicians call a "random walk." Thus, disciples of the EMH reject out of hand the possibility of exploitable patterns in historical market prices—the very basis of technical analysis.

Despite recent proposals of alternative hypotheses, the EMH remains deeply ingrained in the culture of academic finance, a rigorous and highly mathematical discipline that has become central to the financial industry. This state of affairs stands in sharp contrast to technical analysis, which attempts to divine market direction based on past prices and volume. As we saw in the previous two chapters, this involves searching with the naked eye for certain patterns in price histories that are believed to embody the prime mover of all market action: crowd psychology.

The EMH was formally developed in the 1960s, but its roots go back much further in time. Its earliest beginnings can be traced back to the 1565 manuscript *Liber de Ludo Aleae* (*The Book of Games of Chance*) in which the prominent Italian mathematician Girolamo Cardano (1501–1576) first proposed an elementary theory of gambling. In this remarkably prescient volume, Cardano described the basic logic of the "martingale"—a precursor to the EMH—in the following way:

> The most fundamental principle of all in gambling is simply equal conditions, e.g., of opponents, of bystanders, of money, of situation, of the dice box, and of the die itself. To the extent to which you depart from that equality, if it is in your opponent's favour, you are a fool, and if in your own, you are unjust.[1]

This notion of a "fair game," a gamble that is neither in your favor nor your opponent's, has the interesting implication that the best forecast of either party's total wealth tomorrow is simply equal to today's total wealth, which sounds a lot like the EMH.

When the martingale hypothesis is applied to the prices of financial securities, some rather surprising implications follow. For example, if stock prices are a martingale, it can be mathematically proven that no linear forecasting rule based solely on historical prices can forecast future price changes—thus ruling out the efficacy of moving-average rules, regression models, trendlines, and other staples of technical analysis. Such are the sweeping statements of academic finance that have become anathema to the practicing technician.

A more modern version of the EMH originated in the mid-nineteenth century in the French popular investment literature. It was formalized mathematically by Louis Bachelier half a century later (see Chapter 8), five years before Albert Einstein proposed essentially the same model for Brownian motion, and six decades before Paul Samuelson and Eugene Fama formulated the version used today.

More recently, departures from the EMH have been documented in the behavioral finance literature, providing theoretical grounding for technical analysis and paving the way for its formalization and synthesis. Nevertheless, efforts to incorporate technical analysis into the theory of financial markets are in many ways just getting underway. This is due not only to cultural biases but also to historical limitations in areas other than finance that help bring financial ideas to fruition. In the mid-twentieth century, two theories of financial markets were proposed roughly simultaneously—Simon's theory of bounded rationality and Paul Samuelson's and Eugene Fama's theory of market efficiency. Both had merit, but only the latter had a clean mathematical representation; the former would require greater understanding of human psychology and computation that simply didn't exist at the time. Now that the notion of adaptative markets and computationally bounded algorithms are available, though not yet fully developed, reinterpreting market efficiency in computational and evolutionary terms might well be able to bridge the gap between academic finance and technical analysis.

In the next chapter we will look at some of the reasons to doubt strong interpretations of the EMH, as well as evidence supporting the methods of technical analysis and a theoretical framework in which such techniques can add value. In the present chapter we recount the rise of academic finance and how it eclipsed other approaches, including technical analysis and behavioral approaches. And because the EMH implies that the stock market's ups and downs are indistinguishable from randomness, at the end of the chapter we reexamine the very meaning of "random."

Prices As Objects of Study

As we saw in the early chapters, the history of technical analysis is inextricably tied to the history of behavioral finance—the use of social, cognitive, and emotional factors to explain and predict market activity. Such practices originated in the price diaries of the ancient Babylonians 2,700 years. They evolved through centuries and civilizations, with ancient Athenians devising price-based market sentiment measures; with medieval merchants relying on a combination of prices and planets' orbits, which they believed had an effect on human behavior, to forecast future price; and with sophisticated speculative techniques that took into account human psychology flourishing on the seventeenth-century Bourse of Amsterdam. This long, folkloristic tradition of recognizing prices as a reflection of minds and actions of people and using them to forecast the future price was formalized to some extent in the eighteenth century by Munehisa Homma in Japan and in the early twentieth century by Charles Dow and his successors in the United States, molding the legacy of times past into a distinct craft of technical analysis.

All these, however, are popular developments—practical solutions to concrete everyday problems, which were often passed on from generation to generation through word of mouth, and sometimes documented in the astronomical price diaries, newspaper articles, and merchant and investor manuals. These practices belong to the realm historians of economic thought call "low" or vernacular economics. This stands in contrast with its "high" or academic counterpart, of which the EMH is a central element. While academic economics is "a body of homogeneous, abstract, and formalized explanations of economic processes," vernacular economics "is understood to comprise heterogeneous sets of practices, know-how techniques, and rationalization procedures that help social actors make sense of their economic environment and of the economic consequences of their own actions," Preda explains.[2]

As we saw in Chapters 4 and 5, the nineteenth century witnessed a general shift in worldview toward systematic, formal modeling, and as part of this shift, the economy came to be seen as a natural, law-based system that can be mathematically rationalized. And as described in Chapters 1–3, people had been recording prices since ancient times, but price had always stood on an equal footing with other types of data, such as political, climatic, and even astronomical, on which it was often superimposed with the goal of detecting causal relationships. For example, James Vansommer, the secretary of the Committee of the London Stock Exchange, in 1843 published a collection of charts in which he correlated bond price movements with political events over a 44-year period, and nineteenth-century British geographers would routinely superimpose the prices of wheat and bonds with measures of temperature.[3] It comes as no surprise that at the time when price recording was difficult and unreliable, as was especially the case with higher frequency intraday records, prices were often tied to political events in the popular press; newsletter writers would simply add an additional column in the table of price quotations to indicate the political event that happened on a day when the price reached a particular level.[4] As Preda points out, if economic and political events occurred less frequently than price variations, they could not have explained them.[5]

But by the end of the nineteenth century prices had come to be regarded as more than just a useful lens on the market; they increasingly came to be seen as the ultimate embodiment of every possible kind of information that influenced them, including investor psychology, market sentiment, and all other behavioral factors. With the advent of technology it became possible to record and accurately disseminate prices in real time, the causal explanation of price movements fell by the wayside, and technical analysis, which stresses pure price movements, advanced.

Financial markets are to be "approached in a functionalist, not in a causal, manner," argued investment writers of that time.[6] For example, in his 1874 investor manual, *Principles of the Science of the Stock Exchange*, Henri Lefevre depicted prices themselves as autonomous, living organisms by defining them via biological analogies, as opposed to focusing on causal explanations of price movements; what mattered was "to explain the functions fulfilled by markets in the society at large":[7]

> The stock exchange is a circulation organ; its function is to make [things] circulate, not to appraise the quality of the materials submitted to its action. When you introduce poison, venom, in the veins of an animal, the heart makes it circulate through

the entire organism. More or less grave disorders result, and the heart becomes a victim, but, again, its role is to produce movement, and not to make chemical analyses. This is why most criticisms of the bourse are off the mark, like the legal dispositions they pretended to impose upon [the bourse]. It will go on like that as long as we continue to believe that society is a mechanism whose movements and wheels can be controlled at will, when in fact it is a natural *organism* whose spontaneous functioning must be studied with the aim of supporting its development.[8]

In rejecting the causal explanation of price movements, the functionalists highlighted the importance of their visual representation: "The public does not need definitions and formulas; it needs images that are fixed on its mind [esprit], and with the help of which it can direct its actions. Images are the most powerful auxiliary of judgment; thus, whatever properties of a geometric figure result from its definition and are implicitly contained within, it would be impossible to extract them without the help of the eyes, that is, of images, in order to help the mind," wrote Lefevre. He further emphasized that "especially in the case of stock exchange operations, where the developments are so rapid, where the decisions must sometimes be so prompt, it matters if one has in his mind clear images instead of more or less confused formulas, because the slightest hesitation or a false movement may cause considerable damage in some cases."[9] This insistence on visualization naturally gave an impetus to technical analysis, which together with the ticker ushered in what Preda calls "cognitive standardization," where price charts serve as a standardized mode of visualization and technical analysis jargon as the standardized language of chartists.[10]

By the 1900s, technical analysis became institutionalized, with investor magazines regularly publishing detailed charts, chart rooms growing into fixtures of brokerage houses, and technical analysis jargon of head and shoulders, triangles, and rectangles becoming commonplace.[11] "This self-styled 'science of financial markets' promoted the notion that financial markets are governed by principles that are not controlled by any single individual or group," explains Preda.[12] That markets are governed by universal principles had been well recognized for hundreds of years. By the early twentieth century, this attitude was reinforced in technical analysis circles. Although big traders and bankers might be able to manipulate prices, the movements they induce were deemed only temporary, it was believed; as Nelson argued, "in the long run, it is the investor who establishes the price of a stock based on its value."[13]

Similarly, Pierre-Joseph Proudhon's realization of the ubiquitous and omniscient nature of the markets inspired him in 1854 to proclaim that restricting market operations would be absurd and even unfeasible:

> Let the press be muzzled, a tariff be put on the library, let the post be spied on, the telegraph exploited by the state, but speculation, by the anarchy that constitutes its essence, escapes all state and police regulations. To try putting a control on this last and infallible interpreter of opinions would mean to govern in the darkness of Egypt, which, according to the rabbis, was so thick that even candles and lanterns went out. How, for example, to forbid *options markets*? To forbid options markets, they should stop the oscillations of *demand* and *supply*, that is, guarantee to the trade the production, the quality, the placement, and the invariability of commodities' prices and at the same time eliminate all the aleatory conditions of the production, circulation, and consumption of goods, which is impossible and even contradictory.[14]

The popular science of financial markets provided practical solutions to everyday problems; the point was to reach the masses, not elite academic circles. But as a side effect, argues Preda, popular financial writers prepared the ground for rigorous theoretical treatment of financial markets. The EMH, he continues, was a result of a "slow evolution of popular knowledge into an academic, formalized science," not due to bursts of isolated genius.[15]

The Emergence of Efficient Markets

In describing how the movement of investing toward science led to the EMH, Preda notes that "irrational mass psychology was superseded as an explanatory variable by the informed decisions of individuals."[16]

While this conclusion is largely justified given the enormous success of the EMH both in academia and in industry, it does a disservice to the technical analysts of the early twentieth century, many of whom acknowledged the forces of irrationality explicitly, and dissected these forces and developed heuristics for dealing with them. Eventually, these practical rules of thumb took on a life of their own without reference to the psychological and economic milieu that gave rise to them.

Interestingly, the EMH came to France first, where the ticker was slow to be adopted and, as a result, the uncertainty about prices was especially high. For example, in the unofficial French bond options markets, traders would often negotiate directly with each other, without an auctioneer acting as a central clearing house, causing conflicting prices to be posted simultaneously for the same securities and rendering detailed price charts an impossible endeavor.[17] In the absence of charts, speculators relied on abstract models to reduce market risks. While, in France, the absence of the ticker gave an impetus to theoretical models of market behavior, its presence in the United States made it possible to understand investor behavior by charting and analyzing the price data through which it was reflected.

Moreover, just as "the popular science of financial investments provided the cognitive and cultural background against which elaborate theories and models, like Louis Bachelier's [model of market efficiency], could appear" in the early twentieth century, as Preda suggests, we argue that technical analysis has provided the background against which a rigorous theory of behavioral finance could take shape.[18] When Nobel Prize–winning economist Herbert Simon in 1955 proposed his model of financial markets based on the idea of bounded rationality— according to which humans are naturally limited in their computational resources and therefore bound to make choices that are merely satisfactory and not necessarily optimal—he was not working in a vacuum. Simon's ideas were as much a product of the cognitive and cultural background in which he operated as they were of his genius; the long legacy of technical analysts lies precisely in their recognition of human inability to consistently make optimal decisions and in the heuristics they developed to deal with that inability. However, the lack of appropriate technology inhibited the materialization of Simon's ideas. Though immediately compelling—even earning Simon a Nobel Prize—his work has not yet been operationalized nor made rigorous. One possible cause was the lack of the necessary concepts in the economics and computer science literatures: The notions of adaptive markets (see Chapter 8) and computationally constrained algorithms (see below) did not exist in his time, and still have not been fully developed to this day.

Around the same time as Simon, the now-familiar ideas of market efficiency were taking shape. While Paul Samuelson and Eugene Fama are credited with this important milestone in financial economics, the notion of efficiency began taking shape in the 1950s and 1960s. For example, a British statistician by the name of Maurice G. Kendall (1953) presented a paper, *The Analysis of Economic Time-Series—Part I: Prices*, to the Royal Statistical Society, in which he insisted that "there [was] no hope of being able to predict movements on the exchange for a week ahead without extraneous information."[19] Rather, it was "almost as if once a week the Demon of Chance drew a random number from a symmetrical population of fixed dispersion and added it to the current price to determine the next week's price."[20] In other words, predicting future stock prices based on past prices alone, without insider information or knowledge of a company's fundamentals, was deemed a futile endeavor. It is from this rediscovery that the EMH stems.[21]

Also, in Paul Cootner's classic 1964 volume *The Random Character of Stock Market Prices*, a collection of academic studies by a number of prominent economists and statisticians, he summarizes Harry Roberts's (1959) motivation for the random walk model for stock prices in the following passage:

> The basic proposition depends upon a characteristic of competition in perfect markets: That participants in such a market will eliminate any profits above the bare minimum required to induce them to continue in the market, except for any profits which might accrue to someone who can exercise some degree of market monopoly. There is, for example, no reason why a trader with special information about future events cannot profit from that monopolized knowledge. On the other hand, we should not expect, in such a market, that traders could continue to profit from the use of a formula depending only upon past price data and generally available rules of "technical analysis." If

this is so, all changes in prices should be independent of any past history about a company which is generally available to the trading public.[22]

This summary is a strikingly contemporary and practical view of market efficiency that anticipates Samuelson's (1965) and Fama's (1970) more formal analyses. And note that even as the EMH was being developed, disdain for technical analysis was already building!

The concept of market efficiency has a counter-intuitive and Zen-like contradictory flavor to it: the more efficient the market, the more random the sequence of price changes generated by such a market must be, and the most efficient market of all is one in which price changes are completely random and unpredictable. Unlike the motivation for Brownian motion in the physical and biological sciences—typically a weak statement of general ignorance regarding the dynamics of interactions—the motivation for randomness in financial markets is the direct outcome of many active participants attempting to profit from their information. Unable to curtail their greed, an army of investors aggressively pounces on even the smallest informational advantages at their disposal, and in doing so, they impound their information into market prices and quickly eliminate the profit opportunities that gave rise to their actions. If this occurs instantaneously, which it must in an idealized world of "frictionless" markets and costless trading, then prices must always fully reflect all available information and no profits can be garnered from information-based trading (because such profits have already been captured).

With the benefit of hindsight and the theoretical insights of LeRoy (1973) and Lucas (1973), it is now clear that efficient markets and the random walk hypothesis are two distinct ideas, neither one necessary nor sufficient for the other. The reason for this distinction comes from one of the central ideas of modern financial economics: the necessity of some trade-off between risk and expected return. If a security's expected price change is positive, it may be just the reward needed to attract investors to hold the asset and bear the corresponding risks. Indeed, if an investor is sufficiently risk averse, he might gladly *pay* to avoid holding a security that has unforecastable returns. In such a world, prices do not need to be perfectly random, even if markets are operating efficiently and rationally.[23]

Cootner and the other early contributors can hardly be faulted for not appreciating the distinction between efficient markets and the random walk. By itself, the notion of market efficiency is not a well-posed and empirically refutable hypothesis. To make it operational, we must specify additional structure, such as investors' preferences, the information they each possess, their current financial circumstances, and so on. But then a test of market efficiency becomes a test of several auxiliary hypotheses as well, and a rejection of such a joint hypothesis tells us little about which aspect of the joint hypothesis is inconsistent with the data. The hypothesis that investors are fully rational agents that instantaneously and correctly process all available information is clearly unrealistic—rationality is difficult to define, human behavior is often unpredictable, information can be difficult to interpret, technology and institutions change constantly, and there are significant "frictional" costs to gathering and processing information, and to transacting. But how can we take all the complexities of the real world into account? We tackle this issue in the next chapter. Before doing so, however, we take a short detour to review the historical origins of randomness, a concept that is central not only to quantitative finance, but also to the skepticism surrounding technical analysis.

What Is Random?

The concept of randomness is directly related to the evolution of the probability theory, and here again, popular science paved the way for its academic counterpart. The nineteenth-century popular financial writer Henri Lefevre was also an inventor of instruments for conducting probabilistic calculations for gamblers, such as the *autocompteur*, his 1871 creation intended as an aid in horse-race betting.[24] Probabilistic modeling was not limited to gambling outcomes, but was also applied to financial speculation with the aim of reducing the risks and making it more acceptable to investors. As Preda points out, "While investor behavior was reduced to decisions according to certain given situations, decisions were reduced to calculations. In order to decide, the investor needs to compute possible outcomes."[25] Lefevre, for example, in addition to his horse-race gambling device, also invented the "abacus of the speculator," a wooden board divided into squares and equipped with movable letters, where by moving the letters one could see the outcomes of decisions for different options contracts.[26] And in his 1891 business manual *The Mathematical Theory of Long-Term Investing*, Adolphe Pierre Brasilier presented a framework in which French corporate bonds were to be treated as a lottery problem because of their structure—periodically a certain number of bonds would be drawn by lottery and reimbursed at a premium above the issue price, and the rest of the bonds would continue to receive interest until the next drawing date—and analyzed Parisian bonds from 1855 to 1860 in that framework.[27]

Using past prices, business manuals also suggested computing the probabilities that the securities would attain certain price levels in the future. One method was to take the difference between the yield of a given security and the state bond yield—the latter was used as a reference point because it was guaranteed and slow varying; then, based on past variations of these differences, future variations were predicted.[28] As the probability theory was making the inroads into the analysis of price fluctuations, it provoked hot debates in the investor manuals, such as the 1854 *La Bourse de Paris*:

> I do not know about the power of probabilistic calculus applied to the operations of the stock exchange, but I know that Condorcet and the Marquis of Laplace failed on all their calculations on the probability of moral events, on judgments on a plurality of votes, and on the results of parliamentary votes. A moral event depends on a thousand unknown causes that cannot be submitted to any calculus. If we would want to try our fortune by some calculus, the method of the Viscount Saint-André would be better. The Marquis of Laplace has made a science out of probability calculus. This science can be applied to life insurance, to ship insurance; it has a basis in the mortality tables and the number of ships that are stranded every year, but it is impossible to find it in the lows and highs of bonds. What produces the movements of these bonds is as variable as the golden arrow on the palace of the bourse.[29]

The credit for the first formal study of the mathematics of probability belongs to the same Italian mathematician who gave us the martingale, Girolamo Cardano. His treatise *Liber de Ludo Aleae* went far beyond simple games of chance, and also contained many of the basic concepts of formal probability theory. As was the case with many of his contemporaries, Cardano's interest in this subject was sparked by his passion for gambling; he believed that there was a sense in which, when throwing a pair of dice, some numbers were more likely to come up than others, and that he could use this insight to make money. However, the addiction for gambling proved stronger than his rationality, apparently driving him to squander the money his family had left him, and, on one occasion, cutting with a knife the opponent whom he thought had cheated at cards.

A century later the study of probability was taken over by the French. Chevalier de Méré, another gambler, devised in 1654 a system for gambling which he thought would win him money; when it did not, he asked the mathematician Blaise Pascal (1623–1662) why. After some analysis, Pascal noticed that, in fact, Chevalier's system would lose more often than not. This event fostered Pascal's interest in probability theory, leading to an intense correspondence with Pierre de Fermat (1601–1665) which laid the foundations of probability theory. After having learned of this correspondence, a Dutch scientist, Christiaan Huygens, published *De Ratiociniis in Ludo Aleae*, the first book on probability. The theory was further developed in the seventeenth and eighteenth centuries by Daniel Bernoulli and Abraham de Moivre. Then in 1812 Pierre de Laplace published his *Théorie Analytique des Probabilités*, which, unlike previous works, did not focus on games of chance but developed a general theory of probability applicable to many practical problems, even catching the eye of Napoleon.

According to Laplace's notion of probability—which we term the "classical approach to randomness"—a certain probability is assigned to each possible outcome of an experiment. For example, when tossing a coin, heads has probability 1/2, and tails has the same. Classical probability theory develops many sophisticated ways to compute these probabilities, but at the core is the underlying assumption that the outcomes of experiments have certain inherent or fundamental probabilities: The fact that heads has probability 1/2 is axiomatic, and the theory allows us to compute more complicated probabilities, such as that of obtaining heads 10 times in a row, which is $(1/2)^{10}$.

This classical notion of probability is used today in nearly every branch of science. However, it is in some sense unsatisfactory because it does not capture people's intuitive notion of "random." This is best understood by considering the following paradox. Suppose a friend tells you: "I have tossed a die 10 times and I have gotten 6, 6, 6, 6, 6, 6, 6, 6, 6, 6." You would probably think he is lying, or that he was using a nonstandard die. But what if the same friend tells you: "I have tossed a die 10 times and I have gotten 1, 3, 4, 3, 6, 2, 5, 4, 2, 5"? You would probably harbor no suspicions about that sequence; it "looks random." Intuitively, the second sequence of outcomes looks more random than the first. The paradox is that, according to the classical theory of probability, both sequences have the same probability: $(1/6)^{10} = 0.00000001653 \ldots$. Thus, the classical notion of randomness does not match human intuition.

A solution to this paradox had to wait until the beginning of the twentieth century, when what we refer to as "the ontological approach to randomness" emerged. The idea is to note that 6, 6, 6, 6, 6, 6, 6, 6, 6, 6 is very regular—it is the repetition of the number 6—whereas the second sequence, 1, 3, 4, 3, 6, 2, 5, 4, 2, 5, appears irregular. The ontological approach to randomness declares a sequence of outcomes random if the outcomes are not regular. This notion is indeed ontological because it refers to a quality that is intrinsic to an object: A fixed string can be random or not. At first sight, it seems problematic to make sense of this approach, since it is not clear what "regular" may mean. One person might see regularity in 2, 3, 5, 7, 11, 13, recognizing the sequence of prime numbers, but others may not. Arbitrarily complicated regularity may be created. Thus, how can we be sure that the second sequence our friend shows us—1, 3, 4, 3, 6, 2, 5, 4, 2, 5—is indeed random?

To answer this question, one needs a precise definition of "regular." This definition was made possible in the first half of the twentieth century with the development of computer science. The work of Gödel (1931), Church (1936), Kleene (1936), Post (1936), and Turing (1937) gave strong evidence that computers form a universal language in which every possible regularity can be programmed (this is known as the Church-Turing thesis). This computational framework is central to the ontological definition of randomness, which appeared in the 1960s, most notably in the works of Ray Solomonoff (1960, 1964) and Andrey Kolmogorov (1965).[30]

According to this theory, we consider a string regular, and so nonrandom, if there is a way to generate the string with a computer program that is shorter than the string itself; in other words, the program is "compressing" the string. For example, the 20-character string 6, 6, 6, 6, 6, 6, 6, 6, 6, 6, 6, 6, 6, 6, 6, 6, 6, 6, 6, 6 is nonrandom because the computer program "Print '6' 20 times" generates it and is much shorter than the string itself. Conversely, the string 1, 3, 4, 3, 6, 2, 5, 4, 2, 5, 2, 6, 4, 4, 3, 2, 1, 4, 2, 3 is random because the shortest computer program generating it is "Print 1, 3, 4, 3, 6, 2, 5, 4, 2, 5, 2, 6, 4, 4, 3, 2, 1, 4, 2, 3," which contains the string inside it and in particular is longer than the string it outputs. The shorter the computer program generating the string, the more regular and less random the string is.

The need for a third definition of randomness is clear. Modern computer systems routinely need large amounts of random numbers to carry through simulations of probabilistic models in a variety of fields including finance, physics, and biology—a paradigm known as Monte Carlo simulation. Moreover, the explosion of electronic commerce also requires a large quantity of random numbers, which are used to encrypt our credit card numbers every time we make a purchase online. As it turns out, neither the classical definition of random nor the ontological one are of much use to generate these numbers. The classical definition of random gives no way to generate randomness, but rather assumes that certain experiments, such as tossing a coin, have random outcomes; certainly we don't expect computers to toss coins to obtain random numbers. Even other experiments whose outcomes are believed to be random, for example, those involving radioactive decay, usually cannot be performed sufficiently fast by computers to be of use in applications (though sometimes they are used as the starting point or "seed" for the procedures we describe in Note 31); today we use procedures, or algorithms, that quickly output a stream of pseudorandom numbers. The ontological approach to randomness does not help either in this enterprise: It declares a string to be random precisely when there is no way to generate it using a computer program!

The way around this is given by what we call the modern or "behavioral" approach to randomness. This approach comes with a twist on our original question: Rather than asking what "is" random, we should ask what "looks" random. We have already encountered an example of how such a reformulation could make a difference. A mathematician could spot the prime numbers in the sequence 2, 3, 5, 7, 11, 13, and because of this regularity would deem the sequence to be nonrandom. But somebody who is not familiar with prime numbers might very well think of this sequence as random; the sequence may not be random, but looks random to him.[31]

This behavioral perspective on randomness suggests that a more direct "test" of the efficacy of technical analysis might be to ask whether humans can distinguish actual market data from randomly generated numbers. Now this is a horse race that technicians should care about!

The conviction that humans cannot distinguish market returns from randomly generated ones is widespread.[32] It is clearly at odds with technicians, who study past returns with the aim of forecasting future returns—a task that is impossible for randomly generated returns and, therefore, should not be possible for market returns either.

As we briefly discussed in Chapter 6, in an experimental study co-authored by us and Emanuele Viola, we test this simple hypothesis by recruiting human subjects to play a Web-based video game (http:// arora.ccs.neu.edu) in which individuals are shown two dynamic price series side by side, both evolving in real time (a new price is realized each second)—but only one of which is a "replay" of actual historical price series, the other series being constructed from a random shuffling of the actual series (see figure).[33] On each trial, subjects are asked to press a button indicating which price series they think is the real one, and they are given immediate feedback as to whether they were correct or incorrect. In a sample of 78 subjects participating in up to 8 different contests (using different types of financial data), with each contest lasting two weeks and concluding with prizes awarded to top performers, we obtained 8,015 human-generated guesses for this real-time choice problem. The results provided overwhelming statistical evidence (less than 1 percent probability of the findings being generated by pure chance) that humans can quickly learn to distinguish actual price series from randomly generated ones.

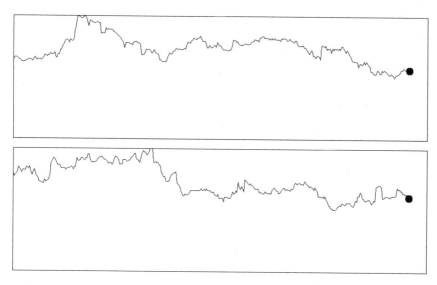

Real and simulated financial prices—can you tell which one is which? See Note 34 for the answer.

This experiment can be viewed as the financial version of the Turing test, an idea proposed by Alan Turing (1950) for deciding whether a computer program can be considered truly intelligent. In Turing's scenario, a human subject interacts with two other agents— one machine, one human—via written correspondence; the computer will have passed the test if the subject cannot correctly identify which correspondent is artificial. To date, no computer has passed the Turing test. Similarly, our video-game experiments show that financial markets have not passed the financial Turing test either, which is encouraging news for technical analysis.

The financial Turing test is just one example of how computer science can change the way we think about economics and finance. More broadly, the notion of computationally bounded algorithms may be an important missing piece in Simon's theory of bounded rationality. Although there are many early examples of scientists distinguishing between "efficient" and "inefficient" algorithms—where efficiency is now used in a completely different sense than the EMH—it was not until the 1960s that Cobham (1964), Edmonds (1965), and Hartmanis and Stearns (1965), as part of the early development of computational complexity theory, identified the class of computationally bounded algorithms today known simply as "P" (for polynomial-time algorithm).[35] To model Simon's bounded rationality, we need to understand what can be computed efficiently; in other words, how good a decision can be made in a limited amount of time and/or with a limited amount of memory. This amounts to understanding what algorithms lie in P. Although the class P was put forth already in the 1960s, its understanding still baffles researchers to this day.

The study of the power of algorithms that use limited resources has proved a daunting task that has arguably seen very little progress. It is, in fact, one of the seven "millennium problems" for which the Clay Mathematics Institute offers a prize of one million dollars to the first person to come up with a solution. Undoubtedly, progress in the theory of bounded rationality in economics will go hand-in-hand with the progress in the theory of computationally bounded algorithms. And tagging right along will be the analytical future of technical analysis.

Chapter 8

Academic Approaches to Technical Analysis

Big strides have been made toward the standardization of technical analysis in recent years.[1] The impetus for statistically evaluating technical analysis naturally comes from academia, with studies yielding evidence of its validity in wide-ranging areas, such as moving averages (Brock, Lakonishok, and LeBaron, 1992), genetic algorithms to discover optimal trading rules (Neely, Weller, and Dittmar, 1997), and the Dow theory (Brown, Goetzmann, and Kumar, 1998), to name a few. In their quest to quantify technical analysis, academics have turned, too, to the most controversial of its techniques: geometric patterns. Finding patterns in price charts is a subjective endeavor that relies on the natural smoothing filter of the human eye (which, needless to say, is vastly more sophisticated than a moving average); therefore, a main challenge in quantifying the patterns lies in modeling the way in which eyes smooth the data they view. Academics such as Chang and Osler (1994) and Lo, Mamaysky, and Wang (2000) take on this challenge by smoothing the data using statistical filtering techniques. They then develop algorithms to automatically identify technical patterns in those data and finally evaluate the information content of the patterns thus found; these works, too, find proof of the potential value of technical analysis.

In this chapter we survey these and other relevant works. Our purpose is to review the main trends rather than provide an all-inclusive encyclopedia of academic research.

Theoretical Underpinnings

While the idea that stock market prices follow a random walk was anticipated in the nineteenth-century popular investment literature by French authors such as Henri Lefevre, the steps toward its mathematical formalization were first made in 1900 by the French graduate student Louis Bachelier (1870–1946) in his doctoral dissertation, *Théorie de la Spéculation*. Unfortunately, the dissertation, now deemed the "origin of mathematical finance," fell into oblivion until the statistician L.J. Savage rediscovered his thesis and contacted Paul A. Samuelson, who immediately recognized its significance.[2]

As we saw in Chapter 6, a great deal of research has been devoted ever since to formulating theoretically the efficient market hypothesis, building up market efficiency—the idea that "prices fully reflect all available information"—into one of the most important concepts in economics. Since Samuelson's and Fama's landmark papers, many others extended their original framework, yielding a "neoclassical" version of the efficient market hypothesis, where price changes, properly weighted by aggregate marginal utilities, must be unforecastable.[3] In markets where, according to Lucas (1978), all investors have "rational expectations," prices do fully reflect all available information and marginal-utility-weighted prices follow martingales. Market efficiency has been extended in many other directions, including the incorporation of nontraded assets such as human capital, state-dependent preferences, heterogeneous investors, asymmetric information, and transaction costs.[4] But the general thrust is the same: Individual investors form expectations rationally, markets aggregate information efficiently, and equilibrium prices incorporate all available information instantaneously.[5]

But the EMH is not the unassailable edifice it is often made out to be. For example, consider situations of asymmetric information. It has been argued that even if market inefficiencies could be induced by asymmetric informedness of market participants, they would be instantly eliminated. In Fischer Black's (1986) presidential address to the American Finance Association, he argued that financial market prices were subject to "noise," which could temporarily create inefficiencies that would ultimately be eliminated through intelligent investors competing against each other to generate profitable trades. Since then, many authors have modeled financial markets by hypothesizing two types of traders—informed and uninformed—where informed traders have private information better reflecting the true economic value of a security, and uninformed traders have no information at all, but merely trade for liquidity needs.[6] In this context, Grossman and Stiglitz (1980) suggest that market efficiency is impossible because if markets were truly efficient, there would be no incentive for investors to gather private information and trade, and DeLong et al. (1990, 1991) provide a more detailed analysis in which certain types of uninformed traders can destabilize market prices for periods of time even in the presence of informed traders.[7]

More direct evidence against the EMH and in favor of technical analysis emerged in the work of Treynor and Ferguson (1985), who show that it is not only the past prices, but the past prices plus some valuable nonpublic information, that can lead to profit. A more basic challenge to market efficiency was proposed by Lo and MacKinlay (1988), who strongly reject the efficient market hypothesis for weekly stock market returns by using a simple volatility-based specification test.

Empirical Evaluation

The early empirical testing of the EMH turned out in its favor, though this was as much due to the cultural attitudes toward technical analysis as to the scientific results. For example, in their important study, Fama and Blume (1966) investigate whether one can exploit the degree of dependence between successive price changes of individual securities by following a mechanical trading rule. Independence here refers to a situation where successive price changes are independent in a probabilistic sense. For example, if today's price is higher than yesterday's, that makes it neither more nor less likely for tomorrow's price to be higher than today's. If, on the other hand, a positive price change increases the likelihood of observing a positive (negative) price change in the future, that is called positive (negative) dependence. The trading rule they consider is known as Alexander's filter technique, and they measure its profitability by comparing its expected returns to those of a passive buy-and-hold strategy. More precisely, in their 1966 paper, "Filter Rules and Stock-Market Trading," Fama and Blume investigate whether the random walk model of price movements is meaningful from an investor's viewpoint. They start by noting that the degree of dependence between successive price changes of individual securities may simultaneously be meaningful to some and insignificant to others—it all depends on the specific case. For example, for an investor, the independence assumption becomes meaningful if it can make expected profits from some mechanical trading rule greater than those of a buy-and-hold strategy.

With this in mind, the authors evaluate Alexander's filter technique, a mechanical trading rule developed by Sidney Alexander to test whether or not prices move in trends. According to the filter of size x percent, if the daily closing price of a particular security moves up at least x percent, one buys and holds the security until its price moves down at least x percent from a subsequent high, at which time one sells and goes short and maintains the short position until the price moves up at least x percent above a subsequent low, at which time one covers and buys.

The authors apply Alexander's filter technique to a series of daily closing prices for each of the individual securities of the Dow Jones Industrial Average from 1956 to 1962 using various values for x. They find that even when the commissions are omitted, the average returns from the filter rules are inferior to the returns from the buy-and-hold strategy. This stands in contrast to the findings of Alexander, who, according to the authors, wrongly concluded that the filter rule was superior to the buy-and-hold rule. The reason for his misinterpretation lies in his improper adjustment for dividends, Fama and Blume explain. They also point out that even if the filter technique were restricted to the more profitable long positions, it would not consistently outperform the buy-and-hold

strategy, and that, naturally, the inclusion of commissions further empha-
sizes the superiority of the buy-and-hold strategy. Fama and Blume hence
conclude that "even on extremely close scrutiny" the results "[do] not
yield evidence of dependence."[8]

The authors do find, however, that slight amounts of both positive
and negative dependence are present in the price changes. Specifically,
for the filter sizes of 0.5 percent, 1.0 percent, and 1.5 percent, the average returns per security on long positions are greater than the average
return from buy-and-hold, and the average losses on short positions
are smaller than the gains from buy-and-hold. The opposite is true for
filter sizes that are larger than 1.5 percent and smaller than 5 percent,
constituting evidence for positive dependence in very small movements
of stock prices and for the negative dependence in the intermediate
movements. However, the authors deemphasize this evidence by arguing that the degree of the dependences is so small that it is easily offset
by the transaction costs, making it impossible, even for a floor trader,
to profit from the filter rule. Since the marginal transaction costs of
the floor trader are the minimum trading costs, the authors again conclude that the market is indeed efficient and that, even from an investor's viewpoint, the random walk model is an adequate description of
the price behavior. Such conclusions rule out the possibility that technical analysts, whose principal assumption is that past prices contain
information for predicting future returns, can add value to the investment process. Consequently, for a long time technical analysis has been
largely discredited in the academic world, with Burton G. Malkiel, the
author of the influential *A Random Walk Down Wall Street* (1973), concluding that "under scientific scrutiny, chart-reading must share a ped-
estal with alchemy."

To this day many academics remain critical of the discipline.
However, an increasing number of studies suggest, either directly or
indirectly, that "technical analysis may well be an effective means for
extracting useful information from market prices."[9] A growing number
of finance academics are coming to recognize that efficient markets are
not an adequate model of reality. Thus, a crack in the door has been
opened for academic considerations of technical analysis.

An early (though in its time largely ignored) study by Granger
and Morgenstern (1963) finds that the random walk model ignores

the possibly important low-frequency (long-run) components of the time series of stock market prices. Specifically, in their 1963 paper, "Spectral Analysis of New York Stock Market Prices," Granger and Morgenstern test how well the random walk model fits the specified sample of New York Stock Exchange prices and also promote the idea that "the most appropriate statistical techniques to be used [in the analysis of stock market data] are the recently developed spectral methods."[10] Spectral analysis, in this case, refers to a statistical procedure known as the Fourier transform, which, loosely speaking, decomposes a time series into cycles of different frequencies. This procedure is used to obtain a frequency spectrum of the time series—its representation in the frequency domain—which shows how much of the series lies within different frequency bands over a range of frequencies.

The authors start by suggesting that the random walk model may ignore the possibly important low-frequency (long-run) components of the time series. For example, let $\{X_t\}$ denote a time series of prices generated by a random walk model, ω a small frequency value, and a some constant term. Then, the first differences of $\{X_t\}$ are virtually indistinguishable from the first differences of $\{Y_t\}$, where $Y_t = X_t + a \cos(\omega t)$, even though the latter contains a low-frequency (long-run) component specified by a cosine of a small ω. The authors then test whether their data contain long-run components of greater importance than the random walk hypothesis would imply. They hence estimate the frequency spectrum of the data and compare them to the expected spectrum if the random walk hypothesis were true. They find that, while most of the frequency bands of the estimated spectra parallel their expected counterparts, certain bands are significantly greater than what the random walk model would lead us to expect. The authors conclude that the random walk model, "although extremely successful in explaining most of the spectral shape, does not adequately explain the strong long-run (24 months or more) components of the series."[11]

The controversy of the EMH in the theoretical literature has also paved the way for more direct studies of the validity of various technical analysis techniques and systems: The natural starting point was the most readily quantifiable of them, such as technical trading systems and moving averages. For example, Pruitt and White (1988) test the performance of a technical trading system and conclude that it does better than a simple buy-and-hold strategy to an extent that could not be attributed to chance alone.

And in their 1992 paper, "Simple Technical Trading Rules and the Stochastic Properties of Stock Returns," Brock, Lakonishok, and LeBaron test "two of the simplest and most popular trading rules"— moving average and trading range break—based on the data of the Dow Jones Index from 1897 to 1986. Two moving average varieties are considered: the "variable length moving average," which initiates buy (sell) signals when the short moving average is above (below) the long moving average by an amount larger than the specified band, and the "fixed length moving average," which initiates buy (sell) signals when the short moving average cuts the long moving average from below (above) and keeps that position for the next 10 days. In a trading range break-out rule, a buy (sell) signal is generated when the price penetrates the resistance (support) level, as defined by a local maximum (minimum). It is found that the buy signals select periods with higher conditional returns and lower volatilities, while the sell signals select periods with lower conditional returns and higher volatilities; the fact that the higher returns for buys do not arise during riskier periods indicates that the difference in returns between buys and sells is not easily explained by risk.

Overall, these results indicate that the technical rules explored do possess some predictive power. Consistently, buy (sell) signals provided by the trading rules generate returns that are higher (lower) than unconditional returns. Moreover, the returns generated from the buy and sell signals are unlikely to be generated by the random walk or other popular null models, suggesting that the empirical foundations of the EMH may not be as strong as is generally believed.

Attention turned next to the most controversial of technical analytic practices, chart-pattern reading, for patterns are the most subjective and hardest to quantify of technical indicators. One of the first rigorous studies of patterns was initiated by Charles Kirkpatrick, who convinced his then employer, Arthur Little Corporation, to hire Robert Levy to conduct the study. The results are summarized in Levy's 1971 paper, "The Predictive Significance of Five-Point Chart Patterns." Studying 32 possible forms of five-point chart patterns in the daily closing prices of 548 New York Stock Exchange securities from 1964 to 1969, Levy finds that after accounting for transaction costs none of the patterns show profitable forecasting ability. He concedes that changing the parameters of his pattern definitions and the type of data on which they are based, and most significantly specifying patterns not only in terms of price but also in terms of volume, may alter the conclusions.

The next important step in this direction was made by Chang and Osler, who in their pioneering work, "Evaluating Chart-Based Technical Analysis: The Head-and-Shoulders Pattern in Foreign Exchange Markets," evaluate the predictive power of the head-and-shoulders pattern using daily dollar exchange rates of the dollar vs. the yen, mark, Canadian dollar, Swiss franc, French franc, and pound during what at the time constituted the entire floating rate period, from March 1973 to June 1994. Chang and Osler's head-and-shoulders pattern identification algorithm starts by tracing out a zigzag pattern in the data, then scans the thus smoothed data for the evidence of the defining characteristics of the head-and-shoulders pattern (see Chapter 6). Importantly, the position is entered after the breaking of the neckline and exited when a new peak or a new trough is reached, and the profits are calculated as the gain or loss between entry and exit. The results indicate that the profits are significantly greater than what a random walk model would suggest, albeit only for the mark and the yen. Nonetheless, this suggests that the head-and-shoulders pattern has some predictive power. The authors also note that while profitable for the mark and the yen, the head-and-shoulders pattern is "extremely risky." Namely, the standard deviation of returns across positions ranged from 2 to 4 times the mean return. However, Chang and Osler argue that it is still likely that investors would find the profits from the head-and-shoulders pattern attractive in the context of a diversified portfolio, given that they are often more concerned with systematic risk than with absolute risk.

Further work in the pattern quantification was done by Lo, Mamaysky, and Wang (2000), who in an attempt to transform the "art" of technical analysis into more of a science, propose in their paper, "Foundations of Technical Analysis: Computational Algorithms, Statistical Inference, and Empirical Implementation," an algorithm which aims to formalize and automate the highly subjective and controversial practice of detecting, with the naked eye, the geometric patterns that appear in price charts and are believed to have predictive value. They start by recognizing that the evolution of prices over time is not random, but that it contains certain regularities or patterns, and they then attempt to identify, or extract, these nonlinear patterns from the historical time series of prices. Here it is important to realize that identifying patterns directly from the raw price data would not be sensible. When professional technicians study a price chart, their eyes naturally smooth the data, while their cognitive faculties discern regularities. Moreover, many would argue that much of this process takes place on an intuitive and subconscious level, making it even harder to quantify. Hence, natural candidates for modeling the process by which technicians look for patterns in a price chart are pattern-recognition techniques known as smoothing estimators, which estimate nonlinear relationships by averaging the data in sophisticated ways to reduce the observational errors. In particular, Lo, Mamaysky, and Wang (2000) automate technical analysis using a smoothing estimator known as kernel regression.

In an attempt to answer the question of whether or not this aspect of technical analysis "works," they apply kernel regression to the daily returns of individual NYSE/AMEX and Nasdaq stocks from 1962 to 1996. The kernel regression function is then analyzed for the occurrence of each of the 10 technical patterns under consideration in the experiment: head-and-shoulders, triangles, rectangles, broadening and double formations, and their inverse or "bottom" counterparts. After the technical patterns have been obtained, their information content is examined by comparing the unconditional empirical distribution of returns with the corresponding conditional empirical distribution, conditioned on the occurrence of a technical pattern. If technical patterns are informative, conditioning on them should alter the empirical distribution of returns; in other words, if the information contained in such patterns has already been incorporated into returns, there should not be much difference between the conditional and unconditional distribution of returns.[12]

They find that certain technical patterns, when applied to many stocks over many time periods, do provide incremental information, especially for Nasdaq stocks, supporting the claim that technical analysis can add incremental value to the investment process.[13] The authors conclude that although there will probably always be demand for talented technical analysts, the benefits of transparency and low cost associated with its automation suggest that algorithms should play some role in an investor's portfolio and may also bring technical analysis closer to other forms of systematic financial analysis. The same conclusions are reached by Hasanhodzic (2007), who conducts the robustness test of the Lo, Mamaysky, and Wang results by replacing the kernel regression smoothing algorithm with the neural network one.

"The proof is in the pudding," respond successful technicians when faced with skepticism about their craft. Rather than simply dismissing as exception bias the track records of winning technicians, some academics have evaluated them statistically. One such technician, the legendary early-twentieth-century Dow theorist William Hamilton, is the subject of Brown, Goetzmann, and Kumar's 1998 paper, "The Dow Theory: William Peter Hamilton's Track Record Reconsidered." In particular, Brown, Goetzmann, and Kumar reevaluate Alfred Cowles's (1933) test of the Dow theory, which provided "strong evidence" against the ability of the theory to forecast stock market prices. The authors test whether Hamilton's interpretation of the Dow theory can predict stock market movements and attempt to uncover the rules of the Dow theory (as interpreted by Hamilton) and to understand its implications for the EMH. To this end, they label as bullish, bearish, neutral, or indeterminate the 255 editorials Hamilton published in *The Wall Street Journal* during his tenure as its editor from 1902 to 1929, and then calculate the frequency with which the Dow theory beats the risk-free rate (assumed to be at 5 percent per annum) over the interval following an editorial, conditional upon bull or bear call.

Brown, Goetzmann, and Kumar (1998) find that the proportion of successful up calls is greater than the proportion of the failed up calls, and that the proportion of successful down calls is much greater than the proportion of failed down calls. In fact, their contingency table analysis shows strong evidence of an association between Hamilton's calls and subsequent market performance. In addition, the proportion of correct bear calls is found to be much higher than what could be attributed to chance alone. To make these observations more concrete, they simulate a trading strategy based on Hamilton's editorials—going long the market on a bullish signal and shorting the market on

a bearish one. They find that over the 27-year period under consideration, the Hamilton strategy yields a very similar average annual return to
the Standard & Poor's Composite Index but with lower volatility,
resulting in a superior risk-adjusted return.

To test the validity of Hamilton's forecasts out of sample (that is,
for the Dow Jones Industrial Average from 1930 to 1997 for which
Hamilton did not generate any forecasts), Brown, Goetzmann, and
Kumar (1998) first reduce the dynamics of past price series to basic
trend shapes such as rising trends, falling trends, head-and-shoulders,
and resistance levels. These trend shapes are then used as inputs to a
neural network that is trained on the 27 years' worth of Hamilton editorials data to identify a nonlinear mapping from features to Hamilton's
recommendation.

The success of the in-sample performance (that is, for the 1902–1929
period for which Hamilton's forecasts are available) of the neural network
indicates that Hamilton did rely on structures that resemble positive and
negative trends and reversals. The out-of-sample performance is evaluated on the September 1930–December 1997 period, and returns of the
buy-and-hold strategy are compared to those of the "next day Hamilton
strategy" and the "second day Hamilton strategy." The "next day
Hamilton strategy" refers to investing at the opening-of-the-day prices of
the day on which the neural network forecast comes out—for example,
an investor who bought the paper before the opening of the market can
take advantage of the signal immediately or as soon as the market opens.
And the "second day Hamilton strategy" refers to investing at the close-
of-the-day prices of the day on which the neural network forecast comes
out—for example, an investor who bought the paper before the opening of the market cannot take advantage of the signal until the end of the
day. The authors find that while the returns of the second day strategy
are almost exactly equal to the buy-and-hold returns (but would be less
than that after transaction costs), they do exhibit less variance and lower
systematic risk compared to the buy-and-hold.

Such results are comparable to those obtained during Hamilton's
lifetime: returns that are close to a buy-and-hold strategy, but that are
characterized with lower levels of risk. The next-day Hamilton strategy has much higher returns than the second-day Hamilton strategy;
however, even the next-day strategy does not dominate buy-and-hold

in the 1980s. The results suggest that the Dow theory is not entirely consistent, and it would not be able to generate large excess returns due to transaction costs and other trading frictions. However, these results also indicate that the Dow theory was more than random decision making on the part of Hamilton. In particular, the Hamilton strategy appears to reduce portfolio volatility and, in the case where the immediate execution of the sell signal is possible, to yield profits that are higher than those of the buy-and-hold. Again, this implies that the empirical foundations of the EMH may not be as strong as long believed.

The observation that human nature never changes, and that consequently technical indicators designed to measure the reflection of human nature in market prices never change either, is a notable argument in favor of technical analysis, but one that at the same time underscores its main shortcoming: Technical analysis has not kept up with technological advances. Of course, charting and data collection have become automated, but most popular patterns and heuristics of today were developed in the precomputing age when calculating a simple moving average was a formidable task. For example, the 10-day moving average became popular not because it was optimal, but simply because it was trivial to compute. The 10-day moving average remains in common use today in spite of the fact that computers can calculate a moving average for *any* time scale with equal ease.

Suboptimal parametrization is only a symptom of a chronic disease afflicting technical analysis: Its static nature cannot account for the ever-changing character of financial markets. In the past, when execution was manual and costly, and financial systems were far less connected and complex, "static" used to be a prerequisite for practical use; now it is more often a recipe for failure. As markets evolve and trading strategies become more sophisticated, the need for new, dynamic indicators is apparent. Never has this need been more urgent than now, in the wake of the financial crisis of 2007–2009.

Some authors have taken steps in this regard by investigating the form of an optimal trading rule that can be revealed by the data themselves, rather than evaluating the commonly used technical indicators. For example, in their 1997 paper, "Is Technical Analysis on the Foreign Exchange Markets Profitable? A Genetic Programming

Approach," Neely, Weller, and Dittmar use genetic programming to discover trading rules that are most profitable given the data with which they are dealing. The purpose of such an approach is to reduce the risk of the out-of-sample bias, which arises when the trading rules are selected ex post, rather than at the beginning of the sample period (the authors claim that the results of previous studies that sought to document the existence of excess returns to various types of trading rules in the foreign exchange market are all biased in this way). Six exchange rate time series are considered: dollar/German mark, dollar/yen, dollar/pound, dollar/ Swiss franc, German mark/yen, and pound/Swiss franc, and the rules are obtained over the period 1975–1980.

When the performance of these rules is examined over the period 1981–1995, strong evidence of economically significant out-of-sample excess returns after the adjustment for transaction costs is found for each of the six exchange rates. Since technical analysts commonly claim that their rules exploit general features of financial markets, rather than being specific to any particular market, the authors run the dollar/German mark rules on the data of other markets under consideration and conclude that there is a significant improvement in performance in the vast majority of cases.

Finally, the trading rules that emerge from their research approximate well the rules commonly used by technical analysts, they argue. The rules that at first sight might appear complicated are often highly redundant; for example, the rule that was represented by a tree with 10 levels and 71 nodes turned out to be equivalent to the following simple advice: "Take a long position at time t if the minimum of the normalized exchange rate over periods $t - 1$ and $t - 2$ is greater than the 250-day moving average."[14]

Adaptive Markets and Technical Analysis

Even though the craft of technical analysis is deeply rooted in human civilization, serious efforts to formalize and statistically evaluate it have been launched only in the last two decades. The cultural biases of finance academics are, at least in part, responsible. In his autobiography, *Education of a Speculator*, the renowned trader and one-time finance professor, Victor Niederhoffer, paints an irreverent picture of the kind of forces at work in creating such biases at the University of Chicago where he was a finance Ph.D. student in the 1960s:

> This theory and the attitude of its adherents found classic expression in one incident I personally observed that deserves memorialization. A team of four of the most respected graduate students in finance had joined forces with two professors, now considered venerable enough to have won or to have been considered for a Nobel Prize, but at that time feisty as Hades and insecure as kids on [their] first date. This elite group was studying the possible impact of volume on stock price movements, a subject I had researched. As I was coming down the steps from the library on the third floor of Haskell Hall, the main business building, I could see this Group of Six gathered together on a stairway landing, examining some computer output. Their voices wafted up to me, echoing off the stone walls of the building. One of the students was pointing to some output while querying the professors, "Well, what if we really do find something? We'll be up the creek. It won't be consistent with the random walk model." The younger professor replied, "Don't worry, we'll cross that bridge in the unlikely event we come to it."
>
> I could hardly believe my ears—here were six scientists openly hoping to find no departures from ignorance. I couldn't hold my tongue. "I sure am glad you are all keeping an open mind about your research," I blurted out. I could hardly refrain from grinning as I walked past them. I heard muttered imprecations in response.[15]

One reason the EMH took such a stronghold in the academic community is because it was the first to be formalized and operationalized; although economists, including Nobel laureates, have proposed behavioral theories of financial markets—such as Simon's theory of bounded rationality (see Chapter 7)—over half a century ago, their ideas were not as directly implementable using the mathematical and computational tools available at the time. Now that the notions of adaptive markets and computationally bounded algorithms are available, a reinterpretation of market efficiency in evolutionary and computational terms might be the key to reconciling this theory with the possibility of making profits based on past prices alone. From an engineer's perspective, the efficiency of a device or system is rarely an all-or-nothing condition, but is more likely to be a continuum that captures the degree to which energy is transformed from one type to another. Just as air conditioners and hot-water heaters have efficiency ratings that fall somewhere between 0 and 100 percent—with higher ratings implying better cooling and heating abilities per unit of input power—financial markets differ in their ability to transform information into market prices, with more efficient markets impounding greater information into prices over a fixed time interval. The relevant question is not whether a market is efficient, but rather what its *relative degree of efficiency* is when compared to other alternatives.

Moreover, it makes little sense to talk about market efficiency without taking into account that market participants have bounded resources and adapt to changing environments. Instead of saying that a market is "efficient," we should say, borrowing from theoretical computer science, that a market is efficient with respect to certain resources, such as time or memory, if no strategy using those resources can generate a substantial profit. Similarly, it may be misleading to say that investors act optimally given all the available information; rather, they act optimally within their resources. This allows for markets to be efficient for some investors but not for others; for example, a computationally powerful hedge fund may extract profits from a market that looks very efficient from the point of view of a day trader who has fewer resources at his disposal—arguably the status quo.[16]

Human behavior is central to the limitations of the EMH, but the debate between disciples of market efficiency and proponents of behavioral finance have created a false dichotomy between the two schools of thought—in fact, both perspectives contain elements of truth, but neither is a complete picture of economic reality. Markets do function quite efficiently most of the time, aggregating vast amounts of disparate information into a single number—the price—on the basis of which millions of sound decisions are made. This remarkable feature of capitalism is an example of Surowiecki's (2004) "wisdom of crowds." But every so often, markets can break down, and the wisdom of crowds can quickly become the "madness of mobs."

Why do markets break down? Animal spirits! Recent neuroscientific research has shown that what we consider to be "rational" behavior is the outcome of a delicate balance among several distinct brain functions, including emotion, logical deliberation, and memory.[17] If that balance is upset—say, by the strong stimulus of a life-threatening event—then reason may be cast aside in favor of more instinctive behaviors like herding or the fight-or-flight response. Although few of us encounter such threats on a daily basis, much of our instincts are still adapted to the plains of the African savannah 50,000 years ago, where survival was a full-time occupation. Brain scans have shown that these same instincts can be triggered by more modern threats such as shame, social rejection, and financial loss. And as social animals, humans will react en masse if the perceived threat is significant enough, occasionally culminating in lynch mobs, riots, bank runs, and market crashes. Markets are not always efficient, nor are they always irrational—they are adaptive.

This "adaptive markets hypothesis" of Lo (2004, 2005)—essentially an evolutionary biologist's view of market dynamics—is at odds with the current economic orthodoxy, which has been heavily influenced by mathematics and physics (see, for example, Lo and Mueller, 2010). This orthodoxy has emerged for good reason: Economists have made genuine scientific breakthroughs, including general equilibrium theory, game theory, portfolio optimization, and derivatives pricing models. But any virtue can become a vice when carried to an extreme. The formality of mathematics and physics, in which mainstream economics is routinely dressed, can give outsiders—especially business leaders, regulators, and policymakers—a false sense of precision regarding our models' outputs (recall Samuelson's admonition that "macroeconomists have predicted 5 out of the past 3 recessions"). From an evolutionary perspective, markets are simply one more set of tools that *Homo sapiens* has developed in his ongoing struggle for survival. Occasionally, even the most reliable tools can break or be misapplied.

The adaptive markets hypothesis offers an internally consistent framework in which the EMH and behavioral biases can coexist. Behavior that may seem irrational is, instead, behavior that has not yet had sufficient time to adapt to modern contexts. For example, the great white shark moves through the water with fearsome grace and efficiency, thanks to 400 million years of natural selection. But take that shark out of water and onto a sandy beach, and its flailing undulations will look . . . irrational! The origins of human behavior are similar, differing only in the length of time we have had to adapt to our environment (about 2 million years) and the speed with which that environment is now changing.

Like the six blind monks who encountered an elephant for the first time—each monk grasping a different part of the beast and coming to a wholly different conclusion as to what an elephant is—disciples of the EMH and behavioral finance have captured different features of the same adaptive system.

The implications of the adaptive markets hypothesis for technical analysis are significant. Markets can be trusted to function properly during normal times, but when humans are subjected to emotional extremes (either pleasure or pain), animal spirits may overwhelm rationality, even among seasoned investors. Therefore, fixed investment rules that ignore changing environments will almost always have unintended consequences, and pattern recognition—in any form—may yield important competitive advantages.

Languishing for too long in the murky waters of part art, part science, technical analysis is finally starting to develop a more rigorous foundation. Although the fortress walls separating technicians from the adherents of modern finance still stand tall, they are not insurmountable, and we hope that the recognition of the thousands-of-years-long legacy of technical analysis and the role it has played in shaping the behavioral theory of financial markets will awaken some of the skeptics and open the door for a more constructive dialogue between the two communities.

Notes

Introduction

1. A. W. Lo and J. Hasanhodzic, *The Heretics of Finance: Conversations with Leading Practitioners of Technical Analysis* (New York: Bloomberg Press, 2009), 100.

2. Throughout the manuscript, when referencing academic papers in the text, we will use the "author lastname (publication year)" convention commonly followed in the academic finance literature.

3. W. Bingyuan, *Maoyi xuzhi yaoyan* (1900), 15; as quoted in R.J. Lufrano, *Honorable Merchants: Commerce and Self-Cultivation in Late Imperial China* (Honolulu: University of Hawai'i Press, 1997), 133.

4. J. de la Vega, *Confusion de Confusiones* (Boston: Harvard University Printing Office, 1957), 35.

5. A. Sapori, *The Italian Merchant in the Middle Ages* (New York: W. W. Norton, 1970), 38.

Chapter 1

1. G. A. Wright, *Obsidian Analyses and Prehistoric Near Eastern Trade: 7500 to 3500 B.C.* (Ann Arbor: University of Michigan, 1969), 57–62.

2. Ibid., 62–67.

3. Ibid., 70.

4. L. L. Orlin, *Assyrian Colonies in Cappadocia* (The Hague: Mouton, 1970), 49–50.

5. H. W. F. Saggs, *The Greatness That Was Babylon* (London: Sidgwick and Jackson, 1988), 237–238.

6. H. Parkins and C. Smith, eds., *Trade, Traders, and the Ancient City* (New York: Routledge, 1998), 23.

7. Saggs, *Greatness That Was Babylon*, 246–247.

8. M. Rowlands, ed., *Centre and Periphery in the Ancient World* (Cambridge: Cambridge University Press, 1987), 67.

9. Ibid., 72–73.

10. J. P. Lévy, *The Economic Life of the Ancient World* (Chicago and London: University of Chicago Press, 1967), 9–10.

11. M. Silver, *Economic Structures of Antiquity* (Westport, CT: Greenwood Press, 1995), 154.

12. *CAD* s.v. e; as quoted in Silver, *Economic Structures*, 155.

13. Silver, *Economic Structures*, 155.

14. K. R. Veenhof, *Aspects of Old Assyrian Trade and Its Terminology* (Leiden: Brill, 1972), 376–377; as quoted in Silver, *Economic Structures*, 98.

15. Silver, *Economic Structures*, 103.

16. B. Kienast, *Die altassyrischen Texte des orientalischen Seminars der Universitat Heidelberg und der Sammlung Erlenmeyer-Basel* (Berlin: De Gruyter, 1960), 47; as quoted in Silver, *Economic Structures*, 98.

17. 2 Kings 7:1; as quoted in Silver, *Economic Structures*, 104.

18. W. Goetzmann, *Financing Civilization*, http://viking.som.yale.edu.

19. The oldest known diary to contain market values of the six commodities is the second-oldest surviving diary, which dates back to 567 B.C. The oldest surviving diary does not contain such information, but, as Slotsky speculates, this may be due to the fact that "the tablet is broken off precisely where such information would have been inscribed." A. L. Slotsky, *The Bourse of Babylon* (Bethesda, MD: CDL Press, 1997), 7.

20. Slotsky, *Bourse*, 5–6.

21. Ibid., 8–9.

22. Ibid., 8.

23. Ibid., 8–9.

24. Ibid., 11. Note that the conversion is as follows: 1 *pān* ≈ 30 liters, 1 *sūt* ≈ 5 liters, 1 *qa* ≈ 1 liters (Slotsky, *Bourse*, 46).

25. Ibid., 17.
26. Ibid., 6.
27. Ibid., 6–7.
28. H. M. Gartley, *Profits in the Stock Market* (Pomeroy, WA: Lambert-Gann Publishing, 1981), 81.
29. R. W. Schabacker, *Stock Market Theory and Practice* (New York: Forbes, 1930), 591.
30. Slotsky, *Bourse*, 22.
31. Diary -87 VI (Gotarzes); as quoted in Slotsky, *Bourse*, 21.
32. H. D. Schultz and S. Coslow, eds., *A Treasury of Wall Street Wisdom* (Palisades Park, NJ: Investors' Press, 1966), 214.
33. Schabacker, *Stock Market Theory*, 592.
34. Schultz and Coslow, *A Treasury*, 245.
35. Gartley, *Profits*, 35.
36. Slotsky, *Bourse*, 20.
37. Schabacker, *Stock Market Theory*, 593–594.
38. Ibid., 594.
39. Slotsky, *Bourse*, 21.
40. Ibid.
41. Ibid., 22.
42. Schabacker, *Stock Market Theory*, 594.
43. Slotsky, *Bourse*, 22.
44. Diary of -164 XII; as quoted in Slotsky, *Bourse*, 22.
45. Diary of -62 I; as quoted in Slotsky, *Bourse*, 22.
46. Diary of -324 II; as quoted in Slotsky, *Bourse*, 22.
47. Slotsky, *Bourse*, 25–29.
48. Ibid., 29–33.
49. Ibid., 40.
50. Ibid., 25.
51. Ibid., 29.
52. Ibid., 37.
53. Ibid., 19–20.
54. Ibid., 105.
55. W. I. Davisson and J. E. Harper, *European Economic History* (New York: Appleton-Century-Crofts, 1972), 90–91.

56. Ibid., 112.

57. Ibid., 115–120.

58. Ibid., 120. The markets at Sardis and Corinth actually preceded the market at Athens; however, it was at Athens that the market became well-established and visible to other parts of the Mediterranean, many of which adopted this innovation (Davisson and Harper, *European Economic History*, 121).

59. G. Glotz, *Ancient Greece at Work* (New York: The Norton Library, 1967), 290.

60. Davisson and Harper, *European Economic History*, 108.

61. Ibid., 110.

62. Glotz, *Ancient Greece*, 303.

63. Davisson and Harper, *European Economic History*, 159.

64. G. M. Calhoun, "Risk in Sea Loans in Ancient Athens," *Journal of Economic and Business History 2* (1930): 110.

65. Glotz, *Ancient Greece*, 304.

66. Ibid., 306.

67. F. Meijer and O. van Nijf, *Trade, Transport and Society in the Ancient World: A Sourcebook* (New York: Routledge, 1992), 9.

68. Glotz, *Ancient Greece*, 306–307.

69. Ibid.

70. Lévy, *Economic Life*, 27.

71. M. Whitby, "The Grain Trade of Athens in the Fourth Century BC," in *Trade, Traders, and the Ancient City*, ed. H. Parkins and C. Smith (New York: Routledge, 1998), 119.

72. P. D. Curtin, *Cross-Cultural Trade in World History* (Cambridge: Cambridge University Press, 1984), 80.

73. Davisson and Harper, *European Economic History*, 151.

74. Glotz, *Ancient Greece*, 364.

75. Davisson and Harper, *European Economic History*, 151.

76. Glotz, *Ancient Greece*, 364.

77. N. Morley, *Trade in Classical Antiquity* (Cambridge: Cambridge University Press, 2007), 32.

78. Dem. 56.8; as quoted in Morley, *Trade in Classical Antiquity*, 32.

79. Whitby, "Grain Trade of Athens," 119.

80. Ibid.

81. Silver, *Economic Structures*, 5.

82. Ibid., 6.

83. H. H. Scullard, *Festivals and Ceremonies of the Roman Republic* (Ithaca, NY: Cornell University Press, 1981), 122; as quoted in Silver, *Economic Structures*, 5.

84. Davisson and Harper, *European Economic History*, 206.

85. P. Temin, "The Economy of the Early Roman Empire," *Journal of Economic Perspectives* 20, no. 1 (2006), 139. Temin suggests that market buildings that housed numerous merchants and different kinds of merchants promoted communication and exchange of information—this was one way in which problems of incomplete information were remedied.

86. Morley, *Trade in Classical Antiquity*, 80–81.

87. Temin 2006, 149.

88. Ibid., 134.

89. See, e.g., Duncan-Jones 1974.

90. D. Rathbone, *Economie antique: Prix et formations des prix dans les economies antiques*, vol. 3 (1997), 211; as quoted in P. Temin, "A Market Economy in the Early Roman Empire," Massachusetts Institute of Technology Working Paper 01-08 (February 2001), 19.

91. Temin 2001, 25.

92. Ibid.

93. Ibid., 28.

94. H. Heaton, *Economic History of Europe*, rev. ed. (New York: Harper and Brothers, 1948), 163.

95. Xen. *Mem* 3.4; cf. Plato, *Laws* 831; as quoted in Morley, *Trade in Classical Antiquity*, 83.

96. *Mem.* 2.6; as quoted in Morley, *Trade in Classical Antiquity*, 83.

97. Cic. *Off.* 1.150; as quoted in Morley, *Trade in Classical Antiquity*, 84.

98. Hes. *WD* 320–5; as quoted in Morley, *Trade in Classical Antiquity*, 84–86.

99. Morley, *Trade in Classical Antiquity*, 86.

Chapter 2

1. A. Sapori, *The Italian Merchant in the Middle Ages* (New York: W.W. Norton, 1970), 68.

2. Ibid., 69.

3. H. Heaton, *Economic History of Europe*, rev. ed. (New York: Harper and Brothers, 1948), 162.

4. Ibid., 173.

5. S. B. Clough and C. W. Cole, *Economic History of Europe* (Boston: D.C. Heath, 1941), 50.

6. Cipolla 1972, 303.

7. H. Pirenne, *Economic and Social History of Medieval Europe* (New York: Harcourt, Brace, 1937), 96–98.

8. Heaton, *Economic History*, 169–170.

9. R. Cameron, *A Concise Economic History of the World: From Paleolithic Times to the Present*, 2nd ed. (New York: Oxford University Press, 1993), 65.

10. Clough and Cole, *Economic History*, 52.

11. Ibid., 53.

12. Heaton, *Economic History*, 171.

13. Pirenne, *Economic and Social History*, 122–123.

14. A. Birnie, *An Economic History of Europe: 1760–1939*, 7th ed. (London: Methuen, 1957), 51.

15. F. L. Nussbaum, *The Triumph of Science and Reason: 1660–1685* (New York: Harper, 1953), 245.

16. Ibid., 203–206.

17. N. Rosenberg and L. E. Birdzell, *How the West Grew Rich* (New York: Basic Books, 1986), 80, 139.

18. Ibid., 11.

19. W. C. Scoville and J. C. la Force, eds., *The Economic Development of Western Europe: The Sixteenth and Seventeenth Centuries*, vol. 2 (Lexington, MA: D.C. Heath, 1969), 8.

20. F. Braudel, *The Wheels of Commerce: Civilization and Capitalism, 15th–18th Centuries*, vol. II (New York: Harper and Row, 1982), 97.

21. Ibid.

22. Cippola 1972, 311.

23. Heaton, *Economic History*, 179.

24. Cippola 1972, 328.

25. Ibid., 327.

26. D. Herlihy, R. S. Lopez, and V. Slessarev, eds., *Economy, Society, and Government in medieval Italy: Essays in memory of Robert L. Reynolds* (Kent, OH: Kent State University Press, 1969), 36.

27. W. N. Goetzmann, *Fibonacci and the Financial Revolution*, NBER Working Paper Series (March 2004), 2–3.

28. J. J. Murphy, *Technical Analysis of the Financial Markets* (New York: New York Institute of Finance, 1999), 322.

29. Herlihy, Lopez, and Slessarev, eds., *Economy, Society*, 40–41.

30. Ibid., 41.

31. V. Barbour, *Capitalism in Amsterdam in the 17th Century* (Ann Arbor: University of Michigan Press, 1963), 74.

32. Ibid., 78–79.

33. Ibid., 75.

34. J. de la Vega, *Confusion de Confusiones* (Boston: Harvard University Printing Office, 1957), 35.

35. N. W. Posthumus, "The Tulip Mania in Holland in the Years 1636 and 1637," in Scoville and la Force, eds., *Economic Development*, 140.

36. Ibid., 141.

37. Ibid., 142.

38. Ibid.

39. See also Lo 2005, 34.

40. R. Ehrenberg, *Capital and Finance in the Age of the Renaissance*, translated from German by H. M. Lucas (London: Jonathan Cape, 1928), 240; as quoted in G. Poitras, *The Early History of Financial Economics, 1478–1776* (Cheltenham, UK: Edward Elgar Publishing, 2000), 251.

41. C. Kurz, as quoted in E. Chancellor, *Devil Take The Hindmost: A History Of Financial Speculation* (New York: Plume, 2000), 8.

42. Ehrenberg, as quoted in Poitras, *Early History*, 251.

43. Ibid.

44. C. Kurz's report to Tucher, quoted in Ehrenberg, as quoted in Poitras, *Early History*, 251–252.

45. Poitras, *Early History*, 252.

46. Preda 2001, 212.

47. Ibid., 226–227.

48. Clough and Cole, *Economic History*, 66–68.

49. Ibid., 82.

50. Ibid., 55.

51. Cippola 1972, 311.

52. Clough and Cole, *Economic History*, 82.

53. Ibid.

54. Nussbaum, *Triumph*, 1.

55. Ibid., 2, 26.

56. The relationship between the rise of capitalism in Europe and the Protestant Reformation has been a controversial topic. One point of contention is that England, the least Protestant of the Protestant countries, was the frontrunner

in the development of capitalism. See K. Fullerton, "Calvinism and Capitalism," in Scoville and la Force, eds., *Economic Development*, 16, for more details.

57. Rosenberg and Birdzell, *How the West Grew Rich*, 132–133.

58. Nussbaum, *Triumph*, 207–208.

59. A. Toynbee, "The Classic Statement of the Industrial Revolution," in C. S. Doty, ed., *The Industrial Revolution* (New York: Holt, Rinehart and Winston, 1969), 11.

60. Preda 2001, 216.

61. H. Lefevre, *Traité des valeurs mobilières et des opérations de Bourse. Placement et spéculation* (*Treatise on financial securities and stock exchange operations. Placement and speculation*) (Paris: E. Lachaud, 1870), v–vii; as quoted in Preda 2001, 215.

62. *The Shareholder's Circular and Guardian: A General Compendium of Stock Exchange News and of All Matters Relating to Joint-Stock Companies* (London, 1863), 1(1), 5, as quoted in Preda 2001, 215.

63. Preda 2001, 228.

64. *Manuel du spéculateur à la Bourse* (*Manual of the stock exchange speculator*) 1854. (Paris: Garnier Frères, 1854), 4, as quoted in Preda 2001, 218.

65. Preda 2001, 228.

Chapter 3

1. S. Nison, *Japanese Candlestick Charting Techniques*, 2nd ed. (New York: Prentice Hall, 1991), 13.

2. J. Hirschmeier and T. Yui, *The Development of Japanese Business, 1600–1973* (Cambridge, MA: Harvard University Press, 1975), 18.

3. Nippon Technical Analysis Association, *Analysis of Stock Prices in Japan* (Tokyo: Nippon Technical Analysis Association, 1989), 12.

4. Nippon Technical Analysis Association, 12.

5. Nison, *Japanese Candlestick*, 14.

6. Nippon Technical Analysis Association, 12.

7. Nison, *Japanese Candlestick*, 14.

8. Ibid., 15.

9. Ibid., 15–16.

10. Nippon Technical Analysis Association, 12–13.

11. S. Nison, *Beyond Candlesticks: New Japanese Charting Techniques Revealed* (New York: Wiley, 1994), 14.

12. Ibid., 14.

13. R. Russell, *Dow Theory Today* (Flint Hills, VA: Fraser Publishing, 1997), 17.

14. As quoted in Nison, *Beyond Candlesticks*, 14.

15. Nippon Technical Analysis Association, 12.

16. Ibid., 13.

17. R. Rhea, *The Dow Theory* (Flint Hill, VA: Fraser Publishing, 1994), 103.

18. Nison, *Beyond Candlesticks*, 16.

19. Ibid., 15.

20. Nippon Technical Analysis Association, 13.

21. H. M. Gartley, *Profits in the Stock Market* (Pomeroy, WA: Lambert-Gann Publishing, 1981), 192.

22. Nison, *Beyond Candlesticks*, 16–18.

23. Nison, *Japanese Candlestick*, 14.

24. Nippon Technical Analysis Association, 13.

25. Rhea, *Dow Theory*, 101–102.

26. Nippon Technical Analysis Association, 13.

27. Nison, *Beyond Candlesticks*, 18.

28. Translation from R. Wilhelm, *The I Ching or Book of Changes*, trans. C. F. Baynes (New York: Bollingen/Pantheon, 1961), Book II, 129; as quoted in S. Yoshinobu, *Commerce and Society in Sung China* (Ann Arbor: Center for Chinese Studies at the University of Michigan, 1970), 140.

29. M. Elvin, *The Pattern of the Chinese Past* (Stanford, CA: Stanford University Press, 1973), 164.

30. J. K. Fairbank and E. Reischauer, *China: Tradition and Transformation* (Boston: Houghton Mifflin, 1989), 132–134.

31. See W. K. K. Chan, *Merchants, Mandarins, and Modern Enterprise in Late Ch'ing China* (Cambridge, MA: Harvard University East Asian Research Center, 1977), 15–21 for more details about the traditional Chinese dislike of trade.

32. Fairbank and Reischauer, *China*, 134.

33. Yoshinobu, *Commerce and Society*, 142.

34. Ibid., 164.

35. Ibid., 156–157.

36. Ibid., 158–162.

37. As quoted in Yoshinobu, *Commerce and Society*, 160.

38. Yoshinobu, *Commerce and Society,* 165.

39. Ibid., 169.

40. Ibid., 173–176.

41. As quoted in Yoshinobu, *Commerce and Society*, 170.

42. Elvin, *The Pattern*, 175.

43. R. Latham, trans., *The Travels of Marco Polo* (London: 1958), 188; as quoted in Elvin, *The Pattern*, 177.

44. Elvin, *The Pattern*, 177.

45. As quoted in Elvin, *The Pattern*, 268.

46. Elvin, *The Pattern*, 268–269.

47. Ibid., 270.

48. S. Shigeo. *Mindai ni okeru shōzei to zaisei to no kenkyūi* (The Business Tax and Financial Administration in the Ming Period), *Shigaku zasshi* LXV.i and ii (1956): ii, 23. As quoted in Elvin, *The Pattern*, 269.

49. Elvin, *The Pattern*, 276–277.

50. Ibid., 284.

51. R. J. Lufrano, *Honorable Merchants: Commerce and Self-Cultivation in Late Imperial China* (Honolulu: University of Hawai'i Press, 1997), 137.

52. Ibid., 137.

53. Ibid., 2, 51.

54. Ibid., 52.

55. Ibid., 10.

56. W. Bingyuan, *Maoyi xuzhi yaoyan* (1900), 15; as quoted in Lufrano, *Honorable Merchants*, 133.

57. Ibid.

58. M. Masaaki, *Shinan gemban shishō ruiyō ni tsuite*, 104; as quoted in Lufrano, *Honorable Merchants*, 133.

59. C. Egerton, trans., *The Golden Lotus*, vol. 3, 41; as quoted in Lufrano, *Honorable Merchants*, 133.

60. Lufrano, *Honorable Merchants*, 133.

61. W. Zhongfu, *Shanggu bianlan*, vol. 2, 4; as quoted in Lufrano, *Honorable Merchants*, 136.

62. Lufrano, *Honorable Merchants*, 134.

63. W. Qi, ed., *Shishang yaolan*, vol. 3, 3; as quoted in Lufrano, *Honorable Merchants*, 135.

64. Lufrano, *Honorable Merchants*, 134–135.

65. Ibid., 136.

66. Ibid.

Chapter 4

1. D. Colbert, *Eyewitness to Wall Street: 400 Years of Dreamers, Schemers, Busts, and Booms* (New York: Broadway Books, 2001), 10.

2. J. S. Gordon, *The Scarlet Woman of Wall Street* (New York: Weidenfeld and Nicolson, 1988), 10.

3. Ibid., 28.

4. Colbert, *Eyewitness*, 10.

5. Ibid., 11.

6. Ibid.

7. Ibid.

8. Ibid.

9. Gordon, *Scarlet Woman*, 11.

10. R. Sobel, *The Big Board: A History of the New York Stock Market* (New York: The Free Press, 1965), 15.

11. Gordon, *Scarlet Woman*, 11.

12. Sobel, *The Big Board*, 15.

13. C. R. Geisst, *Wall Street: A History* (New York: Oxford University Press, 1997), 9.

14. Gordon, *Scarlet Woman*, 11.

15. Ibid., 12.

16. Ibid.

17. Ibid., 12–13.

18. J. E. Meeker, *The Work of the Stock Exchange* (New York: The Ronald Press Company, 1923), 28.

19. Ibid., 29.

20. Sobel, *The Big Board*, 25.

21. Ibid.

22. Ibid., 20–21.

23. Meeker, *The Work*, 29.

24. Sobel, *The Big Board*, 21.

25. Ibid., 30.

26. Ibid.

27. Meeker, *The Work*, 30.

28. Sobel, *The Big Board*, 31.

29. Ibid.

30. Ibid., 30 – 31.

31. As quoted in Meeker, *The Work*, 30.

32. Sobel, *The Big Board*, 30–31.

33. Gordon, *Scarlet Woman*, 14.

34. J. K. Medbery, *Men and Mysteries of Wall Street*, 21; as quoted in Gordon, *Scarlet Woman*, 14.

35. Gordon, *Scarlet Woman*, 14.

36. H. M. Wachtel, *Street of Dreams—Boulevard of Broken Hearts: Wall Street's First Century* (London; Sterling, VA: Pluto Press, 2003), 146.

37. Medbery, *Men and Mysteries of Wall Street*, 130–131; as quoted in Wachtel, *Street of Dreams*, 147.

38. Gordon, *Scarlet Woman*, 14.

39. As quoted in Gordon, *Scarlet Woman*, 115.

40. Wachtel, *Street of Dreams*, 148–149.

41. Ibid., 149.

42. Gordon, *Scarlet Woman*, 14.

43. Geisst, *Wall Street*, 37.

44. Ibid., 38.

45. Wachtel, *Street of Dreams*, 138.

46. Ibid.

47. Ibid., 141.

48. Ibid., 157; Preda 2002, 12–13.

49. Preda 2002, 13.

50. *The Magazine of Wall Street* 40 (9), August 25, 1927, 753; as quoted in Preda 2002, 13.

51. E. C. Stedman (ed.), *The New York Stock Exchange. Its History, Its Contribution to the National Prosperity, and Its Relation to American Finance at the Outset of the Twentieth Century* (New York: New York Stock Exchange Historical Company, 1905), 441; as quoted in Preda 2002, 13.

52. Preda 2002, 13.

53. Ibid., 14.

54. Ibid.

55. Wachtel, *Street of Dreams*, 158–159.

56. *Guide to Investors. Haight & Freese's Information to Investors and Operators in Stocks, Grain and Cotton*, 385, 396; as quoted in Preda 2002, 16.

57. Preda 2002, 18.

58. Ibid., 18–19.

59. Ibid., 27.

60. *The Ticker* 1 (4), February 1908, 7; as quoted in Preda 2002, 26–27.

61. Gordon, *Scarlet Woman*, 28.

62. O. W. Holmes, Sr., writing in 1835; as quoted in Sobel, *The Big Board*, 27.

63. Gordon, *Scarlet Woman*, 47.

64. Ibid., 32.

65. Ibid., 47.

66. Ibid., 42.

67. Ibid.

68. Ibid.

69. Ibid., 47–48.

70. E. D. de Haurame, *Lettres et notes de voyage*; as quoted in Gordon, *Scarlet Woman*, 34–35.

71. A. Trollope, *North America*; as quoted in Gordon, *Scarlet Woman*, 34.

72. J. D. McCabe, *Lights and Shadows of New York Life*; as quoted in Gordon, *Scarlet Woman*, 35.

73. Gordon, *Scarlet Woman*, 48.

74. de Goede 2005, pp. 90–92. See also W. Kula, *Measures and Men*, trans. R. Szreter (Princeton: Princeton University Press, 1986), 13–14.

75. D. Campbell and M. Dillon, 1993. "The End of Philosophy and the End of International Relations," in *The Political Subject of Violence*, ed. D. Campbell and M. Dillon (Manchester: Manchester University Press, 1993), 6; as quoted in de Goede 2005, 91.

76. Campbell and Dillon, "The End of Philosophy," 36; as quoted in de Goede 2005, 91.

77. W. S. Jevons, "On the Study of Periodic Commercial Fluctuations," in *The Foundations of Econometric Analysis*, ed. M. S. Morgan and D. F. Hendry (Cambridge: Cambridge University Press, 1995 [1862]), 113; as quoted in de Goede 2005, 93.

78. W. S. Jevons, *The Theory of Political Economy* (London: MacMillan, 1911 [1871]), 21; as quoted in de Goede 2005, p. 93.

79. W. Stanley Jevons, "On the Variations of Prices and the Value of the Currency since 1782," *Journal of the Statistical Society of London* 28, no. 2 (1865), 302; as quoted in de Goede 2005, 93.

80. As quoted in de Goede 2005, 102.

81. de Goede 2005, 102.

82. As quoted in de Goede 2005, 102.

83. de Goede 2005, 114.

84. R. W. Schabacker, *Stock Market Profits* (Wells, VT: Fraser Publishing, 1967 [1934]), 3, 6; as quoted in de Goede 2005, 114.

85. "Why Not Investment Experts? Demand for Advice and Opinions on Investments, Suggests the Establishment of a New Profession," *The Ticker* 1, no. 6 (April 1908), 35; as quoted in Preda 2002, 20.

86. Preda 2002, 17–19.

87. Geisst, *Wall Street*, 35.

88. Ibid., 31.

89. Ibid., 32.

90. Ibid., 33.

91. Ibid.

92. Ibid., 36.

93. Ibid., 64.

94. Pujo Committee, *Money Trust Investigation: Investigation of Financial and Monetary Conditions in the United States under House Resolution Nos. 429 and 504, before the Subcommittee on Banking and Currency* (Washington, DC: Government Printing Office, 1912), 6; as quoted in de Goede 2005, 96.

95. S. Untermyer, "Speculation on the Stock Exchanges and Public Regulation of the Exchanges," *American Economic Review* 5, no. 1 (1915), 24–68; as quoted in de Goede 2005, 96.

96. As quoted in Schultz and Coslow, *A Treasury of Wall Street Wisdom* (Palisades Park, NJ: Investors' Press, 1966), 34.

Chapter 5

1. D. L. Thomas, *The Plungers and the Peacocks: An Update of the Classic History of the Stock Market*, rev. ed. (New York: William Morrow, 1989), 119.

2. Thomas, *The Plungers*, 121; H. D. Schultz and S. Coslow, eds., *A Treasury of Wall Street Wisdom* (Palisades Park, NJ: Investors' Press, 1966), 3.

3. Schultz and Coslow, *A Treasury*, 10.

4. As quoted in Schultz and Coslow, *A Treasury*, 15.

5. Ibid.

6. As quoted in R. Russell, *Dow Theory Today* (Flint Hill, VA: Fraser Publishing, 1997), 17.

7. As quoted in H. M. Gartley, *Profits in the Stock Market* (Pomeroy, WA: Lambert-Gann Publishing, 1981), 177.

8. As quoted in Schultz and Coslow, *A Treasury*, 11.

9. W. P. Hamilton, *The Stock Market Barometer: A Study of Its Forecast Value Based on Charles H. Dow's Theory of the Price Movement* (New York: Harper and Brothers, 1922), 5.

10. Thomas, *The Plungers*, 120; Gartley, *Profits*, 54.

11. As quoted in de Goede 2005, 104.

12. C. H. Dow, *Scientific Stock Speculation: A Condensed Statement of the Principles upon Which Successful Stock Speculation Must Be Based*, ed. G. C. Selden (New York: The Magazine of Wall Street, 1920), 15; as quoted in de Goede 2005, p. 108.

13. Schultz and Coslow, *A Treasury*, 14.

14. As quoted in Russell, *Dow Theory Today*, 19.

15. For more information about the Wyckoff method see H. Pruden, *The Three Skills of Top Trading: Behavioral Systems Building, Pattern Recognition, and Mental State Management* (Hoboken, NJ: Wiley, 2007) and R. D. Wyckoff, under the pseudonym Rollo Tape, *Studies in Tape Reading* (Burlington, VT: Fraser Publishing Co., 1982 [1910]).

16. S. A. Nelson, *The ABC of Stock Speculation* (Flint Hill, VA: Fraser Publishing, 1997), 7.

17. S. A. Nelson, *The ABC of Stock Speculation*. (Wells, VT: Fraser Publishing, 1964 [1903]), 24; as quoted in de Goede 2005, 105.

18. As quoted in Schultz and Coslow, *A Treasury*, 37–38.

19. Schultz and Coslow, *A Treasury*, 37–38.

20. Nelson, *ABC*, 31.

21. Ibid., 37–38.

22. As quoted in Schultz and Coslow, *A Treasury*, 99–100.

23. Gartley, *Profits*, 174.

24. Schultz and Coslow, *A Treasury*, 46.

25. As quoted in Schultz and Coslow, *A Treasury*, 46.

26. Hamilton, *Stock Market Barometer* 4; as quoted in de Goede 2005, p. 105.

27. Schultz and Coslow, *A Treasury*, 52.

28. Hamilton, *Stock Market Barometer* 4; as quoted in de Goede 2005, p. 105.

29. Ibid.

30. Gartley, *Profits*, 176.

31. Russell, *Dow Theory Today*, 8.

32. Schultz and Coslow, *A Treasury*, 80; Russell, *Dow Theory Today*, 7.

33. Russell, *Dow Theory Today*, 15.

34. Ibid., 116.

35. As quoted in Schultz and Coslow, *A Treasury*, 95–96.

36. Schultz and Coslow, *A Treasury*, 95–96.

37. Gartley, *Profits*, 176.

38. Ibid.

39. As quoted in Schultz and Coslow, *A Treasury*, 34.

40. Schultz and Coslow, *A Treasury*, 90–92.

41. As quoted in Schultz and Coslow, *A Treasury*, 92.

42. W. S. Jevons, "Commercial Crises and Sun-Spots," *Nature* 19 (November 14, 1878), 36; as quoted in de Goede 2005, p. 103.

43. W. S. Jevons, "Sun-Spots and Commercial Crises," *Nature* 19 (April 24, 1879), 588; as quoted in de Goede 2005, 103.

44. Dow, *Scientific Stock Speculation*, 97–98; as quoted in de Goede 2005, 103.

45. Hamilton, *Stock Market Barometer* 27; as quoted in de Goede 2005, 103.

46. Dow, *Scientific Stock Speculation*, 97; as quoted in de Goede 2005, 103.

47. C. H. Dow, "Review and Outlook," *The Wall Street Journal* (April 21, 1899), 1; as quoted in de Goede 2005, 104.

48. R. R. Prechter, ed., *R. N. Elliott's Masterworks: The Definitive Collection* (Gainesville, GA: New Classics Library, 1996), 50.

49. Prechter, *R. N. Elliott's Masterworks*, 52.

50. As quoted in J. A. Hyerczyk, *Pattern, Price and Time* (New York: Wiley, 1998), 9.

51. Prechter, *R. N. Elliott's Masterworks*, 53, 59.

52. C. Lebeau and D. W. Lucas, *Technical Traders Guide to Computer Analysis of the Futures Market* (Homewood, IL: Business One Irwin, 1992), 32.

53. Prechter, *R. N. Elliott's Masterworks*, 53.

54. Schultz and Coslow, *A Treasury*, 239–241; Schabacker 1930, pp. 656–657.

55. Preda 2002, 11.

56. Schultz and Coslow, *A Treasury*, 228–230.

57. Ibid., 235–238.

58. J. E. Meeker, *Measuring the Stock Market*. Address before the American Statistical Association, Cleveland, Ohio, December 30, 1930, 3; as quoted in de Goede 2005, 106.

59. Meeker, *Measuring the Stock Market*, 18; as quoted in de Goede 2005, p. 106.

60. Meeker, *Measuring the Stock Market*, 19–20; as quoted in de Goede 2005, 106.

61. Schultz and Coslow, *A Treasury*, 246.

62. Gartley, *Profits*, 299.

63. As quoted in Gartley, *Profits*, 192.

64. Ibid.

65. Ibid.

66. Ibid.

67. Gartley, *Profits*, 192.

68. Ibid., 193.

69. Ibid.

70. Ibid., 391.

71. Ibid., 325.

72. Hyerczyk, *Pattern, Price*, 19.

73. H. Weingarten, *Investing by the Stars: Using Astrology in the Financial Markets* (New York: McGraw-Hill, 1996), 29–30.

74. Weingarten, *Investing*, 29.

75. Ibid., 31.

76. Ibid., 29–30.

77. Ibid., 45.

78. Ibid., 27.

79. Hyerczyk, *Pattern, Price*, 21.

80. G. Marisch, *The W. D. Gann Method of Trading* (Brightwaters, NY: Windsor Books, 1990), 2–3.

81. Marisch, *Gann Method*, 3.

82. As quoted in Hyerczyk, *Pattern, Price*, 11.

83. Weingarten, *Investing*, 66.

84. Hyerczyk, *Pattern, Price*, 12.

85. Weingarten, *Investing*, 66.

86. As quoted in Marisch, *Gann Method*, 3.

87. Hyerczyk, *Pattern, Price*, 12–13.

88. As quoted in Hyerczyk, *Pattern, Price*, 9.

89. Ibid., 9–11.

90. Ibid.

91. Ibid., 19–20.

92. Ibid., 9.

93. T. Plummer, *Forecasting Financial Markets: The Truth Behind Technical Analysis* (London: Kogan Page, 1989), 233.

94. Ibid.

95. As quoted in Hyerczyk, *Pattern, Price,* 11.

96. R. W. Colby, *The Encyclopedia of Technical Market Indicators,* 2nd ed. (New York: McGraw-Hill, 2003), 109.

97. Weingarten, *Investing,* 20, 24–25.

Chapter 6

1. For more information about the point-and-figure charting methods, see A. W. Cohen, *How to Use the Three-Point Reversal Method of Point and Figure Stock Market Trading* (Larchmont, NY: Chartcraft, 1968) and J. du Plessis, *The Definitive Guide to Point and Figure: A Comprehensive Guide to the Theory and Practical Use of the Point and Figure Charting Method* (Petersfield: Harriman House Publishing, 2005).

2. G. A. Chestnutt, Jr., *Stock Market Analysis: Facts and Principles* (Larchmont, NY: American Investors Corporation, 1965), 19; as quoted in R. A. Levy, *The Relative Strength Concept of Common Stock Price Forecasting* (Larchmont, NY: Investors Intelligence, 1968), 89.

3. Chestnutt, *Stock Market Analysis,* 28; as quoted in Levy, *The Relative Strength Concept,* 89–90.

4. R. W. Colby, *The Encyclopedia of Technical Market Indicators,* 2nd ed. (New York: McGraw-Hill, 2003), 177.

5. C. Kirkpatrick, "Charles Dow Looks at the Long Wave," *Journal of Technical Analysis* 57 (Winter–Spring 2002), 6–8.

6. Lo and Hasanhodzic 2009, 148.

7. C. R. Geisst, *Wall Street: A History: From Its Beginings to the Fall of Enron* (New York: Oxford University Press, 2004), 280–281.

8. E. W. Tabell and A. W. Tabell, "The Case for Technical Analysis," *Financial Analysts Journal* 20, no. 2 (March–April 1964), 67.

9. Lo and Hasanhodzic 2009, 244–245.

10. Ibid., 14–15.

11. R. Sobel, *The New Game on Wall Street* (New York: Wiley, 1987), 20.

12. *The Institutional Investor,* as quoted in J. Brooks, *The Go-Go Years* (New York: Weybright and Talley, 1973), 147.

13. I. Friend, F. E. Brown, E. S. Herman, and D. Vickers, *A Study of Mutual Funds* (Washington, DC: Government Printing Office, 1962), x–xi; as quoted in R. A. Levy, *The Relative Strength Concept,* 245.

14. Sobel, *The New Game,* 7.

15. Geisst, *Wall Street: A History,* 366–368.

16. Lo and Hasanhodzic 2009, 15–16.

17. Cf. Chapter 4.

18. Sobel, *The New Game*, 15.

19. Geisst, *Wall Street: A History*, 306.

20. Sobel, *The New Game*, 15.

21. Lo and Hasanhodzic 2009, 14.

22. Geisst, *Wall Street: A History*, 303.

23. Ibid., 305.

24. Ibid., 307.

25. Lo and Hasanhodzic 2009, 68.

26. Ibid., 146–147.

27. Geisst, *Wall Street: A History*, 308.

28. W. Christie and P. Schultz, "Why Do NASDAQ Market Makers Avoid Odd-Eighth Quotes?" *Journal of Finance* 49, no. 5 (1994), 1813–1840.

29. Geisst, *Wall Street: A History*, 368–369, 384.

30. Lo and Hasanhodzic 2009, 98.

31. Geisst, *Wall Street: A History*, 383.

32. Ibid., 370.

33. Ibid., 384.

34. Lo and Hasanhodzic 2009, 145–146.

35. D. L. Thomas, "Calculating Risks," *Barron's* XLV, no. 26 (June 28, 1965), 3, 19; as quoted in Levy, *The Relative Strength Concept*, 13.

36. Thomas, "Calculating Risks," 3, 19; as quoted in Levy, *The Relative Strength Concept*, 13.

37. R. E. Blodgett, "Wall Street Computers Begin Analyzing Stocks to Select 'Best' Buys," *The Wall Street Journal* (August 10, 1965), 1; as quoted in Levy, *The Relative Strength Concept*, 14.

38. Ibid., 144.

39. Ibid., 156.

40. Ibid., 149.

41. Ibid., 102.

42. Smith 1968, 172–173.

43. Ibid., 176.

44. Bloomberg 1997, 42.

45. Ibid., 51–52.

46. Ibid., 42.

47. Lo and Hasanhodzic 2009, xxi.

48. Ibid., 156.

49. The game is available at http://arora.ccs.neu.edu.

50. J. Hasanhodzic, A. W. Lo, and E. Viola, "Is It Real, or Is It Randomized? A Financial Turing Test". Available online at http://ssrn.com/abstract=1558149 (2010).

51. Ibid., 237.

Chapter 7

1. O. Ore, *Cardano: The Gambling Scholar, with a Translation from the Latin of Cardano's Book on Games of Chance by Sydney Henry Gould*, Princeton: Princeton University Press, 1953.

2. Preda 2004, 354.

3. Ibid., 367–368, footnote 12.

4. Ibid., 370–371.

5. Ibid., 371.

6. Preda 2004, 371. Over a century later, the functional approach to finance has become a reality with R. Merton and Z. Bodie, 1993, "Deposit Insurance Reform: A Functional Approach", Carnegie-Rochester Conference Series on Public Policy 38, 1–34, and R. Merton and Z. Bodie, 1995, "Financial Infrastructure and Public Policy: A Functional Perspective", in D. Crane, K. Froot, S. Mason, A. Perold, R. Merton, Z. Bodie, E. Sirri, and P. Tufano, 1995, *The Global Financial System: A Functional Perspective* (Boston, MA: Harvard Business School Press), Chapter 8.

7. Preda 2004, 371.

8. H. Lefevre, *Principes de la science de la Bourse: Méthode approuvée par la chamber syndical des agents de change de la Bourse* [Principles of the science of the stock exchange: A method approved by the Union of Stock Brokers] (Paris: Publications de l'Institut Polytechnique, 1874), 13; as quoted in Preda 2004, 371.

9. H. Lefevre, *Traité des valeurs mobilières et des operations de Bourse: Placement et speculation* [Treatise of financial securities and stock exchange operations] (Paris: E. Lachaud, 1870), 184–185; as quoted in Preda 2004, 372.

10. Preda 2002, 27.

11. Preda 2004, 368.

12. Ibid., 360.

13. As quoted in Schultz and Coslow, *A Treasury*, 34.

14. P.-J. Proudhon, *Manuel du spéculateur à la Bourse* (Paris: Garnier frères, 1854), 31; as quoted in Preda 2004, 375.

15. Preda 2004, 356.

16. Ibid., 363.

17. Ibid., 367.

18. Ibid., 380.

19. M. G. Kendall and A. Bradford Hill, "The Analysis of Economic Time Series Part I: Prices," *Journal of the Royal Statistical Society* 116, no. 1 (1953), 11–34, 11.

20. Ibid., 13.

21. R. A. Brealey and S. C. Myers, *Principles of Corporate Finance* (New York: McGraw Hill Higher Education, 2000), 354.

22. P. H. Cootner, ed., *The Random Character of Stock Market Prices* (Cambridge, MA: MIT Press, 1964).

23. Although this distinction between efficient markets and the random walk may seem to be a subtle one, it underscores an important current in the finance literature that has become even more pronounced today—the increasing gulf between purely statistical and mathematical models of financial markets (now known as "mathematical finance"), and models firmly grounded in economic theory. Classic examples of the latter approach are the equilibrium models of Sharpe (1964) and Lintner (1965) in which risk and expected return are related to each other through the forces of supply and demand—expected return being the necessary reward to cause investors to bear undiversifiable risk. It is notable and curious that Cootner did not see fit to include either of these papers in his volume, and it is one of the few gaps in the volume's coverage of the most important research topics of that era. Indeed, although many of the chapters make oblique references to risk aversion, the dynamics of buyers and sellers, and market competition, it is apparent that the notion of an equilibrium trade-off between risk and expected return was still in its embryonic stages. The more typical world view was the kind espoused by Bachelier (1900) in his doctoral dissertation in which he developed the mathematics and statistics of Brownian motion without delving into the economic underpinnings.

24. Preda 2004, 352.

25. Ibid., 362–363.

26. Ibid., 374.

27. Ibid., 379.

28. Ibid., 377.

29. A. G. de Mériclet, *La Bourse de Paris: Moeurs, anecdotes, speculations, et conseils* (Paris: D. Giraud, 1854), 88–89; as quoted in Preda 2004, 377.

30. See also M. Li and P. Vitanyi, *An Introduction to Kolmogorov Complexity and Its Applications* (New York: Springer Verlag, 2008).

31. This twist is closely related to the development, in the second half of the twentieth century, of computational complexity theory, which is the study of what can be solved by a computer in a limited amount of time. A striking outcome of recent research is that (assuming widely believed conjectures) it is possible to generate strings that look random for all practical purposes, in the sense that no human being nor computer could tell the strings apart from coin tosses in less than, say, a billion years. In other words, the task of distinguishing one of these strings from a hypothetical string made of truly random coin tosses is infeasible for computers, even in an astronomical amount of time. Such are the strings used in all computer systems mentioned before, such as Monte Carlo simulations or online purchases; their adequacy for these simulations precisely relies on the fact that no computer can tell them apart from coin tosses. The computer will behave as if it were tossing coins to obtain random numbers. See also O. Goldreich, *Foundations of Cryptography: Volume 1, Basic Tools* (Cambridge: Cambridge University Press, 2001).

32. For example, Malkiel (1973) discusses an experiment in which students were asked to generate returns by tossing fair coins, which yielded observations that were apparently indistinguishable from market returns (p. 143). Kroll, Levy, and Rapoport (1988) conduct an experiment of a portfolio selection problem, where 40 subjects are asked to choose between two assets whose returns are sampled randomly and independently from normal distributions, and given the option of viewing the assets' past return series. The authors find that "even in the extreme case of our experiment, where the subjects were instructed and could actually verify that the stock price changes were random, many of them still developed, maintained for a while, discarded, and generated new hypothesis about nonexistent trends" (p. 409). The same conclusions are reached by De Bondt (1993), who in a series of experiments about forecasting stock prices and exchange rates, including what he calls a "technical analysis game," finds that "people are prone to discover 'trends' in past prices and to expect their continuation," even when "stock prices changes are highly unpredictable" as is the case over short horizons (p. 357). Similar experiments were reported in Roberts (1959), Keogh and Kasetty (2003), and Swedroe (2005), and summarized in Warneryd (2001).

33. Shuffling the actual historical price series preserves the marginal distribution of the returns but eliminates any time-series properties, effectively creating a random walk for prices.

34. Gold spot price tick data (1–60 sec.), June–October 2009. Real data is in the top panel. See also Hasanhodzic, Lo, and Viola (2009).

35. For an introduction to this exciting active area of research see J. E. Hopcroft and J. D. Ullman, *Introduction to Automata Theory, Languages and Computation* (Reading, MA: Addison-Wesley Publishing Company, 1979); M. Sipser, *Introduction to the Theory of Computation* (Boston: PWS Publishing Company,

1997); O. Goldreich, *Computational Complexity: A Conceptual Perspective* (New York: Cambridge University Press, 2008); S. Arora and B. Barak, *Computational Complexity: A Modern Approach* (New York: Cambridge University Press, 2009).

Chapter 8

1. See, for example, D. Aronson, *Evidence-Based Technical Analysis: Applying the Scientific Method and Statistical Inference to Trading Signals* (Hoboken, NJ: Wiley, 2007) and C. Kirkpatrick and J. Dahlquist, *Technical Analysis: The Complete Resource for Financial Market Technicians* (Upper Saddle River, NJ: FT Press, 2006).

2. J.-M. Courtault, Y. Kabanov, B. Bru, P. Crepel, I. Lebon, and A. Le, "Louis Bachelier: On the centenary of 'Théorie de la Spéculation,'" *Mathematical Finance* 10, no. 3 (2000) 339–353.

3. See, for example, S. F. LeRoy, "Risk aversion and the martingale property of stock returns," *International Economic Review* 14 no. 2 (1973), 436–446; M. Rubinstein, "The valuation of uncertain income streams and the pricing of options," *Bell Journal of Economics* 7 (1976), 407–425; R. Lucas, "Asset Prices in an Exchange Economy," *Econometrica* 46 (1978), 1429–1446.

4. See A. W. Lo, ed., *Market Efficiency: Stock Market Behaviour In Theory and Practice, Volumes I and II.* (Cheltenham, UK: Edward Elgar Publishing Company, 1997), 50–67 for a representative collection of papers in this literature.

5. See A. W. Lo, "Effcient Markets Hypothesis," in L. Blume and S. Durlauf, eds., *The New Palgrave: A Dictionary of Economics*, 2nd ed., (New York: Palgrave McMillan, 2007) for a more detailed summary of the market efficiency literature in economics and finance.

6. See, for example, S. Grossman and J. Stiglitz, "On the Impossibility of Informationally Efficient Markets," *American Economic Review* 70 (1980), 393–408; D. W. Diamond and R. E. Verrecchia, "Information Aggregation in a Noisy Rational Expectations Economy," *Journal of Financial Economics* 9 (1981), 221–235; A. R. Admati, "A Noisy Rational Expectations Equilibrium for Multi-Asset Securities Markets," *Econometrica* 53, no. 3 (1985), 629–657; A. S. Kyle, "Continuous Auctions and Insider Trading," *Econometrica* 53, no. 6 (1985), 1315–1336.; and J. Y. Campbell and A. S. Kyle, "Smart Money, Noise Trading and Stock Price Behavior," *Review of Economic Studies* 60 (1993), 1–34.

7. More recently, studies by G. Luo, "Evolution and Market Competition," *Journal of Economic Theory* 67 (1995), 223–250; G. Luo, "Market Efficiency and Natural Selection in a Commodity Futures Market," *Review of Financial Studies* 11 (1998), 647–674; G. Luo, "Natural Selection and Market

Efficiency in a Futures Market with Random Shocks," *Journal of Futures Markets* 21 (2001), 489–516; G. Luo, "Evolution, Efficiency and Noise Traders in a One-Sided Auction Market," *Journal of Financial Markets* 6 (2003), 163–197;), D. Hirshleifer and G. Luo, "On the Survival of Overconfident Traders in a Competitive Securities Market," *Journal of Financial Markets* 4 (2001), 73–84; and L. Kogan, S. A. Ross, J. Wang, and M. M. Westerfield, "The price impact and survival of irrational traders," *Journal of Finance* 61 (2006), 195–229 have focused on the long-term viability of noise traders when competing for survival against informed traders. While noise traders are exploited by informed traders as expected, certain conditions do allow them to persist, at least in limited numbers, these authors argue.

8. E. Fama and M. Blume, "Filter Rules and Stock Market Trading," Journal of Business 39 (1966), 236.

9. A. W. Lo, H. Mamaysky, and J. Wang, "Foundations of Technical Analysis: Computational Algorithms, Statistical Inference, and Empirical Implementation," *Journal of Finance* LV, no. 4 (August 2000), 1705.

10. C. W. J. Granger and O. Morgenstern, "Spectral Analysis of New York Stock Market Prices," *Kyklos* XVI (1963), 3.

11. Granger and Morgenstern, "Spectral Analysis," 11.

12. The distance between the two distributions is measured in two ways: (1) by a goodness-of-fit test, which compares the deciles of conditional returns with their unconditional counterparts, and (2) by the Kolmogorov-Smirnov test.

13. It is important here to distinguish between evaluating the "profitability" of technical trading rules and evaluating the "information content" of technical analysis; the former necessitates the modeling of the trading implementation and risk management, whereas the latter detects supply/demand imbalances regardless of whether one can profitably act on that information.

14. C. Neely, P. Weller, and R. Dittmar, "Is Technical Analysis in the Foreign Exchange Market Profitable? A Genetic Programming Approach," *Journal of Financial and Quantitative Analysis* 32 (1997), 405–426, p. 420.

15. V. Niederhoffer, *Education of a Speculator* (New York: Wiley, 1997), 270.

16. J. Hasanhodzic, A. W. Lo, and E. Viola, "A Computational View of Market Efficiency," Available online at http://arxiv.org/abs/0908.4580 (2009).

17. A. Damasio, *Descartes' Error: Emotion, Reason, and the Human Brain* (New York: Avon Books, 1994).

Bibliography

Allen, F. and R. Karjalainen. "Using Genetic Algorithms to Find Technical Trading Rules." *Journal of Financial Economics* 51 (1999): 245–271.

Bachelier, L. *Théorie de la Spéculation*, trans. A. J. Boness, Paris: Gauthiers-Villars, 1900. In P.H. Cootner, ed., *Random Character of Stock Market Prices*. Cambridge, MA: MIT Press, 1964.

Black, F. "Noise." *Journal of Finance* 41 (1986): 529–544.

Blomquist, T. W. "The Dawn of Banking in an Italian Commune: Thirteenth Century Lucca." In *The Dawn of Modern Banking*, 53–72. Center for Medieval and Renaissance Studies. New Haven, CT: Yale University Press, 1979.

Bloomberg, M. *Bloomberg by Bloomberg / with invaluable help from Matthew Winkler*. New York: J. Wiley, 1997.

Bretz, W. G. *Juncture Recognition in the Stock Market*. New York: Vantage Press, 1972.

Brock, W. A., J. Lakonishok, and B. LeBaron. "Simple Technical Trading Rules and the Stochastic Properties of Stock Returns." *Journal of Finance* 47 (1992): 1731–1764.

Brown S. J., W. N. Goetzmann, and A. Kumar. "The Dow Theory: William Peter Hamilton's Track Record Reconsidered." *Journal of Finance* 53, no. 4 (1998): 1311–1333.

Cameron, R. E. "Banking in the Early Stages of Industrialization: A Preliminary Survey." In *The Economic Development of Western Europe: The Late Nineteenth and Early Twentieth Centuries*, edited by W. C. Scoville and J. C. la Force, 120–136. Lexington, MA: D.C. Heath, 1969.

Campbell, J. Y., A. W. Lo, and A. C. MacKinlay. *The Econometrics of Financial Markets*. Princeton: Princeton University Press, 1997.

Cary, M. and H. H. Scullard. *A History of Rome Down to the Reign of Constantine*. London: Macmillan Press, 1975.

Cerny, J. "Fluctuations in Grain Prices during the Twentieth Egyptian Dynasty." *Archiv. Orientalni* 6 (1933).

Chancellor, E. *Devil Take The Hindmost: A History Of Financial Speculation*, New York: Plume, 2000.

Chang, K. and C. Osler. "Evaluating Chart-Based Technical analysis: The Head-and-Shoulders Pattern in Foreign Exchange Markets." Federal Reserve Bank of New York Working Paper (1994).

Chang, K. and C. Osler. "Methodical Madness: Technical Analysis and the Irrationality of Exchange-Rate Forecasts." *The Economic Journal* 109 (1999): 636–661.

Church, A. "An Unsolvable Problem of Elementary Number Theory." *American Journal of Mathematics* 58, no. 2 (1936): 345–363.

Cippola, C. M., ed. *The Fontana Economic History of Europe*. London: Collins/ Fontana Books, 1972.

Cobham, A. "The Intrinsic Computational Difficulty of Functions." In Y. Bar-Hillel, ed., *Proceedings of the 1964 Congress for Logic, Mathematics, and Philosophy of Science II*, 24–30. Amsterdam: North-Holland, 1965.

Cowles, A. "Can Stock Market Forecasters Forecast?" *Econometrica* 1 (1933): 309–324.

Damasio, A. *Descartes' Error: Emotion, Reason, and the Human Brain*. New York: Avon Books, 1994.

de Balzac, H. *Gaudissart II*. World Wide School Library (published electronically at www.worldwideschool.org).

———. *The Illustrious Gaudissart*. World Wide School Library (published electronically at www.worldwideschool.org).

De Bondt, W. P. M. "Betting on Trends: Intuitive Forecasts of Financial Risk and Return." *International Journal of Forecasting* 9 (1993): 355–371.

de Goede, M. *Virtue, Fortune, and Faith: A Genealogy of Finance*. Minneapolis, MN: University Of Minnesota Press, 2005.

DeGroot, M. H. *Probability and Statistics*. Reading, MA: Addison-Wesley, 1975.

DeLong, B., A. Shleifer, L. Summers, and M. Waldman. "Noise Trader Risk in Financial Markets." *Journal of Political Economy* 98 (1990): 703–738.

DeLong, B., A. Shleifer, L. Summers, and M. Waldman. "The Survival of Noise Traders in Financial Markets." *Journal of Business* 64 (1991): 1–19.

de Roover, R. *Gresham on Foreign Exchange*. London: Harvard University Press, 1949.

Dines, J. *How the Average Investor Can Use Technical Analysis for Stock Profits*. New York: Dines Chart Corporation, 1972.

Duncan-Jones, R. *The Economy of the Roman Empire: Quantitative Studies*. Cambridge: Cambridge University Press, 1974.

Edmonds, J. "Paths, Trees, and Flowers." *Canadian Journal of Mathematics* 17 (1965): 449–67.

Edmonds, J. "Minimum Partition of a Matroid into Independent Sets." *Journal of Research of the National Bureau of Standards, Section B* 69 (1965): 67–72.

Edwards, R. D. and J. Magee. *Technical Analysis of Stock Trends*. 6th ed. Boston: John Magee, 1992.

Ehrenberg, R., *Capital and Finance in the Age of the Renaissance*, translated from German by H.M. Lucas. London: Jonathan Cape, 1928.

Fama, E. "The Behavior of Stock Market Prices." *Journal of Business* 38 (1965a): 34–105.

———. "Random Walks in Stock Market Prices." *Financial Analysts Journal* 21 (1965b): 55–59.

———. "Efficient Capital Markets: A Review of Theory and Empirical Work." *Journal of Finance* 25 (1970): 383–417.

Fama, E. and M. Blume. "Filter Rules and Stock Market Trading." *Journal of Business* 39 (1966): 226–241.

Francis, J. C. *Management of Investments*. New York: McGraw-Hill, 1983.

Freeman, K. *Greek City-States*. New York: The Norton Library, 1950.

Geisst, C. R. *Wheels of Fortune: The History of Speculation from Scandal to Respectability*. Hoboken, NJ: John Wiley & Sons, 2002.

Geisst, C. R. *Wall Street: A History: From Its Beginings to the Fall of Enron*. New York: Oxford University Press, 2004.

Gernet, J. *A History of Chinese Civilization*. Cambridge: Cambridge University Press, 1982.

Gödel, K. "Über formal unentscheidbare Sätze der Principia Mathematica und verwandter Systeme I" ("On Formally Undecidable Propositions of Principia Mathematica and Related Systems I"). *Monatshefte für Mathematik und Physik* 38 (1931): 173–98. Translation in J. van Heijenoort, ed., *From Frege To Gödel: A Source Book in Mathematical Logic, 1879-1931*, Cambridge, MA: Harvard University Press, 1967.

Granger, C. W. J. and O. Morgenstern. "Spectral Analysis of New York Stock Market Prices." *Kyklos* XVI (1963): 1–27.

Grossman, S. and J. Stiglitz. "On the Impossibility of Informationally Efficient Markets." *American Economic Review* 70 (1980): 393–408.

Hartmanis, J. and R. E. Stearns. "On the Computational Complexity of Algorithms." *Transactions of the American Mathematical Society* 117 (1965): 285–306.

Hasanhodzic, J. "Investments Unwrapped: Demystifying Technical Analysis and Hedge-Fund Strategies." Massachusetts Institute of Technology Ph.D. thesis (2007).

Hasanhodzic, J., A. W. Lo, and E. Viola, "A Computational View of Market Efficiency." Available online at http://arxiv.org/abs/0908.4580 (2009).

Hasanhodzic, J., A. W. Lo, and E. Viola, "Is It Real, or Is It Randomized? A Financial Turing Test." Available online at http://ssrn.com/abstract=1558149 (2010).

Herlihy, D., R. S. Lopez, and V. Slessarev, eds. *Economy, Society, and Government in Medieval Italy: Essays in Memory of Robert L. Reynolds.* Kent, Ohio: Kent State University Press, 1969.

Henderson, W. O. *The Industrialization of Europe: 1780–1914.* New York: Harcourt, Brace and World, 1969.

Kaufman, P. *Trading Systems and Methods.* New York: John Wiley & Sons, 1998.

Keogh, E. J. and S. Kasetty. "On the Need for Time Series Data Mining Benchmarks: A Survey and Empirical Demonstration." *Data Mining and Knowledge Discovery* 7 (2003): 349–71.

Kleene, S. C. "General Recursive Functions of Natural Numbers." *Journal Mathematische Annalen* 112, no. 1 (1936): 727–42.

Knapp, A. B. *The History and Culture of Ancient Western Asia and Egypt.* Chicago: Dorsey Press, 1988.

Kolmogorov, A. N. "Three Approaches to the Quantitative Definition of Information." *Problems of Information and Transmission* 1, no. 1 (1965): 1–7.

Kroll, Y., H. Levy, and A. Rapoport. "Experimental Tests of the Mean-Variance Model for Portfolio Selection." *Organizational Behavior and Human Decision Processes* 42 (1988): 388–410.

Laurence Holt Books. *Stikky Stock Charts.* New York: Laurence Holt Books, 2003.

LeRoy, S. "Risk Aversion and the Martingale Property of Stock Returns." *International Economic Review* 14 (1973): 436–46.

Levy, R. A. "The Predictive Significance of Five-Point Chart Patterns." *Journal of Business* 44, no. 3 (1971): 316–323.

Lintner, J. "The Valuation of Risk Assets and the Selection of Risky Investments in Stock Portfolios and Capital Budgets." *Review of Economics and Statistics* 47, no. 1 (1965): 13–37.

Liu, J. T. C. and W. Tu. *Traditional China*. Englewood Cliffs, NJ: Prentice-Hall, 1970.

Lo, A. W. "The Adaptive Markets Hypothesis: Market Efficiency from an Evolutionary Perspective." *Journal of Portfolio Management* 30 (2004): 15–29.

Lo, A. W. "Reconciling Efficient Markets with Behavioral Finance: The Adaptive Markets Hypothesis." *Journal of Investment Consulting* 7 (2005): 21–44.

Lo, A. W. and J. Hasanhodzic. *The Heretics of Finance: Conversations with Leading Practitioners of Technical Analysis*. New York: Bloomberg Press, 2009.

Lo, A. W. and A. C. MacKinlay, 1988. "Stock Market Prices do not Follow Random Walks: Evidence from a Simple Specification Test." *Review of Financial Studies* 1, no. 1 (1988): 41–66.

Lo, A. W., H. Mamaysky, and J. Wang. "Foundations of Technical Analysis: Computational Algorithms, Statistical Inference, and Empirical Implementation." *Journal of Finance* LV, no. 4 (2000): 1705–1765.

Lo, A. W. and M. Mueller. "WARNING: Physics Envy May Be Hazardous To Your Wealth." *Journal of Investment Management* 8 (2010): 13–63.

Lucas, R. "Asset Prices in an Exchange Economy." *Econometrica* 46 (1978): 1429–46.

Malkiel, B. G. *A Random Walk Down Wall Street*. New York: W.W. Norton & Co., 1973.

Marx, K. and F. Engels. *Selected Works*, vol. 1. Moscow: Foreign Language Publishing House, 1962.

Meadows, A. and K. Shipton. *Money and Its Uses in the Ancient Greek World*. New York: Oxford University Press, 2001.

Meskill, J., ed. *An Introduction to Chinese Civilization*. New York: Columbia University Press, 1973.

Millett, P. "Sale, Credit and Exchange in Athenian Law, Politics and Society." In *Nomos: Essays in Athenian Law, Politics and Society*, 167–94. Cambridge: Cambridge University Press, 1990.

Montet, P. *Everyday Life in Egypt in the Days of Rameses the Great*. Philadelphia: University of Philadelphia Press, 1981.

Morley, N. *Metropolis and Hinterland: The City of Rome and the Italian Economy*. Cambridge: Cambridge University Press, 1996.

MTA Educational Foundation. *College Level Introduction to Technical Analysis* disk, containing lectures aimed to guide those preparing for the CMT exam.

Neely, C., P. Weller, and R. Dittmar. "Is Technical Analysis in the Foreign Exchange Market Profitable? A Genetic Programming Approach." *Journal of Financial and Quantitative Analysis* 32 (1997): 405–426.

Neill, H. B. *The Art of Contrary Thinking*. Caldwell, ID: Caxton Printers, 1954.

Nelson, S. A. *The ABC of Stock Speculation*. Flint Hill, VA: Fraser Publishing, 1997.

Nemet-Nejat, K. R. *Daily Life in Ancient Mesopotamia*. Westport, CT: Greenwood Press, 1998.

Paterson, J. "Trade and Traders in the Roman World." In *Trade, Traders, and the Ancient City*, 149–167. New York: Routledge, 1998.

Post, E. L. "Finite Combinatory Processes—Formulation 1." *Journal of Symbolic Logic* 1, no. 3 (1936): 103–5.

Powell, M. A. "Identification and Interpretation of Long Term Price Fluctuations in Babylonia: More on the History of Money in Mesopotamia." *Altorientalische Forschungen* 17 (1990).

Preda, A. "The Rise of the Popular Investor: Financial Knowledge and Investing in England and France, 1840-1880." *The Sociological Quarterly* 42 (2001): 205–232.

Preda, A. "On Ticks and Tapes: Financial Knowledge, Communicative Practices, and Information Technologies on 19th Century Financial Markets." http://www.coi.columbia.edu/ssf/papers/preda.doc (2002).

Preda, A. "Informative Prices, Rational Investors: The Emergence of the Random Walk Hypothesis and the Nineteenth-Century 'Science of Financial Investments.'" *History of Political Economy* 36 (2004): 351–386.

Pring, M. *Technical Analysis Explained*. New York: McGraw-Hill, 1991.

Pruitt, S. and R. White. "The CRISMA Trading System: Who Says Technical Analysis Can't Beat the Market?" *Journal of Portfolio Management* 14 (1988): 55–58.

Reed, C. A. *Maritime Traders in the Ancient Greek World*. Cambridge: Cambridge University Press, 2003.

Roberts, H. V. "Stock-Market 'Patterns' and Financial Analysis: Methodological Suggestions." *Journal of Finance* 14 (1959): 1–10.

Robinson, O. F. *Ancient Rome: City Planning and Administration*. New York: Routledge, 1992.

Roelling, W. "Die altmesopotamische Markt." *Welt des Orients* 8 (1976): 286–95.

Ropp, P. S., ed. *Heritage of China: Contemporary Perspectives on Chinese Civilization*. Berkeley, CA: University of California Press, 1990.

Samuelson, P. "Proof that Properly Anticipated Prices Fluctuate Randomly." *Industrial Management Review* 6 (1965): 41–9.

Sharpe, W. F. "Capital Asset Prices: A Theory of Market Equilibrium under Conditions of Risk." *Journal of Finance* 19, no. 3 (1964): 425–42.

Simon, H. A. "A Behavioral Model of Rational Choice." *Quarterly Journal of Economics* 69, no. 1 (1955): 99–118.

Smith, A. *The Money Game*. New York: Dell, 1968 [1967].

Sobel, R. *Inside Wall Street: Continuity and Change in the Financial District*. New York: Norton, 1977.

Solomonoff, R. "A Preliminary Report on a General Theory of Inductive Inference." Zator Company Report V-131 (Cambridge, MA: 1960).

Solomonoff, R. "A Formal Theory of Inductive Inference." *Information and Control*, Part I vol. 7, no. 1 (1964): 1–22 and Part II vol. 7, no. 2 (1964): 224–54.

Surowiecki, J. *The Wisdom of Crowds: Why the Many Are Smarter Than the Few and How Collective Wisdom Shapes Business, Economies, Societies and Nations*. New York: Little, Brown, 2004.

Swedroe, L. E. *The Only Guide to a Winning Investment Strategy You'll Ever Need*. New York: Truman Talley Books / St. Martin's Press, 2005.

Treynor, J. and R. Ferguson. "In Defense of Technical Analysis." *Journal of Finance* 40 (1985): 757–773.

Turing, A. M. "On Computable Numbers, with an Application to the Entscheidungsproblem." *Proceedings of the London Mathematical Society* 2, no. 42 (1937): 230–65.

Turing, A. M. "On Computable Numbers, with an Application to the Entscheidungsproblem: A correction." *Proceedings of the London Mathematical Society* 2, no. 43 (1937): 544–6.

Turing, A. M. "Computing Machinery and Intelligence." *Mind* 59 (1950): 433–60.

Veenhof, K. R. "Prices and Trade: The Old Assyrian Evidence." *Altorientalische Forschungen* 15 (1988).

von Reden, S. "The Piraeus: A World Apart." *Greece and Rome* 42 (1995): 24–37.

Wärneryd, K. E. *Stock-Market Psychology: How People Value and Trade Stocks*. Northampton, MA: Edward Elgar, 2001.

Young, G. K. *Rome's Eastern Trade*. London and New York: Routledge, 2001.

Acknowledgments

We are profoundly grateful to many people whose help, encouragement, and countless discussions with us have made this project possible. Although it is impossible to list all of them here by name, we wish to mention a few in particular.

First, we thank Emanuele Viola for working with us on the connections between finance and computer science. Our discussions and papers co-authored with him have shaped our view of technical analysis, which is clearly reflected in this book. We are particularly indebted to him for writing the first draft of the "What Is Random?" section of Chapter 7.

We owe much to Charlie Kirkpatrick for editing the preliminary version of the manuscript and correcting factual omissions therein. Our treatment in Chapter 6 of the practice of technical analysis over the last fifty years—during which Charlie was active in the markets— has benefited especially from his expert knowledge and first-hand evidence. We also thank John Bollinger for his feedback on the preliminary manuscript. It is at his suggestion that Richard D. Wyckoff's work is properly recognized in Chapter 5. The kind of help we received from these two master practitioners and expositors of technical analysis is more than we could have ever hoped for.

We remain indebted to the leading practitioners of technical analysis who selflessly shared their store of knowledge with us when we interviewed them for our previous book, *The Heretics of Finance*. Ralph Acampora, Laszlo Birinyi, Walter Deemer, Paul Desmond, Gail Dudack, Robert Farrell, Ian McAvity, John Murphy, Bob Prechter, Linda Raschke, Alan Shaw, Tony Tabell, and Stan Weinstein taught us a great deal about technical analysis today and its evolution in recent history. Their genius and passion continues to inspire us as we learn more about this discipline.

Far more than any single individual, the Market Technicians Association and the MTA Educational Foundation have toiled tirelessly over the years to bring recognition to technical analysis in both professional and academic circles. We thank them for supporting our various initiatives and hope this book can further their mission.

We also thank our academic colleagues—Buzz Brock, David Brown, Kevin Chang, Bob Dittmar, Bob Ferguson, William Goetzmann, Bob Jennings, Josef Lakonishok, Blake LeBaron, Harry Mamaysky, Chris Neely, Maureen O'Hara, Carol Osler, Stephen Pruitt, Jack Treynor, Jiang Wang, Paul Weller, and Richard White—for blazing a trail in technical analysis research, despite the potential backlash from the academic community.

We have had a rare opportunity to work with not one but two exceptional publishers in this endeavor—Bloomberg Press and Wiley (the latter acquired the former halfway through the production process). Our book became a reality thanks to the hard work and dedication of the staff at both publishing houses. In particular, we are grateful to Sophia Efthimiatou and Jared Kieling for signing us with Bloomberg Press, Mary Ann McGuigan for terrific editorial support, Pamela van Giessen for enthusiastically embracing and shepherding this project after it moved over to Wiley, and Emilie Herman and Kevin Holm for spearheading our book through development and production at Wiley. We also thank Matthew Blakeslee and Jayna Cummings for proofreading the manuscript and providing additional editorial assistance.

It is hard to find adequate words to acknowledge everything that the late Mike Epstein has done for us and for this project. The initial research for this book was completed at the MIT Laboratory for Financial Engineering during Mike's tenure there as a research associate, and Mike not only provided invaluable input but was also quick to connect us to anyone and everyone in his enormous network of technicians, all of whom treated us like old friends thanks to Mike's introduction. Mike taught us to always keep an open mind and never discredit anything just because it is not in vogue. His boundless enthusiasm for financial markets in general, and technical analysis in particular, and the humor and optimism with which he filled everything that came his way, will be with us always.

Finally, we have dedicated this book to our mothers, a dedication so routine that it sometimes loses all meaning (most people think highly of apple pie too!). The banality of our dedication belies the extraordinary circumstances of the two individuals who have supported us throughout our lives, making untold sacrifices to allow us to pursue our respective dreams. Our achievements are also theirs.

About the Authors

Andrew W. Lo is the Harris & Harris Group Professor of Finance at MIT Sloan School of Management and the director of MIT's Laboratory for Financial Engineering. He has published numerous papers in academic and practitioner journals such as the *Journal of Finance*, *Financial Analysts Journal*, and the *Journal of Investment Management*, and his previous books include *The Econometrics of Financial Markets*, *A Non-Random Walk Down Wall Street*, and *Hedge Funds: An Analytic Perspective*. His awards include the Alfred P. Sloan Foundation Fellowship, the Paul A. Samuelson Award, the Graham and Dodd Award, the James R. Vertin Award, and the American Association of Individual Investors Award. Dr. Lo is currently also a research associate of the National Bureau of Economic Research, a member of the FINRA's Economic Advisory Board, and is Chairman and Chief Investment Strategist of AlphaSimplex Group, LLC.

Jasmina Hasanhodzic is a research scientist at AlphaSimplex Group, LLC, where she develops quantitative investment strategies and benchmarks. She received her Ph.D. from MIT's Department of Electrical Engineering and Computer Science. Her works on alternative market betas and technical analysis have appeared in leading publications such as the *Journal of Investment Management*, and she is the co-author with Andrew Lo of the book *The Heretics of Finance* (Bloomberg Press, 2009). She also serves on the board of directors of the Market Technicians Association Educational Foundation. A summa cum laude graduate of Yale College, Dr. Hasanhodzic is a recipient of a number of awards for academic excellence and a member of several honor societies, such as Sigma Xi.

Index

Aaronson, David, 149n1
ABC of Stock Speculation, The, 86
ABC of Wall Street, The, 86
adaptive markets
    hypothesis, 164
    technical analysis and, 161–165
Admati, A. R., 151n6
Alexander's filter technique, 152
Allen, F., 191
American Economic Review, 80
Ancient Greece, 11–15
    speculation in, 13–14
    technical analysis in, 14–15
Ancient Rome, 15–18
Appel, Gerald, 107
Arora, Sanjeev, 148n35
Art of Contrary Thinking, The, 46
attitudes, societal, 73–80

Babylon, 2–3, 5–10
    diaries, 8
    forecasting, 9–10
    omens, 9–10
    technical analysis, 7–8

    time scale, 8–9
    volatility, 8–9
Bachelier, Louis, 133, 138, 150, 191
Balzac, Honore de, 192
Barak, Boaz, 148n35
Barbour, V., 35n31–33
Bernoulli, 143
Bingyuan, Wang, xiii n3, 55n56–57
Birdzell, L.E., 28n17–18, 41n57
Birinyi, Laszlo, 115, 119
Birnie, A., 26n14
Black, Fischer, 151, 191
Blodgett, Richard E., 125n37
Blomquist, Thomas W., 191
Bloomberg, 127n44–45, 128n46
Bloomberg terminals, 127–128
Bloomberg, Michael, 127–128, 191
Blume, 151–153
Blume, L., 150n5
Blume, M., 153n8, 193
Board of Brokers. *See New York Stock and Exchange Board*
Bodie, Z., 135n6
Bollinger bands, 107

Bollinger John, 107
Book of Changes, The, 49, 55
Book of Games of Chance, The, 132, 143
Book of Marvels, The, 51
bourse, 30
Bradford Hill, A., 139n19
Brasilier, Adolphe Pierre, 142
Braudel, F., 30n20–21
Brealey, R. A., 139n21
Bretz, W. G., 191
Brock, W. A., 155, 191
Bronze Age, 2–3
Brooks, John, 116n12
Brown, 89, 158–159
Brown, F. E., 116n13
Brown, S. J., 192
Bru, B., 150n2

Calahan, Edward A., 70, 138
Calhoun, G. M., 13n64
Cameron, R. E., 25n9, 192
Campbell, David, 77n80–81
Campbell, J. Y., 151n6, 192
candlestick charts, 47–48
Cardano, Girolamo, 132, 143
Carolan, Christopher, xii
Cary, Max, 192
Cerny, Jareslav, 192
Chan, W. K. K., 49n31
Chang, K., 149, 156, 192
chart patterns, 94–96
Chestnutt, George, 111–112
China, 49–57
   technical analysis, 54–57
Christie, William, 122
Church, 144, 192
Church–Turing thesis, 145
Cipolla, C. M., 24n6, 192
Clough, S. B., 24n5, 25n10, 26n11,
   40n48–50, n52–53
Cobham, A., 147, 192
Cohen, Abraham W., 108–109
Colbert, D., 60n1, n4, 61n5–8
Colby, R. W., 103n96, 112n4
Cole, C. W., 24n5, 25n10, 26n11,
   40n48–50, n52–53
Collins, C. J., 90, 98

commissions, negotiated, 118–119
Committee of the London Stock
   Exchange, 135
computers, 124–130
Confusion de Confusiones, 36
*Consolidated Stock Exchange of New York,
   The*, 86
Cootner, P. H., 139, 140n22, 141
Corinth, 11
Corre's Hotel, 64–65
Corre's Hotel pact, 118
Coslow, S., 8n32, 137n13
Courtault, J.–M., 150n2
Cowles, A., 192
Crane, D., 135n6
Crawford, Arch, xii, 103
Crepel, P., 150n2
curbstone brokers, 66–67
Curtin, P. D., 14n72
cycles, 92–94, 112–113

Dahlquist, Julie, 149n1
Damasio, A., 164n17, 192
Davisson, W. I., 11n55–56, 12n57–58,
   n60–61, n63, 14n73, n75, 16n84
De Bondt, W. P. M., 146n32, 192
de Goede, M., 77n79, 78n85–88, 79n94,
   84n11, 93n47, 96n58, 192
de Méré, Chevalier, 143
de Mériclet, A. G., 142n29
de Moivre, 143
du Plessis, Jeremy, 108n1
de Roover, R., 193
decimalization, 122–123
Deemer, Walter, 125
DeGroot, M. H., 192
DeLong, B., 192, 193
Diamond, D. W., 151n6
diaries, 6–8
   as charts, 8
Dillon, Michael, 77n80–81
Dines, J., 193
Dittmar, R., 160, 161n14, 195
Dodd, C. T., 69
Dow Jones Industrial Average, 111
Dow theory, 82–91
Dow Theory Today, The, 89

Dow Theory, The, 88
Dow, Charles, 59, 70, 80, 81–93,
  97–98, 134
*Dow's Theory Applied to Business and
  Banking,* 88
Dudack, Gail, 123
Duncan–Jones, R., 193
Durlauf, S., 150n5

Edmonds, J., 147, 193
Education of a Speculator, 161–162
Edwards, R. D., 109, 193
efficient markets hypothesis (EMH), xi,
  131–134, 137–139, 151, 154–160,
  162–165
efficient markets, emergence, 137–141
Egeron, Clement, 55n59
Ehrenberg, Richard, 37n40, 38n42–43,
  193
electronic markets, 123–123
Elliott wave principle, 113
Elliott, Ralph Nelson, 93–94
Elvin, M., 49n29, 51n42, 52n44–47,
  54n49–50
EMH. *See efficient markets hypothesis (EMH)*
empirical evaluation, 152–161
Encyclopedia for Gentry and Merchants, 55–57
*Encyclopedia of Technical Market Indicators,
  The,* 112
Engels, Friedrich, 195
Essentials for Tradesmen, 55–57
Essentials for Travelers, 54–57
evaluation, emprical, 152–161

Fairbank, J. K., 49n30, n32
Fama, Eugene, xi, 133, 139–140,
  150–153, 193
Farrell, Robert, 128
Ferguson, R., 151, 197
Fibonacci numbers, 113
Financial Times, 78
fixed length moving average, 155
Fontana, 32n22, 33n24–25, 40n51
Forecast Reports, 91
forecasting, 9–10
*Fountain of Gold—The Three Monkey Record
  of Money, The,* 46, 48

Francis, J. C., 193
Freeman, K., 193
Friend, Irwin, 116n13
Froot, K., 135n6
Fullerton, 41n56
*Further Collection of Miscellaneous Items,
  The,* 51

games of chance, 143
Gann, William D., xii, 93–94, 100–104
Gartley, Harold M., 7n28, 8n35, 47n21,
  82n7, 87n23, 88n30, 90, 91n38, 97,
  98n63–69, 99
Gazetteer for Kuei–chi, The, 50
Geisst, C. R., 62n13, 69n43–44,
  76n74–75, 77n76–78, 79n92–93,
  114n7, 117n15, 119n10, 120n22–24,
  122n27, n29, 123n31–33, 193
Gernet, J., 193
Glotz, G., 12n59, 12n62, 13n65–66,
  n68–69, 14n74, n76
Gödel, K., 144, 193
Goetzmann, W. N., 6n18, 34n27, 89,
  158–159, 192
Goldreich, Oded, 146n31, 148n35
Goodman, 126–127
Gordon, J. S., 60n2–3, 61n9, 62n11, n14,
  63n15–17, 66n33, n35, n38, 67n39,
  68n42, 73n61, n63–69, 76n73
Government Bond Department, 67
Granger, C. W. J., 153–154, 193
Granville, Joseph, 107
*Granville's New Key to Stock Market
  Profits,* 107
Greece
  ancient, 11–15
  speculation, 13–14
  technical analysis, 14–15
Groesbeck, David, 70
Grossman, S., 151, 194

Hamilton, W. P., 83, 87, 88n28–29, 93,
  98, 158–160
Harper, J. E., 11n55–56, 12n57–58,
  12n60–61, 63, 14n73, n75, 16n84
Harriman, E. H., 85
Hartmanis, J., 147, 194

Hasanhodzic, J., xin1, 114n6, 115n9–10, 118n16, 119n21, 121n25–26, 123n30, 124n34, 125n38–39, 126n41, 128n47–48, 129n50, 130n51, 147, 163n16, 194, 195
Hayes, Howard, 192
head and shoulders, 94–96, 109–110
Heaton, H., 18n94, 24n3–4, 25n8, 26n12, 33n23
Henderson, W. O., 194
Heretics of Finance, The, 114
Herlihy, D., 33n26, 194
Herman, Edward S., 116n13
Hirschmeier, J., 44n2
Hirshleifer, D., 151n7
Homma, Munehisa, xiii, 45–46, 134
Hopcroft, John E., 148n35
How to Use the Three–Point Reversal Method of Point and Figure Stock Market Trading, 108
Huarame, Ernest Euvergier de, 75n70
Huygens, Christiaan, 143
Hyerczyk, J. A., 94n50, 100–101, n84, n87–88, 102n89–91, 103n92, n95

IMM. *See International Monetary Market (IMM)*
institutional trading, technical analysis and, 116–118
International Monetary Market (IMM), 120
Investment Letters, 90, 98
Iron Age, 11

Japan, 44–48
    market psychology, 45–46
    technical analysis, 45
Jevons, William Stanley, xiii, 77–78, 92
Johnson, Ned, 116
Jones, Edward, 81
Journal of Finance, 122
Juglar wave, 113
Juglar, Clement, 113

Kabanov, Yu., 150n2
Kahn, Otto, 85
Karjalainen, R., 191

Kasetty, S., 146n32, 194
Kaufman, Perry, 106, 194
Keene, James R., 85
Keian, Yodoya, 44–45
Kendall, Maurice, 139
Keogh, E. J., 146n32, 194
Kienast, Burkhart, 5n16
Kirkpatrick, Charles, 113, 125–126, 149n1, 155
Kitchin, Joseph, 113
Kleene, S. C., 144, 194
Knapp, A. B., 194
Kogan, L., 151n7
Kolmogorov, A. N., 194
Kondratieff wave, 113
Kroll, Y., 146n32, 194
Kula, Witold, 77n79
Kumar, A., 89, 158–159, 192
Kurz, Christopher, xii, 37n41, 38n44
Kyle, A. S., 151n6

La Force, J. C., 28n19
Lakonishok, J., 155, 191
Laplace, Pierre de, 143
Latham, R., 52n43
Le Bourse de Paris, 142
Le, Al., 150n2
LeBaron, B., 155, 191
Lebeau, C., 94n52
Lebon, I., 150n2
Lefevre, Henri, 42n61, 135–136, 141, 150
LeRoy, S. F., 140, 150n3, 194
Levy, Gus, 119
Levy, H., 194
Lévy, Jean–Phillipe, 3n10, 14n70, 146n32
Levy, Robert A., 112n2–3, 155–156, 194
Li, Ming, 145n30
Liber Abaci, 33
Lintner, J., 194
Liu, J. T. C., 194
Livermore, Jesse, 85
Lo, Andrew W., xi n1, 37n39, 114n6, 115n9–10, 118n16, 119n21, 121n25–26, 123n30, 124n34, 125n38–39, 126n41, 128n47–48, 129n50, 130n51, 147, 149, 150n4–5,

153n9, 156–158, 163n16, 164, 192, 194–195

Lopez, R. S., 33n26, 194

Lucas, 140, 150

Lucas, D. W., 94n52

Lucas, R., 150n3, 195

Lufrano, R. J., 54n51–54, 55n55, n60, 56n62, n64, 57n65–66

Luo, G., 151n7

MACD. *See moving average convergence/ divergence (MACD)*

MacKinlay, A. C., 192, 195

Magazine of Wall Street. See Ticker Magazine

Magee, J., 193

Malkiel, Burton G., xi, 146n32, 153, 195

Mamaysky, H., 149, 153n9, 156–158, 195

Marconi, Guglielmo, 72

Marisch, G., 100n80–81, 101

market breadth, 99

market cycles, 92–94

market integration, 120–122

market psychology, Japan, 45–46

market waves, 92–94

Marx, Karl, 195

Masaaki, Minuno, 55n58

Mason, S., 135n6

Mathematical Theory of Long–Term Investing, 142

McCabe, James, 76n72

Meadows, A., 195

Medbery, James K., 66n34, n37

Meeker, J. Edward, 63n18, 64n19, 65n23, n27, n31, 96–97

Meijer, F., 13n67

Merchant's Guide, The, 54

merchants, 22–26

Meridian, Bill, 103

Merton, R., 135n6

Meskill, J., 195

middle ages, 22–26
    societal attitudes, 39–40
    technical analysis, 32–35

Millett, P., 195

Money Game, The, 126–127

Monte Carlo simulation, 145

Montet, Pierre, 195

Morgan, J. P., 69, 85

Morgenstern, O., 153–154, 193

Morley, Neville, 15n77–78, 16n86, 18n95–97, 19n98–9, 195

moving average convergence/divergence (MACD), 107

moving averages, 106

Mueller, M., 195

Murphy, J. J., 34n28

Murphy, John, 115, 120, 125

Myers, S. C., 139n21

NASD, 119

National Association of Securities Dealers. *See NASD*

Neely, C., 160, 161n14, 195

negative attitude toward traders, 18–19

negotiated commissions, 118–119

Neiderhoffer, Victor, 161–162

Neill, H. B., 195

Nelson, Samuel A., 80, 82, 86, 87n20–21, 91, 195

Nemet–Nejat, K. R., 195

Neolithic period, 2

New Concepts in Technical Trading Systems, 107

New Netherlands, 60–61

New York, 61

New York Society of Security Analysts, 97

New York Stock and Exchange Board, 65–66

New York Stock Exchange (NYSE), 66–68, 79–80, 96

Niederhoffer, V., 162n15

Nijf, O. van, 13n67

Nippon Technical Analysis Association, 44n3–4, 45n6, n10, 46n15–16, 47n20, 48n24, n26

Nison, S, 44n1, n5, 45n7–9, 46n11–12, n14, n18, 47n19, n22, 48n23, n27

nontechnical analysis, 99–104

Nussbaum, F. L., 26n15, 28n16, 41n54–55, n58

NYSE. *See New York Stock Exchange*

Oda, Nobunaga, 44

Okamota, Hiroshi, 48

omens, 9–10
on–balance volume, 107–108
OPEC, 120
Open Board of Brokers, 67
Ore, Oystein, 132n1
Organization of Petroleum Exporting
    Countries. *See OPEC*
Orlin, L. L., 2n4
Osler, C., 149, 156, 192

Pado, Chester, 116
Parkins, H., 2n6, 14n71
Pascal, Blaise, 143
Paterson, Jeremy, 195
patterns, 109–111
    chart, 94–96
Perold, A., 135n6
Pirenne, H., 25n7, 26n13
Plummer, T., 103n93–94
point and figure chart, 84–85, 108–109
Post, E. L., 144, 196
Posthumus, N. W., 36n35–36, 37n37–38
Powell, Marvin A., 196
Prechter, Robert, 93n48–49, 94, 128
Preda, A., 39n46–47, 41n60, 42n62–65,
    70n49–50, n52, 71–72, 73n60,
    79n90–91, 95n55, 134n2, 135n3–7,
    136–138, 141, 142n25–29, 196
prices, objects of study, 134–137
*Principles of the Science of the Stock
    Exchange*, 135
Pring, Martin, 196
probability theory, 143
Profits in the Stock Market, 97, 99
Proudhon, Pierre–Joseph, 137
Pruden, H., 86n15
Pruitt, S., 196

Qi, Wang, 56n63

*Random Character of Stock Market Prices,
    The*, 139
random walk, 132, 139–141, 150,
    152–156, 162
Random Walk Down Wall Street, A, xi, 153
random, 141–148
randomness, 131–148

Rapoport, A., 146n32, 194
rate of change line (ROC), 107
Rathbone, D., 17n90
Record of the Customs of Wu, A, 52
Reden, S. von, 196
Reed, C. A., 196
Reishauer, E., 49n30, n32
relative strength, 91–92
*Relative Strength Concept of Common Stock
    Price Forecasting, The*, 111
relative strength ratio (RS), 111
renaissance, 26–32
    societal attitudes, 40–42
    technical analysis, 35–39
Reynolds, 34n29–30
Rhea, R., 46n17, 48n25, 84, 88, 91
Roberts, H. V., 146n32, 196
Robinson, O. F., 196
ROC. *See rate of change line*
Roelling, Wolfgang, 196
Rome, ancient, 15–18
Ropp, P. S., 196
Rosenberg, N., 28n17–18, 41n57
Ross, S. A., 151n7
Rowlands, M., 3n8–9
RS. *See relative strength ratio (RS)*
Russell, R., 46n13, 82n6, 84n14, 89, 90, 92

Saggs, H. W. F., 2n5, 3n7
Samuelson, Paul, xi, 133, 139–140,
    150, 196
Sapori, A., xivn5, 22n1–2
Savage, L. J., 150
Schabacker, Richard W., 8n29, n33,
    n37–38, 9n42, 79n89, 95–96
Schultz, 80n96, 82n3–5, 83n8, 84n13,
    86n18–19, 87n22, n24–25, 88n27,
    89n32, 90n35–36, 91n39, 92n40–41,
    95n54, n56, 96n57, 97n61, 137n13
Schultz, H. D., 8n32, n34
Schultz, Paul, 122
Scoville, W. C., 28n19
Scullard, H. H., 16n83
Sharpe, W. V., 196
Shaw, Alan, 125
Shigeo, Sakuma, 53n48
Shipton, K., 195

Shleifer, A., 192, 193
Silver, Morris, 5n11, n13, n15, 15n81, 16n82
Simon, Herbert, 138–139, 148, 196
Sipser, Michael, 148n35
Sirri, E., 135n6
Slessarev, V., 33n26, 194
Sloan, Alfred P., 86
Slotsky, A. L., 6n19–24, 7n25–27, 8n30–31, n36, 9n39–41, n43–49, 10n50–54
small investors, technical analysis and, 114–115
Smith, 127n42–43
Smith, A., 196
Smith, C., 2n6, 14n71
Sobel, R., 61n10, 62n12, 64n20–22, 65n24–26, n28–30, n32, 73n62, 116n11, 117n14, 119n18, n20, 196
societal attitudes, 73–80
    middle ages, 39–40
    renaissance, 40–42
Solomonoff, Ray, 145, 196, 197
speculation, 13–14
Stearns, R. E., 147, 194
Stedman, Edmund Clarence, 70n51
Stiglitz, J., 151, 194
stock market, 64–70
Stock Market Barometer, The, 87, 93
Stock Market Profits, 95
Stock Market Theory and Practice, 8, 95
Stock Market Trading Systems: A Guide to Investment Strategy for the 1980s, 107
stock ticker, 70–73
Story of the Averages, The, 88
strength, 111–112
Stuyvesant, Peter, 61
Sumeria, 2
Summers, L., 192, 193
Surowiecki, J., 197
Swedroe, L. E., 146n32, 197
Swings within Swings, 82–83

Tabell, Anthony W., x–xi, 115, 125–126
Tabell, Edmund W., x–xi, 115
Tape, Rollo. *See Wyckoff, Richard D.*
Technical Analysis and Market Profits, 95

Technical Analysis for the Financial Markets, 115
Technical Analysis: The Complete Resource for Financial Market Technicians, 113
Technical Analysis of Stock Trends, 109
technical analysis
    adaptive markets and, 161–165
    China, 54–57
    empirical evaluation, 152–161
    institutional trading and, 116–118
    Japan, 45
    small investors and, 114–115
    underpinnings, 150–151
technology, impact of, 70–73
telegraph, 70–72
Temin, P., 16n85, 17n87–88, n91–92, 18n93
Thomas, Dana L., 81n1–2, 83n10, 125n35–36
Ticker Magazine, 70, 85
time scale, 8–9
Tokugawa, Ieyasu, 44
Toynbee, A., 41n59
Toyotoi, Hideyoshi, 43–44
traders, 22–26
    negative attitude toward, 18–19
trading volume, 96–98
trends, 46–47, 106–109
Treynor, J., 151, 197
Triumph of Science and Reason, The, 41
Trollope, Anthony, 75n71
Truth of the Stock Tape, 101
Tsai, Gerald, 116
Tu, W., 194
Tufano, P., 135n6
Tunnel Thru the Air, 101
Turing, Alan, 144, 147, 197

Ullman, Jeffrey D., 148n35
underpinnings, 150–151
United States Bank, 63
Untermyer, Samuel, 80

Vansommer, James, 135
variable length moving average, 155
Veenhof, K. R., 5n14, 197
Vega, Joseph de la, xiii, 36n34

Verrecchia, R. E., 151n6
Vickers, Douglas, 116n13
Viola, Emanuele, 129, 146, 163n16
Vitanyi, Paul, 145n30
volatility, 8–9
volume, trading, 96–98

Wachtel, H. M., 66n36, 68n40–41,
　　69n45–47, 70n48, 71n55
Waldman, M., 192, 193
Wall Street, 60–73
Wall Street Journal, 78, 81–82, 87–88, 90,
　　98, 125, 158
Wall Street Selector, 101
Wang, J., 149, 151n7, 153n9,
　　156–158, 195
Wärneryd, K. E., 146n32, 197
waves, market, 92–94
Weingarten, H., 100, 101n83, n85, 103n97

Weller, P., 160, 161n14, 195
Westerfield, M. M., 151n7
Western Europe
　　middle ages, 22–26
　　Renaissance, 26–32
Whitby, Michael, 14n71, 15n79–80
White, R., 196
Wilder, J. Welles, 107
Wilhelm, R., 49n28
Wright, G. A., 2n1–3
Wyckoff, Richard D., 85–86, 108
Wyld, James, xiii

Yoshinobu, 50n33–40, 51n41
Young, G. K., 197
Yui, T., 44n2

Zagros Valley, 2
Zhongfu, Wu, 55n61

Operation Husky

The Untold Story of the Logistics of the Sicily Invasion

The Husky plan is 'a dog's breakfast…it breaks every common-sense rule of practical fighting'.[1]

James Garvey